7- 2 /- 7/

Indian Economic Thought

Joseph J. Spengler

Indian Economic Thought

A Preface to Its History

1971
Duke University Press
Durham, N.C.

© 1971, Duke University Press
L.C.C. card no. 75–142293
I.S.B.N. 0–8223–0245–4

PRINTED IN THE UNITED STATES OF
AMERICA BY KINGSPORT PRESS, INC.

To my parents
who found happiness
in history

Preface

This study of economic thought in what is now India and Pakistan is not a definitive study. It is based on translations and secondary works, and is, as entitled, "a preface." Its purpose is to survey the course of Indian economic thought and stimulate intensive, organized inquiry. Much more remains to be done on the economic and ideational history of the subcontinent before a definitive study can be completed—perhaps by a group of Indian and Western scholars with sufficient funding for (say) a ten-year organized inquiry into the growth of Indian society and the history of the interaction of thought and economic life in India. Such funding would not put much of a strain on the resources of foundations in a nation boasting of its entry into an Age of Opulence and a World of Unpeopled Space.

My obligations are various. Off and on for more than a decade I have had limited financial assistance from the Ford and Rockefeller Foundations. Ford and Guggenheim Fellowships have provided me with time, a portion of which could be devoted to this inquiry. I have had support also from the Duke University Research Council and the Duke University South Asia Committee. Perhaps more precious than money have been the intellectual stimulus and help I have had from colleagues interested in South and East Asia, above all Professors Ralph Braibanti and Robert I. Crane. Finally, I have had the patient and careful secretarial assistance of Mrs. Virginia Skinner, a member of that too-little-sung army which gets untidy manuscript material into deceptively readable form. Yet despite all this help, had it not been for the encouragement of my wife, Dorothy, her continuous facilitation of my research, and her surrounding me with flowers of the Orient, I could not have completed this inquiry. Very great is my indebtedness to the Duke Press, and above all to Mr. J. W. Dowling, for his priceless editorial contributions and assistance.

J. J. S.

July 1970

Contents

Indian Economic Thought

Introduction

Economic science as comprehended by present-day economists emerged in the seventeenth and eighteenth centuries. Then as now, there ran through it two main concerns, an administrative and an ethical. Economics (even in this analytical age) has these two sources, two roots, two components. Sometimes the administrative or political component has been ascendant, sometimes the ethical or moral. Sometimes extraeconomic ideas or influences have flowed into political economy through the administrative channel, and sometimes through the ethical channel.

Long before the seventeenth century the two sets of ideas had made themselves felt. For while nothing approximating modern economic science had been formulated, observations were made in respect of economic behavior, and there was need occasionally to assess this behavior as good or bad in the light of customary or other "ethical" criteria. Similarly, as city-states and later empires came into being, support for the apparatus of state had to be found in the form of taxes and other sources of goods and services, and it became necessary to establish administrative mechanisms and thereafter to assess the efficacy of these and related mechanisms and modify them accordingly.

Those dealing with economic matters had to trouble themselves with one or the other set of economic criteria even though the distinction between the sets was not always clear and did not command attention from men concerned with only one or the other. Those charged with administrative responsibilities had to determine how the various administrative approaches functioned and then settle upon the ones conjectured to be best suited to carry out appointed tasks. Other men inquired into the worthwhileness of the accomplishment of these tasks as well as into what we might call their opportunity costs. Inquiry of this type sometimes merged with inquiries pertaining to administrative efficacy in general in that it brought to the fore questions relating to how an economic society had best be organized—say by a free price system instead of by administrative dictate—and to the extent to which economic outcomes are modifiable by changes in the distribution of political or coercive power.

The history of economics can be written from a variety of points of view—with emphasis upon analytical contributions, or with emphasis upon the filiation of particular ideas, or with emphasis upon other aspects. In the present inquiry, however, it is the quest for economic standards that is most prominent. Pre-eighteenth-century analytical contributions were not important, or if they were, their importance was missed or swamped by subsequent independent inquiries. Furthermore, it is about standards, ethical or administrative or both, that most pre-eighteenth-century, economically oriented discussion revolved, and it is in the course of such discussion that occasional protoeconomic "principles" came to the surface. It was partly through changes in standards, moreover, that redistributions of coercive power made themselves felt, as when control of the school system was removed at least partially from those teaching in a particular tradition (say the scholastic), or when absolutist Roman law was superseded by common law, flexible companion to early laissez-faire and merchant law.

Inquiry into the progress of man's quest for economic standards may reveal how and why his economic concerns and situation changed over time. It reveals the importance attached to both justice and political stability, outside as well as within the classical Greek world of Plato and Aristotle. The quest for standards may also reveal why man's income rose very little and in some places hardly at all, over many centuries; why it did not progress continually upward until the advent of modern times, even in countries where quite high living standards were attained over two millennia ago. Apparently the ratio of aggregate income to aggregate population moved upward somewhat, with the spread of public order, the cumulation of capital, and improvement in communication, technology, and commerce. Yet the average income of the common man, after attaining a kind of level, fluctuated about it over long periods, without rising materially. Even the average income of those who appropriated the social surplus probably did not advance notably over the centuries.

This study is not focused upon the details of diverse movements of average output or even upon their immediate causes. It is concerned rather with the impact of economic opinion, as well as that of current values communicated through economic opinion and practice, upon income-affecting behavior; for, as is fairly evident, capacity for the generation of expanding income was present in a number of centers of civilization. This potential and already proved capacity did not continue to be realized as it might have been. It may be presumed, nonetheless, that what men had to say about economic issues did at times affect the course of economic events insofar as today's ideas give rise to tomorrow's actions.

Students of the history of economic thought have focused their attention mainly upon Europe and Europe Overseas. Here in 1650 lived only about one-fifth of the world's people, a fraction that was somewhat less than that around 1900 but above that at the beginning of the Christian era. Then as in 1650, over half of the world's population lived in Asia, mainly in China and India, where economic concerns aroused interest and prompted inquiry even as they did in Europe. Past concentration upon European economic literature flows from many conditions, among them linguistic and cultural circumstances and the apparent uniqueness of European modes of scientific inquiry. Most important, however, is the recency of the origin of the antecedents of "modern" economic thought and hence of the temporal boundaries within which inquiry into its development has been mainly confined. After all, it is in the seventeenth century that we first encounter effective efforts to explain economic behavior in terms of a small number of principles.

Man's economic concerns long antedate his capacity to conceptualize and analyze economic behavior effectively, animating him to discuss these concerns and reflect them in his laws and customs. We therefore find what may be called a protoeconomic literature in most civilizations in which writing developed and literary remains are extant. This is true of the Indian subcontinent as well as of China, Mesopotamia, Egypt, and the Mediterranean world. While it must have been true of India's first great culture, the so-called Indus civilization, the scant literary remains of this civilization have not yet been deciphered. Therefore, the present study begins only with the second half of the last millennium B.C. and continues down to modern times.

Inquiry into the content and progress of ancient economic opinion has little to contribute to our knowledge of the genesis of modern economic theory, largely confined as it has been to the last two centuries. Such inquiry need not, however, be mere archaism. Not only may it serve as a handmaid to economic history and the sociology of knowledge, helping to give meaning and content to various kinds of evidence; it may also illuminate why premodern South Asian economies, despite their ability to generate a surplus above ordinary needs as well as to make technological improvements, were unable to get self-sustaining growth under way. It reveals how the ruling and the articulate circles believed economies to function; it indicates something of the extent to which the working of simple price and marketing systems was hampered; it discloses how static this-worldly expectations were; and it throws light upon the degree in which economic development was prevented by royal and priestly waste, war, and (contrary to J. M. Keynes's description of it as "fortunate" for Egypt) "pyramid building," all of which absorbed portions of the economic surplus that emerged with the establishment of settled agriculture. It thus helps to explain why most men had to live so long in a "pain economy," life in which apparently became even more severe in India as Moslem rule replaced Hindu rule.

Today the science of economics is independent, even as is the science of physics, of the dimensions and culture of any society in which economic analysis is carried on. The findings of this analysis do, of course, reflect the dimensions and culture of the society and economy subjected to study. In early times, however, what amounted to economic thought or discussion was shaped by the empirics of the day. Economic thought reflected the economic behavior of man, and this in turn reflected the physical as well as the cultural dimensions of the economy within which this behavior took place. Standards of adequacy conformed to these dimensions; for example, in medieval India and earlier, transport facilities were primitive and short in supply even by early-nineteenth-century standards, and yet they sufficed to carry the limited amount of goods, few of them bulky, entering into landborne trade, an amount limited also perhaps by man's failure to apprehend how transport conditioned the extent of markets.

In chapter 1 some of the dimensions of an early economy are identified. These do not *determine* the form that economic thought will assume, any more than a physical environment determines the culture of its occupants; but they do *condition* the images, the expectations, the options that can emerge to animate and guide economic behavior. Inquiry into the development of early economic thought must take these dimensions into account, much as today's students of international trade must take into account variation in the size of trading nations. In chapter 2 this theme is pursued further in respect of India. Were there space and had adequate fundamental information been available, it would have been possible to examine India in terms of a model that allowed for the incidence upon economic discussion there of all possible components of the physical and cultural milieu within which Indian economic thought took form. It might then have been possible to contrast in detail Indian conceptions of economic justice, politico-economic stability, attitude toward change, and so on, with the corresponding conceptions in Chinese or in classical Greek and Roman culture. As it stands, however, chapter 2, together with chapter 1, is intended to be prefatory and suggestive in character.

What is describable as ancient Indian economic thought had two principal overlapping repositories, the works of writers on *arthashastra* and the works of writers on *dharmashastra*. Arthashastra is represented in the main by the work of Kautalya, manifestations of whose influence were still present in medieval India and even in Moslem successor states. Dharmashastra is represented above all by the work of Manu, whose influence persisted through the centuries in much greater measure than that of Kautalya. The persistence of these two bodies of thought is closely associated with the relatively stationary character of Indian society. Differences in the persistence of the two bodies of ideas are similarly traceable to the fact that a larger fraction of arthashastra thought had to do with matters sensitive to external change. The content of these two bodies of thought is described in chapters 3 and 4.

While India (like China) was many times invaded after the day of Alexander the Great, the impact of but two waves of invaders has been overwhelming. The first, the Moslems, accounts for the eventual bifurcation of British India, but did not materially affect the content of economic thinking of India beyond accentuating some internal obstacles to economic growth. The second, the British, together with Western modes of thought and practice, set in motion revolutionary forces of transformation whose course is far from run. Among these modes of thought was economics, born not long before Britain's ascendancy and in part as a response to Britain's penetration into India. Though India was slow at first to adopt this mode of thought, it finally began to flourish there late in the nineteenth century when economists were few everywhere and far fewer still in India. Yet within the present century and in the face of numerous obstacles, the economic mode of thought has progressed until today what is done by the economists of India and Pakistan compares favorably with what is done by economists of the West.

The fifth chapter is devoted to economic thought in medieval and postmedieval India and to the influence of the Moslem invaders, particularly in Mughal times. The sixth chapter is devoted to the modernization of Indian economic thought under the influence of a most remarkable collection of men, the representatives of the East India Company, the later spokesmen for the British Raj, and the Indian nationalists who found in economics an instrument of analysis helpful in their struggle for independence and freedom to substitute an Indian welfare function for a function originating in London.

The concluding chapter is made up rather of interpretation than conclusion. One needs more information than is at hand to set down hypotheses and test them. Even more than usually is true of a prefatory survey, the present monograph does not yield hard and fast conclusions. It may be possible for scholars, however, having got an overview of the terrain, after the manner of that formed by explorers of possibly oil-rich areas, to examine it in microdetail and discover functional connections that developed in the past.

Some repetition will be encountered in chapters 3 to 5. There is considerable similarity in contents between arthashastra literature and early dharmashastra literature. There is also overlap between early and late dharmashastra literature. Attempts to remove the repetition, however, seemed to reduce completeness more than they added to readability.

This study is based upon translations and secondary works. One is never certain how far a translator has caught the precise meaning intended in the original. Nor may a nonspecialist in Indian history assume that he has voiced the consensus of the historians, particularly in view of the accumulation of information and changes in interpretation still going on.

The degree to which diacritical marks should be employed in a work not intended for linguistic specialists—Sanskrit scholars in the present instance—presents a problem. It has been solved by following the practice endorsed by the University of Chicago Press *Manual of Style* (12th ed., 1969, p. 228), namely, to "use a system employing as few diacritics as possible, except in linguistic or highly specialized studies."

Chapter 1

Economic Dimensions and Economic Thought

The chronic handicap of the ancient economic historian is lack of figures.

M. I. FINLEY

Economic life is constrained by the dimensions of the society within which it is carried on. These dimensions in turn are reflected in the responses that thinking men make to the economic life and problems surrounding them, especially when attempting to interpret this life and solve these problems. As these dimensions change, economic life changes, and with it the responses thereto of its interpreters. Interpreters have differed, of course, respecting the importance of a society's various dimensions. Some social scientists have stressed time to the exclusion of space, whereas others have emphasized the tyranny of space and the importance of abridging distance, while playing down time.

The subject of this monograph requires discussion of more than the temporal and the spatial dimensions of ancient society, even though these are of paramount importance. It is not proposed that a society's dimensions be dealt with merely in the abstract and free of that external observation which is so stimulative of deductive introspection. Only by analysis of the implications of particular dimensions can we estimate whether economic thought may have been affected thereby. At the same time, just as one can infer the behavioral capacity of an animal from its dimensions, so one can roughly infer the potential range of a society's behavior from its dimensions.[1]

There is a difference, however, between drawing inferences from

1. Compare D'Arcy W. Thompson's classic *On Growth and Form*. (For references cited in the notes consult the List of References preceding the Index.)

the dimensions of a present-day society and drawing them from those of a society situated far back in time.[2] Today, we have information regarding many dimensions and, through statistical analysis of temporal and/or international differences, can determine what dimensions are interrelated and estimate these relations in quantitative terms. This is not true for early societies. We have little information, much of it conjectural, and it relates to too few societies to permit statistical analysis. Even so, our understanding of past societies and of their interpreters may be appreciably enlarged through cognizance of the dimensions, real and conjectural, of these societies.

We shall identify a number of dimensions of ancient as of modern societies and suggest their implications for economic activity. We shall assume that the image which an ancient interpreter of his own economic world formed of that world shaped his thought. Such an image could not, of course, determine the content of an author's thought, but it could fix the confines within which these contents were formed.

Perhaps the outstanding difference between ancient societies, among them India, and modern societies is this. Ancient societies rested upon landed wealth; modern societies now rest upon electronic technology, after having rested upon heavy industry for a century or more. In antiquity, exploitation of land and those who worked it was the principal means to income. This situation continued, moreover, until the advent of the modern world. Even the urban medieval bourgeoisie manifested a strong preference for landed assets, investing their urban profits in land: "they were content merely to collect its revenues."[3]

The dimensions of an economy may be variously classified. For the purposes of this study, a threefold classification seems most appropriate: the physical dimensions, the organizational dimensions, and the dimension of distribution of decision-making power. These classifications overlap somewhat: the distribution of decision-making power is conditioned by an economy's organizational dimensions, and the physical dimensions are conditioned, as are the other two sets of dimensions, by the state of a society's arts.

2. On implications of the dimensions of today's nations as well as literature relating thereto, see Jack Sawyer, "Dimensions."
3. See *Cambridge Economic History*, 1:304–5; and Finley, "Technical Innovation."

Physical Dimensions

Agricultural Yield per Acre

The yield per acre influences the magnitude of the urban component of a nation's population in two ways. First, output per capita tends to be positively correlated with yield per acre, by type of crop. Second, where yield is higher, an urban center can draw its subsistence from a smaller area. For example, if yield per hectare is $1.43x$ instead of x, the radius r of the area πr^2 supplying a given city can be reduced by three-tenths, from $\pi r^2/x$ to $\pi r^2/1.43x$, say from 10 to 7.

Our information on yields in antiquity is very limited, and what we have for particular countries may not be generalizable. We may assume them to be low by modern standards. Agriculture was seldom carried on in a way that made it possible for those in charge of cultivation to make efficient use of accumulated agronomic information and worth their while to invest in so doing. Socioeconomic and political conditions essential to the efficient conduct of agriculture were seldom if ever present.

Reports of n-fold yields, e.g., Matthew, 13:8, provide little information regarding actual yields per acre. One must also know the amount of seed sown, the size of the area planted, the type of crop, and how the yield/seed ratio varied with the quantity of seed sown per unit of area. Fold data reported by Roman authors suggest yields ranging from somewhat over 20 (perhaps 26) bushels per acre in very fertile areas to 9 bushels for Italy as a whole, an average apparently above that in Roman Palestine but corresponding to that reported for France in 1789, but somewhat below the output of mixed grain per acre on the best manors in medieval England.[4]

Before considering yield data for particular times, we may note the average yields normal today in the United States. There 100–125 pounds of rice seed per acre normally produce 4,500 pounds, or

4. Farmer, pp. 150–51; M. E. Seebohm, pp. 162, 173, 216; *Cambridge Economic History,* 1:104, 553, and 125–26, where yields of nine to thirteen fold in the fourteenth century are considered good. C. Clark, *Conditions,* 2d ed., p. 227; Michell, pp. 50–52, 86, and notes. Low seeding rates held down yields in Mesopotamia, according to Adams, *Evolution,* pp. 55–57. See also Oppenheim, *Ancient Mesopotamia* passim; Sperber, p. 11 n.

36–45 fold; 60 pounds of seed wheat normally produce 2,400 pounds of harvested wheat, or 40 fold; 8 pounds of hybrid maize per acre produce 100 or more bushels, or 700 fold at least; 20 pounds of peanuts per acre produce 2,000 pounds of harvested nuts, or 100 fold, and 40 pounds of soybeans produce 2,400 pounds of harvested seed, or 60 fold.

The normal wheat yield in Attica in the fourth century B.C. approximated 0.8 ton per hectare, corresponding to that in modern Greece in 1934–38 but exceeding recent yields in India, about 0.65 ton per hectare. Higher yields were obtained in ancient Egypt, Babylon, and Sicily. In Rome as in England, wheat yields were close to 10 bushels per acre (equivalent to a consumption yield of about 7 bushels per year).[5] They rose in England from less than 10 bushels per acre in 1250, passed the 1963 Indian level (about 12 bushels) in the fifteenth century, and attained a level of 20 bushels per acre around 1700. Rice yield in Japan, about 1,000 pounds per acre in 750 A.D., had doubled by the mid-1700s. Today, of course, British wheat yields are close to 60 bushels per acre, while Japanese rice yields exceed 4,000 pounds per acre. In contrast, in India the yield per acre of milled rice declined from 286 kilograms in the late 1890s to 253 in 1931–35, but thereafter rose; that of wheat, 270 kilograms in 1896–1900, varied between 283 and 321 in 1901–40.[6]

How many persons will a hectare support? The answer, of course, depends on average consumption and average yield. Minimum requirements in terms of kilograms wheat equivalent per head per year range from 230 for small-bodied people in a hot climate to 275 for fairly large-bodied people in a cold climate. If one adds a minimum requirement of textile fibers, the total amount needed per person ranges from 245 to 290 kilograms wheat equivalent.[7] Until consumption approximates 350 kilogram wheat equivalent, most of the increase above the minimum serves to improve the diet if cultivators are free to use it so.[8] In India in the 1930s 0.27 hectare (= ⅔ acre) was required to subsist a person, if he consumed 225 kilograms of milled rice (72½ percent extraction) and if a certain amount was included to exchange for agricultural products other

5. Clark and Haswell, pp. 77–78; Piggott, *Ancient Europe*, pp. 47–49, 68.
6. Lester Brown, chaps. 3, 8, and Appendix.
7. Clark and Haswell, pp. 61–62. Body size probably was smaller in ancient times, given harder conditions of life, than today.
8. Clark and Haswell, p. 53.

than rice.[9] An acre of wheat in antiquity can have supported little more than one person, if that, provided the yield was all used as food except what was used for seed or destroyed by pests; an acre of rice supported only a little more. In medieval Europe around 1300, a man might require as much as 1–3 hectares merely to support himself.[10]

The net amount of grain available for food was less than the gross amount, however. Suppose a gross yield of 900 pounds of wheat per acre. Perhaps 120 pounds or more were used for seed. Storage losses may have amounted to 10–15 percent of the crop stored.[11] An acre might then net only about 700 pounds, or only about 525 pounds if gross yields approximated only 720 pounds. In a good year, then, an acre of wheat would support only between 1 and 1⅓ persons, if so many. An acre of rice with a gross yield of 1,000 pounds would support about 1½ persons. In years when crop yields were reduced by bad weather or plant disease, the carrying capacity of land would be lower.

Agricultural Yield per Cultivator

This average determines both how nonagricultural a society may be and, within limits, how high average output can be. If 1,000 cultivators, together with their families, can produce enough to supply themselves and the equivalent of 200 more families with produce and raw materials, then about one-sixth of a nation's labor force can engage in nonagricultural activities. If a cultivator can supply twenty times as much, those engaged in nonagricultural activities can make up about $^{19}\!/_{20}$ of the labor force. As a result, even if there is no increase in output per nonagricultural worker, overall output per worker will be about five times as high as in the initial situation.

We may infer that output per cultivator was very low in antiquity. "The diets of the broad masses" were "almost exclusively vegetarian" except in areas unadapted to grain production. The golden age of

9. Clark and Haswell, p. 79.

10. *Cambridge Economic History*, 1:670. For a ration of 10 bushels per year, more than an acre per person was required. Piggott, *Ancient Europe*, p. 68. On later English yields, see M. E. Seebohm, pp. 216, 248, 295–96.

11. "Surveys in India show minimum storage losses from all causes of 10 percent for cereals and oil seeds." *World Food Problem*, 2:554. In ancient times birds and wild animals damaged crops in harvesttime. D. R. Das, p. 127.

Athens "was based on 'bread' which now, even in only moderately
civilized countries, would be considered good enough only for
swine." [12] M. K. Bennett conjectures that in the eleventh century
A.D. "roughly a fifth of the world's population," the herdsmen and
the hunters-and-gatherers, had "diets composed almost exclusively
of animal products. The other four-fifths, the townsmen and the
settled agriculturalists and the shifting cultivators, consumed
vegetable products in much larger degree and in some regions
almost exclusively." [13] Most people sought the cheapest of the food
products available to them, and those living in the poorest communities developed diets marked by a high ratio of calories per gram
of wheat equivalent consumed.[14] This ratio had a bearing also on
the transportability of food, conditioning the cost of shipment of
nutrients. Around 1940, for example, while the per capita consumption of food dry-weight ranged, by continent, from 543 pounds in
Asia to 587 in Europe, the wet-weight average ranged from 1,223
pounds in Asia to 1,818 in Oceania. The ratio of dry to wet weight
ranged from around 0.45 in Asia and Africa to 0.31 in Oceania.[15]

Yield per cultivator in ancient times is not easy to get at. Even
today, how much land a cultivator can tend varies greatly, depending as it does upon type of crop, yield, and so on.[16] In a country
like ancient India, total population per 100 members of the agricultural population may have numbered 120 to 140, with 100 agriculturalists supporting as many as 20 to 40 persons in addition to
themselves. Given a gross yield of grain per acre of 720–1,000
pounds and hence a net amount for consumption of 550–800
pounds, a family of five providing support for one or two additional
persons would require 6 or 7 acres in good years. If all of a square
mile were cultivated, population would then number more than
500 per square mile. Yet even in the more densely populated parts

12. Jasny, esp. pp. 229, 244.
13. Bennett, pp. 31–32.
14. Bennett, p. 32; Clark and Haswell, pp. 58–60.
15. Pearson and Harper, p. 12.
16. In India in 1945, at which time about two-thirds of the population were
dependent on agriculture, a fully employed man could look after 2.8 to 8.0
hectares. Clark and Haswell, pp. 119–21. Yet in British India around 1931,
only about five-eighths of the cultivable land was sown, and the area sown per
male agriculturalist averaged only something like 3.5 to 4.0 acres. In 1931 India's
population per square mile was 432 for cultivated land and 213 for all land,
though with density varying widely by province and state. Based on Davis,
chaps. 3 and 21.

of Europe around 1700, population per square mile was in a 105–137 range,[17] and even in India as late as 1941 less than half the country averaged over 200 persons per square mile. If, on an average, one-fourth of each square mile was cultivated each year, density would approximate 160 per square mile, with 115 to 135 engaged in agriculture.

Let us consider the case of contemporary India. There, in 1951, about 83 percent of the population lived in villages and other rural areas, and a corresponding percentage of the labor force carried on its activities in these places; only about 16 percent of the self-supporting population worked in urban centers. While only about two-thirds of the labor force were engaged in agriculture, another one-sixth, or about one-fifth of those employed outside urban centers, carried on nonagricultural activities in rural places. India's orders of magnitude in 1951 are reasonably representative of a country still essentially nonindustrial. If so, we may suppose that in the past at least 65–75 percent of the population and labor force of fairly large countries were engaged in agriculture, with another 15–20 percent living and working in nonurban places (i.e., villages and rural areas), while only 5–20 percent lived in "urban" centers and derived their support there. These proportions might not, of course, fit smaller ancient city-states supported in considerable measure by trade or tribute.

Cost and Speed of Transport

Cost of transport conditioned the size of urban centers and, along with speed of transport, the size and stability of ancient states. Let r represent the distance between an urban center and the perimeter of the area whence it can draw its supply of produce and agricultural raw materials; then this area approximates πr^2. When the distance is 10 miles, the area approximates 201,000 acres; when 20 miles, 804,000 acres. If the support of an individual requires 1 acre, and 75–80 percent of the population are rural, our urban center will number perhaps 50,000 in the one case and 200,000 in the other. These figures are probably too high. After all, even today with modern transport, not much subsistence moves in international trade; around 1940 about 6 percent of world production on a

17. Bowden, p. 3.

dry basis entered trade.[18] It could move less easily in ancient and medieval times. Land transport may have cost 5 or more kilograms grain equivalent per ton-kilometer in ancient times; then the cost of hauling a ton of grain would be 8 percent or more of the value of the ton for a 10-mile journey and 16 percent for a 20-mile journey.[19] While the speed of transport may have conditioned the size and stability of states and the cost of transport, it did not affect the pattern of consumption in ancient times as it would do later when perishables became part of the diet.

Although internal trade in produce and relatively heavy products must have been limited by transport costs in ancient low-energy societies (among them India), this limit applied less markedly to overland trade in which the ratio of value to weight was high, and still less to sea trade. Waterborne trade, mainly by sea, seems to have been of overriding importance, therefore, although subject in greater measure than internal trade to piracy, robbery, and other risks. Waterborne carriage could draw on free energy whereas other carriage could not. The energy cost of building and operating a ship is relatively low; "the surplus energy derived from the sails is potentially enormous as compared with cost of producing the sail and hoisting it." Not at all comparable was the surplus realizable through the use of human power or animal power, which must be fed.[20] As a result, the products that dominated trade were those with high value/weight ratios and those originating close to the sea, or at points on navigable sea-bound rivers, and destined for points near seacoasts.[21] In the Roman world luxury trade in the

18. Pearson and Harper, p. 10.

19. Clark and Haswell give estimates of the cost at various times by various means. Chap. 9, esp. pp. 159–67. See also *Cambridge Economic History,* 1:145 and 389; Goiten, vol. 1, chap. 4, esp. pp. 339–46; Oppenheim, *Ancient Mesopotamia,* passim; Lopez and Raymond, pp. 238–54; Cipolla.

20. Cottrell, chap. 3, esp. pp. 46–49. In the seventeenth century Nehemiah Grew estimated the comparative cost of water, wheeled, and pack-horse carriage at 2, 1, and 16. E. A. J. Johnson, p. 121. Roman sea-transport costs, according to Jasny, "were only about three times those of modern shipping." Clark and Haswell, p. 167. As late as 1830 "the supremacy of the sail was still undisputed on the high seas." L. Gerard, "Transport," in *Cambridge Economic History,* 6, pt. 1:216. See also Goiten, vol. 1, chap. 4.

21. See, for example, Casson; Cottrell, chaps. 3–4. Some ancient transport was not commercial. Long-distance transport of heavy objects, mainly stone, was financed by oppressive governments, not by profit-seeking private enterprisers. See, for example, Heizer. In lower Mesopotamia up-river travel time was about four times down-river travel time. Leemans, pp. 1–2.

aggregate was small in relation to what we should call gross national product. Moreover, "excessive costs of transport by land" made for the diffusion of manufacture as population spread inland. Trade out of a city or region "was economically significant only in the basic foodstuffs (corn, wine, olives), in slaves, and in luxury goods." [22] Even in respect of basic foodstuffs that were low-priced but bulky, the direction of movement was toward and over water, which provided transport far cheaper than that overland. [23]

Some trade took place long before towns, the single most important concomitant of exchange, came into existence in the Fertile Crescent more than a millennium before the Indus Valley civilization began to flourish over four millennia ago. This civilization participated in the trade that began first to develop in the Mesopotamian world. In special shipyards of Sumer quite large wooden boats, some with "a little over five register tons," were constructed for "long sea voyages to Melunna and Dilman"; Dilman is identified as the Indus Valley or the island of Bahrein, which also engaged in some trade with the Indus Valley. [24]

Pattern of Urbanization

How large a fraction of a population can be made available for nonagricultural activities has always depended upon how productive agriculturalists are. This does not tell us, however, where the nonagricultural population will be located. In ancient times much of it, of course, had to be located near the cultivators, in villages, temples, and the like, since transport was expensive. As a rule, the nonagriculturalist resembled a workman living in a city in or before the late 1700s; he had to live in or near his place of work, which was near the agricultural population using his services. He thereby minimized the cost of transporting both his subsistence and what he sold to his agriculturalist clientele. The ratio of villages to towns was therefore very high, as in modern underdeveloped countries—often 200 or more to 1. After all, a draft animal could hardly make a round trip in a day of more than 3 or 4 miles one way, if that far, given the available roads and frequent lack of access to them.

Transport was the key to both the internal structure of cities

22. Finley, "Technical Innovation," pp. 41–42.
23. See Philip Jones's account of trade in medieval Italy, in *Cambridge Economic History*, 1:389.
24. Kramer, *Sumerians*, pp. 104, 276, 279, 281, 289; Glob and Bibby.

and the pattern of urbanization, including city size. When transportation is slow and expensive, workers must remain close to their places of work. In the ancient world's cities, therefore, space was limited, settlement was compact, and numbers were crowded, since multistory structures, being less frequent and less tall than in modern times, did not so greatly increase the ratio of floor to ground space. In Mesopotamia, L. Woolley estimates, population density fell within a range of 120–250 per acre, not greatly different from Aleppo and Damascus around 1900. Density within the walls of Susa around 2000 B.C. may have approximated 160 per acre. By contrast, in the United States density for the whole urban population lay within a range of 4–6 persons per acre in 1790–1950 and averaged only 20 per acre in very large cities, though New York in 1870 had 326 per acre and Old Delhi in 1951 had about 214.[25]

Consider now the impact of transport upon city size and hence upon the distribution of population among cities. The inhabitant of a town or city consumed annually in ancient times the equivalent of 500–600 or more pounds of wheat, and in England in the seventeenth and eighteenth centuries, between 600 and 800 pounds.[26] The weight per inhabitant of what entered into goods produced in a city and normally sold outside the city was much lower. Accordingly, economy was achieved through locating urban and industrial activities in regions where food was abundant and cheap, since transport costs on what flowed into a city and out of it would thus be minimized. Then, "the attraction of food is overwhelming," [27] even as Adam Smith observed nearly two centuries ago.[28] It was

25. C. Clark, *Population Growth*, pp. 339–41; Woolley, esp. pp. 246–48; Galion and Eisner, p. 66; Adams, "Agriculture"; Clawson, pp. 105, 108; Sovani, p. 80.

26. The former figure is in keeping with estimates of Clark and Haswell, pp. 61–62, and 53. The latter figure is from Dean, pp. 25, 27. In medieval England, however, a cultivator's family sometimes averaged as little as 360 pounds of mixed grain per head. Postan, p. 586.

27. Dean, p. 27, and 23–24.

28. Smith wrote that "an inland country, naturally fertile and easily cultivated, produces a great surplus beyond what is necessary for maintaining its cultivators, and on account of the expense of land carriage, and inconveniency of river navigation, it may frequently be difficult to send this surplus abroad. Abundance, therefore, renders provisions cheap, and encourages a great number of workmen to settle in the neighborhood, who find their industry can procure them more of the necessaries and conveniences of life than in other places." These workmen produce goods whose weight is only a very small fraction of their own subsistence. So "corn, which could with difficulty have been carried abroad in its own shape, is in this manner exported in that of the complete manufacture, and may easily be

not possible to set up urban centers where agricultural productivity was low and foodstuffs had to be imported from a distance and hence were expensive. For example, in the sixteenth century, the Iberian Peninsula, unable to support over 50–60 persons per square mile, instead of double that many as in industrial Europe, was under economic pressure to export most of its raw wool to regions richer in food.[29]

This situation did not change greatly until modern times. Urban food imports had to satisfy minimal requirements for all, and for many, demands in excess of minimal requirements. At the same time, output per worker did not rise notably until modern times. When it did, however, the per capita weight of materials used up or incorporated in exports rose above that of the foodstuffs. Hence the locational attraction of cheap food supplies diminished while that of places with relatively low material-shipping costs rose.[30] But this change was not experienced in the ancient world, except possibly in respect of pottery, wine, and oil.

Thus the high cost of land transport, together with the low productivity of agriculture, limited both urban growth and the capacity of cities for growth. Preindustrial cities typically included no more than 5–10 percent of a country's population. Cities of over 100,000 were "sparse," and those of 25,000 to 100,000 were "uncommon." Most common were cities with 10,000 or fewer inhabitants.[31] The local foodshed was too small, as a rule, to support much larger urban concentrations. For example, even a foodshed with a 20-mile radius and a population density of 200 per square mile would hardly support a city of fifty or sixty thousand. Given water transport, however—especially sea transport connecting a city with highly productive food-producing areas—the carriage-cost barrier would be reduced and greater urban growth would

sent to the remotest corners of the world." A. Smith, pp. 382–83. "The sites of the Syrian cities were dictated by the fertility of the soil," Woolley states. Even the Phoenicians, who located cities at points favorable to trade, sought to control enough nearby territory to supply them with foodstuffs. Woolley, pp. 257–59. Adequacy of subsistence was, of course, only a necessary condition; it was not a sufficient condition.

29. Dean, pp. 24–25. On effect of high productivity see Morley, also Millon.

30. Dean, pp. 30–33.

31. Sjoberg, *Preindustrial City*, p. 83. Even in the United States as late as 1910 there were 75,000 places with fewer than 2,500 inhabitants, 974 with 5,000 to 25,000, and 228 with over 25,000. Taeuber, pp. 116–17.

become possible. This barrier was less restrictive also in "tribute states," whose major urban centers were supported in part by tribute that paid its own carriage, especially when it could move by sea, canal, or river.

In the ancient world, cities were, as noted and expected, generally small, and they remained so in the Middle Ages and the early modern period. As late as 1800 only 3 percent of Europe's population and 1 percent of Asia's population lived in cities of over 100,-000.[32] Cities were small even in the Mesopotamian world, where the concepts of urban living and the city-state seem to have originated and whence they spread.[33] Ancient Ur may have numbered only 10,000 people around 2000 B.C., though the city-state at its peak may have included 200,000; while Lagash, with a territory of about 750,000 acres, two-thirds of them "naturally irrigated land," may have had a free population numbering 100,000. This calculated density, 85 per square mile, is too low, of course, since there must have been a considerable number of slaves as well.[34] Densely populated Susa in the second millennium B.C. numbered not over 40,000.[35] Woolley estimates the population of several Assyrian cities as ranging between nine and sixty-five thousand, and that of Syrian and Egyptian cities as small.[36] Phoenician cities too remained small, since the Phoenicians sent out colonies, as did the Greeks, when a city's population became too large.[37] Athens in the fourth century B.C. included something like 124,000 free persons and 20,000 slaves.[38] The city-state Carthage, an exporter of agricultural produce in the fourth century B.C., may have had a population of 400,000 or more at its peak.[39] The city of Rome may have numbered around 300,000, or perhaps not so many; Constantinople

32. Woytinsky, p. 118. There were only 36 cities with over 100,000 inhabitants.
33. On the Sumerian origin of the city-state, see Kramer, *Sumerians*, pp. 288–89. In the third millennium B.C. Sumer "consisted of a dozen or so city-states, each having a large and usually walled city surrounded by suburban villages and hamlets." Ibid., p. 73. See also Jawad, chaps. 1 and 4, pp. 104–16.
34. Kramer, *Sumerians*, pp. 76, 88–89; Sjoberg, "Origin," pp. 56–57, and idem, *Preindustrial City*, pp. 82–83. Babylon covered 2,500 acres; Nineveh, 1,850; Assur, 150. Oppenheim, *Ancient Mesopotamia*, pp. 140–41.
35. Adams, "Agriculture," pp. 114–15.
36. Woolley, pp. 246–48, 250, 252, 256.
37. Woolley, p. 259; Thucydides, *Peloponnesian War*, 1.1; Warmington, pp. 27, 39 ff; A. H. M. Jones, pp. 6, 168–74.
38. A. H. M. Jones, pp. 78–79.
39. Warmington, pp. 150, 153.

never held over 200,000, if that; and Baghdad perhaps 300,000.[40] In China and Japan cities larger than those of Europe and the Middle East came into existence, though hardly as large as often reported.[41] Many centuries later, in and around the later thirteenth century, there were no more than seven or eight European cities with over 50,000 inhabitants.[42] In fourteenth-century England Russell found some evidence of a rank-size rule, but not elsewhere. Here as elsewhere, transport costs (which varied with distance and quality of road or waterway) conditioned the pattern of settlement and limited city size.[43] Eventually transport improved and population increased, with the result that cities grew in size until, by 1800, eighteen European and fourteen Asian cities had more than 100,000 inhabitants each.

Size of State

In the ancient and medieval world, states were usually small. The communications, transport, and common language and culture essential to the maintenance of large states were lacking, with the partial exception of China, the only large ancient state to endure. It is true that great landborne, seaborne, and mixed empires came into existence: Sargon's, the Babylonian, the Egyptian, the Median, the Persian, the Macedonian, the Roman, the Byzantine, the Saracen, the Ottoman. Yet each was but an unstable assemblage of smaller, essentially stable political units and finally collapsed because of internal or external pressure or a combination of these. Presumably, therefore, thinking, policy, and planning tended to be local even within the framework of larger empires. Even so, the size of a state must have influenced a number of conditions found within a state, among them the size of the largest (and probably capital) city which is typically a (somewhat variable) function of a state's size.[44] Among these conditions is the distribution of decision making.

40. Sjoberg, *Preindustrial City*, pp. 82–83; and idem "Origin," p. 6; Russell, "Late Ancient and Medieval Population."

41. Sjoberg, *Preindustrial City*, pp. 81–82.

42. *Cambridge Economic History*, 3:38–39. Several Mughal cities were larger. Naqvi, *Urban Centres*, chaps. 2–3.

43. Russell, "Metropolitan City Region."

44. According to Sawyer ("Dimensions") in the modern world, three dimensions of a nation—size, wealth, and politics—account for 40 percent of the variability in 236 variables. Factors affecting the size of states and empires and accountable for their growth over time have been dealt with by Hart, "Logistic Growth" and idem, *Can World Government Be Predicted*.

Length of Life

Expectation of life at birth must have been very low in the ancient Middle East, mainly because infant and child mortality was very high. An analysis of 250 skeletal remains revealed that 87 percent had died before the age of forty.[45] Given a male life expectancy of 17.55 years at birth, only about 212 of an original 1,000 would be living at age forty.[46] Death would be at the center of life even more than Fourastié interpreted it to be in eighteenth-century France.[47] Where life expectancy is so low, those older than fifty are relatively few and those between ten and twenty-four are relatively many,[48] with the result that earthly time horizons are short, life is cheap, and what counts is the main chance here and sustained chance hereafter. We are not, in ancient times, dealing with a twentieth-century world in which four and even five generations can coexist. There is no point to a fortunate person's troubling greatly about the poverty of an unfortunate person; neither is likely to live long. It is not surprising, therefore, that the ancients, as Finley reports, found wealth, when it came their way, good and in no need of apology or pretense to stewardship.[49]

Population Growth

Population grew very slowly in the ancient and the medieval world. Near the beginning of the first century A.D., the population of the world may have numbered 200–250 million, probably more than double what it had been 800–1,000 years earlier. It was not much larger in the early eleventh century, when the rate of growth accelerated, only to be checked by the Black Death in the fourteenth century. The bulk of the world's population, 1,000–3,000 years ago, lived in Asia, perhaps as much as three-fifths, and this was still true in the seventeenth century, when growth of numbers again began to accelerate. Population progressed slowly and, until

45. Mallowan, p. 96. A life expectancy of less than twenty years is indicated.
46. Coale and Demeny, p. 220.
47. Cf. Fourastié.
48. In ancient times those aged over fifty probably formed only 10 to 14 percent of the population; those between ten and twenty-four, around 28 to 30 percent. The corresponding percentages today may be 30 or slightly higher and around 20. Inferred from tables in Coale and Demeny, pp. 388, 394, 434. I have assumed an expectation of life at birth for males of 17.5 to 25 years and a gross reproduction rate of 2.5 to 3.5.
49. Finley, "Technical Innovation," pp. 31–32.

after the fifteenth century, intermittently, because the causes of high current mortality, together with periodic catastrophes, wiped out all or most of the effects of relatively high gross reproduction rates.

It is perhaps fortunate that population grew so slowly; socio-economic conditions were not favorable to economic growth, even though the potential existed. Yet population pressure periodically became manifest in ancient and medieval times, particularly after numbers had grown for a sustained period, as was quite possible, given the normally high gross reproduction. Colonies were founded, settlement was extended, and indicators of population pressure rose in one or another particular region.[50]

Man's response to population growth in ancient and medieval times was conditioned by the fact that he lived in a quite inelastic agricultural economy, one bearing little resemblance to today's. Thus the response was often really to a worsening of the man-land ratio, a result either of population growth or of a shrinkage in the productivity of land occasioned by soil exhaustion, decline in rainfall, destruction of irrigation systems, or other difficulties. The human response may be examined.

When births continue to exceed deaths in an agricultural economy, population must spread if average income is already at the subsistence level and average output is trending downward. That is, when $O/P = s$, an increase in P must be accompanied by a corresponding increase in O if a decline in s is to be avoided; but this can take place only if P spreads over a greater territory and the man/land ratio P/L is not further reduced. Here O denotes aggregate output; P, population; L, cultivable land; and s, subsistence, where subsistence implies that some though not all inhabitants are at or below the level of subsistence essential to population replacement.

In a modern economy it is usually possible, at least within limits, to increase yield per acre by increasing nonhuman agricultural inputs and/or by utilizing improved methods, plants, and the like. This was seldom possible in ancient economies, at least in the short run; in them the elasticity of agricultural productivity was usually very low or zero. Within limits, of course, as Boserup

50. On the Middle Ages, see *Cambridge Economic History*, vol. 1, chaps. 1, 8, and secs. 2 and 7 of chap. 7.

points out, population pressure may have facilitated technical, economic, and social changes which make for increased productivity. Beyond these limits, an increase in the man-land ratio tended to depress the marginal productivity of agricultural labor and to increase the share claimed by rent as well, unless agricultural labor had an alternative to working in agriculture at a lowered wage. This alternative was seldom present in the ancient or the medieval world. Indeed, in the Graeco-Roman world, Finley believes, dependent labor was abundant.[51]

Economic Growth

We are accustomed, in the modern world, to expect the rate of economic growth to be high, both because the population and the labor force are growing and because output per capita tends to rise. Since population grew very slowly in ancient and medieval times, and average output also grew very slowly for reasons noted below, the rate of aggregate economic growth of states was very low. When a state grew, it usually grew in territorial extent, not in average output, for if external economies were present, they were not effectively exploited.

When the rate of economic growth is very low, policy and expectations are affected. Utopias are distribution-oriented, not production-oriented. It is commonly assumed, at least outside the realm of utility-increasing exchange, that one man's gain is another's loss. No one expects improvement, and there is no scope for an uplifting theory of progress. Conquest and theft come to be looked upon as effective means to wealth, though uncertain.

Barriers to Economic Development

Economic growth proceeded very slowly in ancient and medieval times, and while some people were as well off as many in the nineteenth century, most enjoyed little more than subsistence. Obviously, barriers to growth existed. But were they inherent in ancient economies? Or were they of human origin and did they arise in part at least from man's failure to utilize his productive potential effectively?

Barriers to economic development fall into two categories, the

51. Finley, "Technical Innovation," pp. 43–44. On rent see Clark and Haswell, chap. 6. On the effects of population pressure, see Boserup.

material and the immaterial. Under the heading of the material we may put the physical environment within which a society carries on economic activity, and—the subject we shall next treat —the stock of man-made equipment which the society has at its disposal. Under the heading of the immaterial we may put a society's institutional structure, the state of its arts, its class composition, and its ruling values and value orientations. These distinctions are not as clean-cut, of course, as our simple taxonomy suggests.

First, the magnitude of a society's stock of man-made equipment depends upon the rate at which it augments this stock, and this rate depends upon its social surplus and the uses to which this surplus is put. These uses depend in turn upon the values which animate the ruling circles, since only a minority of a population will receive enough of a low-income society's aggregate output to be able to dispose of a surplus over and above elementary familial and related needs. The values regnant in a society, especially those dominant in ruling circles, play an important part in generating its institutional structure and its class structure, as well as the content of the state of its arts, probably the major component of its immaterial "capital."

In its early preurban stage of material development, a society's rate of material progress is greatly conditioned by the emergence in the agricultural sector of a growing surplus of produce divertible to the support of the nonagricultural sector and nonagricultural activities. Growth of this surplus is a necessary but not a sufficient condition for nonagricultural material progress; it cannot properly be called a cause of such progress. If, however, such a surplus does not emerge and grow, or if, having emerged, it does not in the main support materially productive elements, a society's economy will not develop.[52] Believing that this concept facilitates economic analysis and explanation, we shall suppose that a society's development depends largely upon the magnitude of its "social surplus" and the uses to which this surplus is put. In a modern society we should say that development depends upon the rate of capital formation, material and immaterial, together with

52. Whereas economists regard the emergence of a surplus as essential, anthropologists do not always take this view, presumably because their concern is the total social process of which a surplus is only one of the elements (though a strategic one) constituting the growth process. See Adam Smith, bk. 3, chap. 1; Keyfitz. For the views of anthropologists, see Harris, and the critical comments of George Dalton. See also Polanyi et al., chap. 16, and Childe, *New Light*, passim.

the degree to which this capital is optimally distributed among alternative uses. A surplus available for use outside the sector of elementary want-satisfaction initially came into existence perhaps ten millennia ago and gave rise to an urban civilization about 5,500 years ago, a millennium before the Indus civilization began to develop.[53] Improvement in the climate of the Middle East and perhaps in the Indus Valley may have contributed to the initial emergence of a food surplus.[54]

While surpluses sometimes developed even in primitive societies,[55] they were not of a size and regularity to support an urban society. The requisite degree of support seems to have developed quite gradually,[56] mainly as a result of a number of discoveries in the field of applied science.[57] Supporting surpluses came into existence in India as well as in the Middle East. The productive power of a society should increase faster than its population. If, for example, its productive power per head increased only ¼ percent per year, output per capita would double in about 2¾ centuries. If the "surplus" amounted to 5 percent of the society's annual "net product" and the "productivity" of this increment in "wealth" or "capital" averaged at least 5 percent, output per head would increase about ¼ percent per year, given that population was growing slowly.

Whether an emerging surplus can contribute to the growth of average output in the longer run turns on the uses to which it is put. If it is transformed into increments to a society's population, it cannot contribute to the growth of average income unless this population growth facilitates division of labor and gives rise to economies of scale. Neither can a surplus contribute greatly if it is used to support unproductive wealth and activities. If it is thus used, of course, it may not stimulate population growth, nor intensify population pressure, nor reduce a society's options. It will not, however, increase these options.

It was the unproductive use of emerging surpluses, often to support a prestige economy,[58] that commonly prevented these

53. Braidwood; and Braidwood and Willey; Flannery; Hole; Sjoberg, *Preindustrial City*, passim; Quigley, pp. 70–74.
54. Solecki, p. 192.
55. Herskovits, pt. 5.
56. Zeuner.
57. Childe, *What Happened*, chaps. 2, 5, and 12; and idem, *Man Makes Himself*, chap. 9, pp. 180–81.
58. Polanyi et al., p. 337; Herskovits, pp. 461–86.

surpluses from facilitating even as much as a very slow but continuing increase in average output and income. Indeed, the propensity to use productive power unproductively [59] was dominant in ruling and ecclesiastical circles until modern times and even in the nineteenth century.[60] "All for ourselves, and nothing for other people," observed Adam Smith, "seems, in every age of the world, to have been the vile maxim of the masters of mankind." [61]

In the hierarchical societies that developed in the ancient Middle East, the ruling circles, together with their retainers, devoted their time and effort to war, conquest, the creation of tribute-collecting empires, and other economically unproductive activities.[62] "The upper classes of Ancient Oriental society still wasted a much greater part from the surplus of the production of society to supply their own needs than was justified by the amount of capital at their disposal." [63] In the Graeco-Roman world "funds, manpower and technical skills were made available (and wasted) in vast and ever increasing amounts" by rulers and members of the rentier class.[64] In a world such as the medieval, according to L. Genicot, agriculture, left to itself, "forms little new capital which proprietors can employ in improvements which are often very costly, and such was the medieval social system that the little that was saved from consumption was deflected by the clergy and nobility unto unproductive expenditure. . . . Little or no investment could be expected from the lords," who spent on consumption virtually all that they took in, and "none could be expected from the peasants who had no surplus income available." [65]

The failure of these ancient societies to elevate their incomes

---

59. "No consumption of the class denominated unproductive, has any ulterior effect, beyond the satisfaction of a want by the destruction of existing value." Say, bk. 3, chap. 4, p. 396.
60. "Great inequality of private fortune is hostile to those kinds of consumption that must be regarded as most judicious. In proportion as that inequality is more marked, the artificial wants of the population are more numerous, the real ones more scantily supplied, and the rapid consumption more common and destructive. Say, p. 400.
61. A. Smith, pp. 388–89.
62. Childe, *Man Makes Himself,* chap. 9, and idem, *What Happened,* pp. 219–23, 226–28.
63. Heichelheim, 1:166.
64. Finley, "Technical Innovation," p. 37.
65. L. Genicot in *Cambridge Economic History,* 1:670–71, and 721. In England a peasant who produced, net of seed, 60 bushels of mixed grain had to set aside "at least one half . . . for rent, taxes, and similar outgoings." Ibid., p. 586.

slowly over the centuries is ultimately traceable in considerable part to the values regnant among those who were in possession of the apparatus of state and other sources of power. It is traceable also to the values permeating the culture of the underlying population, often ridden by superstition, and to the constraints under which a small and obviously skilled as well as relatively well-to-do mercantile class functioned.

These values were responsible not merely for the failure to make productive use of the craftsmen released to nonagricultural undertakings by the emergence of a surplus of subsistence above ordinary requirements. They also caused science, scientific method, and invention to be diverted from productive use, and they probably were responsible as well for the fact that efficiency and economic rationalism never took much hold.[66] Utilitarianism never seized the reins.

Organizational Dimensions

The decisions which govern economic and political as well as much other behavior depend upon a society's organizational structure, whose extent, though not its form, is fixed largely by the society's physical dimensions. The capacity of this structure is determined by a number of conditions, among them size of community and markets, state of technology, skill of management, and available means of communication and record keeping. In the ancient world states were far from large, or if large, amounted to unstable collections of small and relatively stable entities. Cities were few and small and, as a rule, the bulk of the population lived in villages. Conditions varied, of course, with the stage of a country's development. Thus, in India, the village-dominated society described in the Rig-Veda gave place to one in which, as population increased to be quite dense in the North, towns grew and markets and trade expanded.

Economies of scale did not flourish in the ancient world. Often they did not exist. When they existed potentially, business firms were usually too small to exploit them fully. Even in the Roman world, Finley reports, there were no long-term private organiza-

66. Finley, "Technical Innovation," pp. 30–37.

tions, partnerships, corporations, or other such investments or effective arrangements for assembling funds.[67]

Distribution of Decision-Making Power

Private decision-making power in the ancient world was widely diffused among the many small decision-making units that made up the private economic sector. Moreover, banking and financial institutions were not organized in a manner suited to augment greatly the capacity for accomplishing decision enjoyed by individual entrepreneurs. Accordingly, when great tasks, public or military, imposed themselves, they could be accomplished only by the state. It alone could mobilize resources on a large scale. Illustrative is the massive transformation of Egypt accomplished by the Ptolemies, which reclaimed land, improved irrigation, introduced new crops and methods, and so on.[68] Perhaps illustrative also is the impact upon private enterprise of concentrated and continuing demands flowing from ancient military establishments.[69]

An economic interpreter or administrator always has an overall image of that which he describes, explains, regulates, or administers, together with lesser images of components of the larger image. He also conceives of his options in terms of these images. The images reflect both objective elements in his physical and organizational environment and subjective elements present in his culture. In this chapter we have indicated some of the physical and organizational constraints present in ancient economies. These were important in shaping the approach of ancient writers to the study of their economies. They did not determine the approach, but they fixed the confines within which it was formed. In the next section we deal with the manifestation of these constraints in India.

67. Finley, "Technical Innovation," pp. 36–38, and idem, "Land, Debt." On the limited scope of economies of scale in underdeveloped societies, see Stolper, chap. 3. On the role of economic mechanisms and bureaucracy in historical bureaucratic societies, see Eisenstadt, pp. 33–49, 105–7; 273–99, 361–72. On the role of writing see Gelb.

68. Rostovtzeff, *Ancient World*, 1:363, and idem, *Hellenistic World*, 1:267–332, 407–15; Finley, "Technical Innovation." See also George, chap. 1.

69. E.g., on the early modern impact, see Nef, chaps. 4–5.

Chapter 2

Civilization, Economy, Economics

The entire course of Indian history shows tribal
elements being fused into a general society.

D. D. KOSAMBI

Every civilization is its own miracle.

ROMILA THAPAR

In the preceding chapter we identified many dimensions that de-
limit the institutions upon which economic discussion may focus.
In chapters to come, we deal initially with representative economic discussion in India before the British became ascendant
and then with the emergence of "modern" economics in British
India. In the present chapter attention is devoted to a variety of
factors that suggest the character of the early Indian economy and
the degree to which the behavior of this economy was subject to
"economic" analysis, an issue concerning which there continued
to be controversy less than two decades before India became politically independent.[1]

The Early Indian Economy

Although the Indian economy underwent some evolution over
the centuries, it remained predominantly rural even into the nineteenth century. Perhaps nine-tenths of the population continued
to live in rural areas, of whom three-fourths or more were directly
engaged in or lived on agriculture. The standard of life, therefore,
depended overwhelmingly upon the efficiency of agriculture and

1. The term "Indian economics" was introduced by nineteenth-century Indian
writers "who supposed that the principles of economics, as they are taught in the
West, did not apply to Indian conditions." Narain, p. xx. Narain adds that there
is "no science of 'Indian economics,'" since Indians have been economically motivated just as have other men. See also Madan, chap. 9.

the distribution of its fruits. Cultivators had to surrender much of their output to other categories in the population, many members of whom were parasitic—to ruling and landowning elements and their bureaucratic and priestly retainers or associates.

While the economic discussion to which this study relates does not greatly antedate the time of Christ, India's first economy is much older, having emerged after several hundred thousand years of primitive life in the subcontinent. This first relatively well-organized and somewhat urban economy came into existence with the Indus civilization which flourished in the Sind and the Punjab roughly between 2300 and 1700 B.C. or later, at a time when the climate may have been more favorable than today.[2] This civilization attained its highest development in its urban centers, above all in Mohenjo-Daro, a city of perhaps 40,000 inhabitants, and Harappa, both of which were more scientifically planned than contemporary Mesopotamian cities and, like some of them, seem to have functioned much as did tributary states. This civilization finally succumbed, in some places apparently to internal decay, flooding, and external onslaughts and in others to replacement by successor cultures. But before it collapsed, it must have produced social practices and usages that persisted through the centuries, as well as material artifactual forms and a capacity for trade which were reflected in later stages of India's civilization. While the requisite information has not yet been assembled and assayed and literary remains have not been diciphered, it may be concluded that conditions essential to the emergence of economic discussion were present in the Indus civilization even as in civilizations to the west.

The Indus civilization, which (Kosambi believes) had much in common with Mesopotamian civilization, was in commercial contact and possibly contact of other kinds with Sumer and Mesopotamia, at least through an urban center on Bahrein in the Persian Gulf.[3]

2. N. R. Banerjee, chap. 4, 13–14; Piggott, *Prehistoric India*, pp. 68, 134–36. Variations in world climate are discussed in J. S. Sawyer, *World Climate*, but not related to the subcontinent. On Indian stone-age cultures, see also Gordon, chaps. 1–3.

3. Glob and Bibby; Jairazbhoy, chap. 1; R. S. Sharma, *Light*, p. 53; Adams, *Evolution*, pp. 154–56; Oppenheim, *Ancient Mesopotamia*, pp. 63–64; Singer et al., 1:45–46, 202, 760; Kane, 5:598–600; Basham, *Wonder*, chaps. 1–2, and pp. 220–31.

Some of the attributes of this civilization were reflected in successor Indian civilizations, though in diluted form. Even today, one finds in India people similar in type to the people apparently predominant in Mohenjo-Daro and Harappa. Conservatism of the sort found in later Indian civilization seems to have characterized the Indus civilization. With the aid of irrigation, however, it apparently generated enough of an agricultural surplus to support a fairly skillful bureaucracy which may have made use of coolie labor and possibly also of slaves. Rudiments of guild and caste organizations appear to have been present as well, together with elements of religion and religious control absorbed into later Hinduism.[4] To what extent Harappan organizations reflected Mesopotamian organizations is not clear.[5]

With the coming of the highly mobile Indo-Iranians to Persia and India near or after the middle of the second millennium B.C.,[6] Indian town life apparently came to an end for over half a millennium, even though plow-equipped Aryan agricultural technology was at least potentially superior to Harappan. In time, however, as the Aryan people settled the land and spread over northern India and as their institutions evolved and their crafts and economic organization improved, urban centers developed again, in and after the sixth century B.C. if not earlier.[7] Iron came into widespread use, rice, sugar, and cotton were widely cultivated, and towns multiplied in northeastern India, together with crafts, guilds, and inland and foreign trade.[8] The success of a town was determined mainly by its suitability for religious or administrative

4. On the Indus civilization, see Banerjee, chaps. 4, 13–14; Kosambi, *Introduction,* chap. 3; R. S. Sharma, *Light,* pp. 53–54; Singer et al., pp. 50, 76, 195, 202–3, 207, 522, 717, 719; Piggott, *Prehistoric India,* esp. chaps. 5–7; Gordon, chaps. 4–5; Jairazbhoy, chap. 1, and p. 25; Wheeler in Piggott, *Dawn,* chap. 8, and Wheeler, *Indus Civilization;* Childe, *New Light,* chaps. 9–10, esp. pp. 170, 186–88, 199–200, 204–6; Sankalia; Dales; Ray, pp. 7–8, 46–47, 124–36; S. D. Singh, *Ancient Indian Warfare,* passim; Mode; Clauson and Chadwick; Casal.
5. On guilds and other institutions in Mesopotamia, see Oppenheim, *Ancient Mesopotamia.*
8. R. S. Sharma, *Light,* pp. 60–65. On the Deccan see D. R. Das, chaps. 4–5, Gimbulas, pp. 827, 834; Gordon, chap. 5; Jairazbhoy, chap. 2; Ruben, "Rgveda"; Chakadar; Banerjee, chap. 5.
7. R. S. Sharma, *Light,* pp. 55–60, esp. p. 59; Kosambi, *Introduction* pp. 126–32, 136–38, 176–77; Bandyopadhyaya, 1:327–333; Wagle, chap. 2.
8. R. S. Sharma, *Light,* pp. 60–65. On the Deccan see D. R. Das, chaps. 4–5, 9, 13.

purposes (inclusive of protection and defense) or for trade, especially at points with water transport. Town size was limited by the accessibility of subsistence.[9] The degree of urbanization, while always low, fluctuated with the prevailing degree of political order and stability; it increased when governments were strong and trade was relatively secure (as under Akbar) and decreased when an opposite set of conditions developed, as in India north of the Vindhyas when Mughal rule weakened.[10] While a first-class city proper had a radius of 2½ to 6 miles, the radius of its jurisdiction extended into the country, perhaps 10 miles or more.[11] The city thus offered workers and the professional and trading classes residence within its jurisdiction and some protection against marauding aristocrats.[12]

While average income may have been higher in late pre-Maurya times than in Indus-civilization times, agriculture and crafts having improved,[13] the standard of life of the Indian masses seems to have been near subsistence, a condition characteristic of most of India's history. Of the land in use in ancient India—perhaps about one-half of that in use in twentieth-century British India—only one-fourth or one-fifth was cropped in any year, Nath believes, though on a basis apparently involving a good deal of conjecture. This amounted to 15–25 acres for the support of the landlord and his family, together with four or five tenant families, or about 1 acre per person, an amount sufficient for the support of one adult, if not taxed.[14] Over the centuries, therefore, the amount of land required to support a family seems to have been around 5 or 6 acres, close to the amount which a family apparently could cultivate. The data suggest, therefore, that between the fifth century B.C. and the nineteenth century, the amount of land required to support an adult was probably in the neighborhood of an

9. R. S. Sharma, *Light*, pp. 62–65; A. Ray, p. 7; Chakraborti, chaps. 3–4; A. N. Bose, 1:193–234. This work deals with the period 600 B.C. to 200 A.D. See also B. B. Dutt; Puri; Cunningham; Niyogi, chap. 5; D. R. Das, chap. 7; Darian.

10. A. Ray, pp. 31–32; also Naqvi, "Progress of Urbanization" and *Urban Centres*.

11. Nath, pp. 66–68. The period referred to is the sixth and seventh centuries A.D. See also A. Ray, pp. 52–62; Basham, *Wonder*, pp. 198–203 and 164.

12. Nath, pp. 133–38. See also A. Bose, vol. 1, bk. 2.

13. R. S. Sharma, *Light*, pp. 60–65, 89; also Kane, 3:162–64, on agriculture, irrigation, and double-cropping.

14. Nath, pp. 40–41, 82–85. In some regions two harvests were gathered annually. D. R. Das, chap. 4.

acre.[15] Around 1930, 0.27 hectare ($=\frac{2}{3}$ acre) was required to
subsist an average person at a minimum level (225 kilograms of
milled rice, 72½ percent extraction) according to Clark and Haswell.[16] Allowance for necessary fibers and for nonfood requirements would raise the minimum support level by one-tenth or
more, say to ¾ acre. Further allowance for seed, crop, food losses,
and so on, raises this amount to about 1 acre. While temples may
have paid comfortable wages, the condition of most tenants, cultivators, and landless laborers must have been miserable.[17]

Not only were yields per acre low over the centuries, manifesting
little improvement; they also varied greatly because rainfall varied
as much as 30 percent or more per year, even in regions of low
rainfall—too much for widespread irrigation to offset. An irregular
monsoon, therefore, periodically condemned parts of India to
famine, in the absence of adequate food reserves. "Moghul India
at the beginning of the 17th century was not a very unhappy India
in ordinary years." [18] Many years, however, were not "ordinary,"
especially in the ages when transport was not good.[19]

Had the average income, together with the condition of the
underlying cultivating masses, improved over time, it would have
been much higher in 1800 than it was. For example, had average
income ($=$ average output) approximated subsistence *s* in 300 B.C.
and then risen 1 percent every twenty years, it would have approximated 1.9*s* by 1000 A.D., and about 3*s* by 1800. Yet it was not
much if any higher in 1800 (or 1600) than in 300 B.C. Pran Nath
describes the "standard of comfort among the labouring classes"
as "very low" in the eleventh century A.D., as well as in Akbar's
time, and implies that it was no better in earlier times, the rise in

---

15. Nath, pp. 84–85; C. S. Sharma, *Light,* pp. 62, 73. The latter makes the
amount required per family—6 *nirvatanas*—approximate 9 instead of 6 acres.
Nath (p. 80) makes it 6 acres. A requirement of but 1 acre per person compares
favorably with requirements in many places. Adams, *Evolution,* pp. 43–45, 55–57.

16. Clark and Haswell, pp. 79 and 61–62.

17. Nath, p. 161. In and around the eleventh century A.D. the annual wage
ranged from 50 *kalams* of paddy per year to 200 for accountants and dancing
masters and 400 for a teacher of Vedanta. Nath, p. 146; R. K. Mookerji, *Local
Government,* pp. 138–39; Nagaswamy, p. 370. See also on the temples Niyogi,
chap. 10, and Gopal, *Economic Life,* passim; and on the importance of the temple-
building industry, Sundaram, p. 22.

18. Narain, p. 85.

19. On famines, see Narain, chap. 5 and p. 29; see also nn. 27 and 28 below. On
rainfall, see Davis, p. 11.

money wages having just about kept pace with the rise in prices.[20] Colin Clark indicates, however, that real wages may have been higher in the eleventh century than in the early seventeenth century, at which time they still were higher than they would be in the eighteenth and the nineteenth centuries.[21]

Three factors contributed to the lowness of average output and its failure to increase notably. One was the misuse of the social surplus and lack of improvements in agriculture. A second was the disesteem in which cultivators were held by the upper classes. The tiller's life was very hard. His social status had been low in the past and continued so, and his material status was little if any better. Thus tillers did not benefit greatly even when weather conditions were good.[22] Edwin Arnold did not write inaccurately when in his *Light of Asia,* he remarked "How the swart peasant sweated for his wage,/Toiling for leave to live." One may, therefore, describe India's economy as a "pain economy," one in which, according to S. N. Patten, coiner of the term, "fear and suffering drive man to his daily tasks." [23] A third barrier to growth was population pressure, described below. When population grew, the living standards of the common man did not rise notably, even though India's age composition was not unfavorable. Its population must have included few old persons—perhaps 3 in 100 were over sixty-five years old [24]—and relatively fewer persons under fifteen than today—perhaps 38 in 100. Its adult fraction—probably around 59 in 100, as a rule—was thus higher than that found in much of today's underdeveloped world.

India's population must have lived in a Malthusian trap. Numbers kept pace with the food supply, increasing, when food sur-

<hr/>

20. Nath, chap. 7, esp. pp. 147–49.
21. C. Clark, *Conditions,* 3d ed., pp. 206–7. Narain describes the "ordinary laborer," the artisan, and the tiller as better off in the sixteenth and seventeenth centuries than in the early twentieth. Narain, chaps. 1–2. Srikantan believes that wages exceeded subsistence in ancient India; but see A. N. Bose, 2:202–13, 254–75.
22. Adhya, pp. 42–45. This work deals with the period 200 B.C. to 300 A.D.
23. See n. 55 below. "It is possible," Narain concedes (pp. 1–2), "that at the time when Bernier visited India (1656–58) the ground 'was seldom tilled except under compulsion,' and the whole country became a desert."
24. The advent of old age was dreaded in ancient India, so much so that death was welcomed. See citations from the sacred books in Hammett, pp. 60–62, 64. A Hindu's acquiescence in withdrawal from social life after having completed his householder–active-worker stage of existence may be traceable in part to the fact that relatively few survived this stage. On the stages, see K. M. Sen, *Hinduism,* chap. 3.

pluses emerged, to depress average income or at least accentuate the forces holding it down. Agricultural methods, the key to advancing income, seem to have improved very little between Maurya times and the ascendancy of the British.[25] Long-run increase in aggregate agricultural output had therefore to come mainly from extension of cultivation into uncultivated areas, a process which may have nearly doubled the land in use between (say) 100 and 1900 A.D.[26] Undoubtedly, the pressure of numbers upon land made for such extension. Mortality must have been very high, of course, with expectation of life at birth not exceeding twenty-five years. Even so, numbers could have increased appreciably; for, given a gross reproduction rate of 3.0, the population would grow about 0.7 percent per year, enough to virtually double the population each century and to augment it over 500 times each millennium. This did not happen, however, since epidemics and famine periodically cut down the population and reduced life expectancy to much below twenty-five years. Epidemics were recurrent, though varying in intensity. Famine, associated mainly with failure of rainfall, had become "a major agrarian problem before the dawn of the Christian era." [27] Indeed, more than two millennia ago men recorded on a limestone slab from Mahasthan "the measures taken by the local authority in the third century B.C. to combat" the earliest known Bengal famine by the "issue of Paddy from reserve stocks." [28] This famine, occurring in the third century B.C., must have had many predecessors as well as many successors. Epidemics may be described similarly.

According to some estimates of India's population, it grew little or not at all between 300 B.C. and 1800. According to others, it grew intermittently. Pran Nath put the figure for the former date

25. Narain, p. 27. "The system of cultivation was not very different from that of the present time," writes Adhya, pp. 42–43. He refers in particular to the types of tools in use. See also Maity, p. 76. Among the tools, instruments, methods, and conveyances persisting since ancient times are a number of Indus Valley origin or vintage. See Singer et al., pp. 45, 46, 195, 202–3, 207, 246, 717, 719; and Clark and Haswell, p. 75, on low productivity of traditional agricultural methods.

26. This is inferable from Nath's data (p. 22). In the seventh century, "the area of cultivated land diminished the further south" one traveled, according to Hsüan Tsang. Thapar, *History*, p. 168.

27. A. N. Bose, 1:134 and 129–50 passim. See also D. R. Das, chaps. 4, 6; Maity, pp. 84–86; Bandyopadhyaya, pp. 324–25; Gopal, *Economic Life*, pp. 248–50. For an account of modern famines see S. Ray.

28. Wheeler in Piggott, *Dawn*, p. 242; compare Kane, 3:163–64. In the sixteenth century "the agricultural Hindu mass remained at a subsistence level, punctuated by famines and floods." Spear, pp. 24, 34.

at 100–140 millions,[29] less than J. M. Datta's estimate of 181 million as of 320 B.C., but more than the "figure of about 100 million or less" which Thapar and others find "more credible." [30] Around 1600 India's population approximated only 100 million, according to W. H. Moreland, and then (according to Colin Clark) grew to 200 million by 1700 only to remain around this figure for a century.[31] By 1800 India's population approximated 120 millions, according to Davis's estimates (based upon those of William Playfair).[32] It had begun to grow with the lessening of warfare and banditry and, subsequently, of famine and disease under newly established European control. Even so, growth was virtually halted as late as in the 1890s by famine, and in 1911–21 by influenza. Yet India's population grew, to exceed 285 million by 1901 and to approximate 306 million by 1921.[33] The marked acceleration of India's population growth since 1800 appears to be mainly a sequel to European rule and order, along with Western influence and practice, even as in the Harappan period it was a response to the introduction of irrigated agriculture and political order. At the same time it is probable that population grew between 300 A.D. and Akbar's time. Cultivation was extended in that interval as well as in 1600–1800. The food supply must therefore have grown, and with it population. After all, even when mortality is very high, it is possible for a population to grow, albeit slowly.

The Indian Polity

One cannot write of India's polity since there was no such thing even in the days of independence. India always consisted of a number of "sovereign" units—kingdoms or republics—comprising

29. Nath, chap. 5; Kingsley Davis (p. 24) finds Nath's estimate acceptable. Until a detailed history of India's settlement is written, information regarding population trends will be deficient.

30. Thapar, *History*, p. 27.

31. Moreland, *India*, pp. 9–22; C. Clark, *Population Growth*, pp. 64, 75–76. Moreland's figure may be too low, Davis believes (p. 24). Clark (p. 64) puts the population of India and Pakistan at 70 million in A.D. 1400 and 79 million in 1500.

32. Davis, p. 25. Bennett (p. 9), who gives 157 million for 1800, puts the population at 48, 68, and 100 million in the periods around 1000, 1600, and 1700, respectively. His estimates, according to which India included about one-sixth of the world's population in 1000 A.D., imply that India's population grew at about the same rate as the world's between 1000 and 1950.

33. Davis, pp. 25, 27, 33.

lesser stable units (especially regions and villages) into which larger unstable units decomposed in times of crisis. Accordingly, the small rather than the large state was the rule. Between 600 and 1000 A.D., India comprised 5 regions and 84 states (*desha*), estimates Pran Nath.[34] Already by 600 B.C. India had developed into a land of small states. In the North, before the emergence of the Maurya Empire, 321–185 B.C., there were sixteen "major states," while in the South in Ashoka's time there were four. Upon its collapse, the Maurya Empire broke up into smaller states, as did the Gupta Empire upon its collapse after attaining sway over much of central India in the fourth and fifth centuries A.D. The last of India's extensive empires, the Mughal, ascendant over much of the subcontinent in the late sixteenth and seventeenth centuries, gave way in the eighteenth century to lesser "states" and British rule.

Because of this instability, the power to decide, together with the task of implementing decision, was lodged for the most part at the local level, with village organizations, castes, guilds, corporations, temples, joint families, and so on. Here this power was, of course, subject to constraints—custom, dharma, and regulations emanating from state or provincial government—and to governmentally imposed burdens designed either to support order and collective needs (e.g., overhead capital) or to supply the military ambitions and requirements of the ruling circles, together with excessive consumption on the part of large landowners. Even so, it was local self-government that generated and continued "associated life in Ancient India." To local self-government India largely owes "the preservation of the integrity, independence, and individuality of Hindu culture, despite the world-shaking and catastrophic political movements to which that culture was frequently exposed in the course of her history." [35] State and society coexisted, "in some degree of independence of each other, as distinct and separate units or entities, as independent centres of national, popular, and collective life and activity." Each was required to confine its activities within defined limits that ideally restricted

34. Nath, pp. 14–16, 18–23. See also T. B. Mukherjee; Jayaswal, pt. 1, chaps. 27–28, pp. 354–63.
35. R. Mookerji, *Local Government*, pp. 1–2. See also Chakraborti, chap. 8, on many corporate activities; also D. R. Das, chap. 12.

the role of the state to the protection of life and property.[36] When the central government proved too weak to control the nobility, the laboring classes, seeking protection, organized themselves under the *kaya;* the industrial and professional classes under the *sreni;* and the trading classes under the *nigama.*[37]

These local institutions are of much earlier origin than the state. Oldest of all those that persisted is the village, the fundamental social and economic unit, which occasionally became transformed into a larger-scale unit, the town. The village was based mainly upon agriculture, though occasionally on crafts.[38] It long met emergency problems (e.g., famines)[39] as well as carried out tasks for central governments and performed day-to-day functions, responsibility for which shifted to municipal bodies or corporations when villages evolved into towns. Even so, the village remains the "nucleus of change," a decentralized base for reform.[40] Of great importance in towns and in suburban and nonagricultural villages were the guilds (sreni), each embracing members of specific industries, crafts, or trades, and responsible for professional, public utility, and banking functions. Craft guilds were responsible for training in the crafts, the rules governing apprenticeship, and a variety of industrial, commercial, legislative, and administrative functions. Their responsibilities thus exceeded those that fell upon merchant guilds, bodies created to perform municipal or collective functions, and more transitory partnerships.[41] All these responsibilities seem to have grown during the Gupta period (A.D. 300–550) which succeeded the rise of the "mercantile community" in 200 B.C.–300 A.D.[42] The guilds had come into existence already

36. R. Mookerji, *Local Government,* p. 3. For a theoretical discussion of the relation of state and community, see MacIver.

37. Nath, p. 138. See also Basham, *Wonder,* pp. 217–18, 222–23.

38. See R. Mookerji, *Local Government,* passim; R. S. Sharma, *Light,* pp. 64, 136–37; Adhya, pp. 33–34; A. Ray, pp. 7, 22–33, 46–62. For an account of the nature of change in the village as a community, change of no importance until recently, see Halpern, pp. 62–77; and Dube.

39. R. Mookerji, *Local Government,* pp. 196–200; Basham, *Wonder,* pp. 104–7.

40. See A. N. Bose, 1:77–90 and 193–99, 225–33 on the shading of the village and its functions into the town and its roles. V. B. Singh, *Economic History,* chap. 4.

41. R. Mookerji, *Local Government,* chaps. 2–4, 6, 8; Gopal, *Economic Life,* chap. 4; Adhya, pp. 82–90; D. R. Das, chap. 12; R. S. Sharma, *Aspects.*

42. Thapar, *History,* chap. 6. On the Gupta period, see Maity, chap. 8; also R. S. Sharma, *Light,* on usury, trade, etc.; Gopal, *Economic Life,* chaps. 4, 6–8; D. R. Das, chaps. 8, 12–13.

during the Vedic period.[43] In the course of time the caste system, incipient already among Aryans outside India,[44] permeated the guild system and transformed many guilds into fossilized "occupational subcastes."[45] Types of feudal relations cut across some of the roles of local organizations between the seventh and the fourteenth centuries and later became bases for military fiefs imposed by Moslem conquerors.[46]

The Indian state came into existence in the last millennium B.C., acquiring an effective administrative apparatus around 500 B.C. in Magadha, predecessor to the Maurya Empire.[47] The subdivision of the empire into provinces and districts may have been influenced by Persian practice and culture in the sixth century and thereafter.[48] The Indian organization of state finance seems to reflect Greek influence,[49] which in general was notable in Indian thought and practice.[50] Despite the strengthening of the administrative apparatus under Maurya rule, custom and usage remained dominant.[51] Moreover, with the disintegration of this empire, much power of decision devolved upon local governmental units, and local interests remained strong even under the Guptas,[52] after whose decline feudal regional states emerged.[53]

43. Bandyopadhyaya, pp. 168, 246–53, 329–32; A. N. Bose, 1:281–97, esp. pp. 281–84.
44. Jairazbhoy, pp. 28–29. See also Hutton; R. S. Sharma, *Light*, pp. 7–8, 15–16. The varna system did not, of course, early and quickly evolve into a caste system. E.g., see Thapar, *History*, pp. 37–39, 121, 123, 153, 189; S. D. Singh, *Ancient Indian Warfare*, pp. 138–41.
45. Gopal, *Economic Life*, p. 82. This book deals with northern India in A.D. 700–1200. Cf. R. Mookerji, *Local Government*, pp. 59–72, on the earlier, less restrictive impact of caste rules.
46. Based on a lecture by Dietmar Rothermund. See also Basham, *Wonder*, pp. 52–58, 93–96, 98.
47. Thapar, *History*, pp. 55–56; Bandyopadhyaya, 1:306–13; V. S. Agrawala, pp. 424–33, 443–54, 477–96; Gonda.
48. Jairazbhoy, chap. 4. Cyrus "adopted in principle the organization first devised by the Assyrians, who replaced the states they had conquered by formal provinces. Each was ruled by a governor with a full staff of subordinates, and all kept in close touch with the central power through a frequent exchange of orders and reports." Olmstead, p. 59.
49. Jairazbhoy, pp. 68–69.
50. Jairazbhoy, chap. 5. See also Banerjee. On Greek-Persian influence, see also N. R. Ray.
51. "Legislation was largely a matter of confirming social usage." Thapar, *History*, p. 82.
52. Thapar, *History*, p. 145.
53. Thapar, *History*, chap. 11; Jayaswal, chaps. 17–20.

Economic Motivation

Throughout most of India's history her economy answered to S. N. Patten's pain economy—an economy "in which fear and suffering drive man to his daily tasks." It is to be distinguished from a pleasure economy "in which the motive of action is the pleasure derived from the goods enjoyed." [54] It is also an economy dominated by "clingers" and hence little prone to progressive change. [55] Of it one may say what Finley said of the Roman world: "There was never the slightest danger in antiquity that the lower classes would be anything but poor." [56]

It would be misleading, however, to infer too much from a distinction between a pain and a pleasure economy. In each the economic motive is overriding, however narrowly the arena within which it operates is circumscribed. Each man is animated, as a rule, by what Adam Smith called the universal "desire of bettering our condition." [57] Indeed, one may assume that even when man's behavior is not very rational in an economic sense, and even though he allocates resources badly, he looks upon wealth as a good thing and as essential to a good life. [58] He is sensitive, therefore, to differences in alternatives, some of which he finds preferable to others. This sensitivity has been demonstrated to be operative even in low-income societies. [59] We may take it for granted, therefore, that, while the welfare indices animating men include noneconomic components (some of which are self-regulating), [60] these indicators are usually dominated by material or economic considerations, above all in economies in which incomes are very low. He who would direct the activities of others effectively must accordingly

54. This distinction, present in Patten's early works, he later (in 1912) modified when he divided "progress into three stages: a pain economy, a pleasure economy and a creative economy." Patten, *Essays,* pp. 337–38. Bahadur describes casteism as a symptom of "pain economy."

55. The "clinger," a product of localities with restricted food supplies, clings to what he has, and develops into a timid, conservative immobile type to whom the utilitarian calculus of pleasures and pains is foreign. Patten, *Development,* pp. 23–25.

56. Finley, "Technical Innovation," p. 43.

57. Adam Smith, p. 324; and pp. 8, 326, 329, 508, 632.

58. E.g., see Finley's analysis, "Technical Innovation," pp. 29–45, esp. pp. 31–32, 36.

59. E.g., W. O. Jones; Bauer and Yamey, pp. 89–101.

60. Even Indian asceticism may be more self-regarding than altruistic. K. M. Sen, *Hinduism,* pp. 24, 64.

take these considerations into account. He who would analyze the
behavior of individuals must do likewise.

Of economic sensitivity we have evidence even in the Rig-Veda,
the first and earliest of the ancient religious books of Hinduism,
composed, possibly as early as the fifteenth century B.C., during the
period of the dispersal of the Aryans from their uncertain region
of origin to western Asia and India.[61] In a secular lyric included
among the Rig-Veda hymns and relating to a period when the
caste barrier was negligible (IX, 112),[62] we read:

> We all have various hopes and plans
>   and many are the ways of men:
> The craftsman seeks for jobs to do,
>   the priest his flock, the leech the sick.

> The arrow-smith with hard dry reeds
>   and feathers from the airy birds,
> Bronze for the tips, and glowing coals,
>   seeks out the man who'll pay him best.

> I am a poet, dad's a leech
>   and mother grinds corn on the quern:
> As cows go following, one on one,
>   we all seek wealth in different ways.

We have much evidence also in the Panchatantra stories dating
from about 200 B.C., though of earlier origin.[63] The importance of
money and money motives are touched upon in many verses:

> A king may scold
>   Yet servant hold
> If but he pay
>   Upon the day.

> Money gets you everything
>   Gets it in a flash:
> Therefore let the prudent get
>   Cash, Cash, Cash.

> The calf deserts the cow
>   whose udder has gone dry.

61. Piggott, *Prehistoric India*, pp. 254–55.
62. Piggott, *Prehistoric India*, p. 272. See the Rig-Veda translated by Griffiths
(1896). Some pandits rejected ascetic values and endorsed the aphorism, "Live
well, as long as you live. Live well even by borrowing." Sen, *Hinduism*, p. 63;
Basham, *Wonder*, pp. 215–16.
63. I have used Ryder's translation of the recension (in Sanskrit) of 1199 A.D.
This is really a nitishastra, or textbook of *niti*, "the wise conduct of life."

The smell of wealth is quite enough
To wake a creature's sterner stuff.

King's favor is a thing unstable
Crows peck at winnings charitable;
You make, in learning the professions,
Too many wearisome concessions
To teachers; farms are too much labor;
In usury you lend your neighbor
The cash which is your life, and therefore
You really live a poor man. Wherefore
I see in trade the only living
That can be truly pleasure-giving.
Hurrah for trade! [64]

The painfulness of poverty is stressed:

No poor man's evidence is heard,
Though logic link it word to word:
While wealthy babble passes muster
Though crammed with harshness, vice, and bluster.

The wealthy, though of meanest birth,
Are much respected on the earth:
The poor whose lineage is prized
Like clearest moonlight, are despised.

The wealthy are, however old,
Rejuvenated by their gold:
If money has departed, then
The youngest lads are aged men.

Since brother, son, and wife, and friend
Desert when cash is at an end,
Returning when the cash rolls in,
'Tis cash that is our next of kin.[65]

The troubles of the perennial poor were summed up not merely in ancient India. An ancient Sumerian writer expressed a universal plaint when he declared:

The poor man is better dead than alive;
If he has bread, he has no salt,

64. Ryder, pp. 49, 196, 201, 374.
65. Ryder, pp. 218, 219. Poverty was looked upon as "living death" and worldly wealth as morally desirable in early Indian literature. Basham, *Wonder*, p. 215.

> If he has salt, he has no bread,
> If he has meat, he has no lamb,
> If he has a lamb, he has no meat.[66]

Until man's minimal material needs are taken care of, man's spiritual aspirations cannot be realized, it was remarked a millennium or more before twentieth-century scholars began to write of a "culture of poverty":

> Until a mortal's belly-pot
> Is full, he does not care a jot
> For love or music, wit or shame,
> For body's care or scholar's name,
> For virtue or for social charm,
> For lightness or release from harm,
> For godlike wisdom, youthful beauty,
> For purity or anxious duty.[67]

It is not surprising, given such folk wisdom respecting the desirability of cash and wealth, that economic incentive was counted upon by administrators and others to mobilize human effort. Even the pyramids of Egypt, some historians now hold, were constructed, not by slaves, but by paid craftsmen and by farmers working off taxes at times when agricultural work was impossible.[68] The importance of economic incentive, not surprisingly, quickly came to be recognized by "economical" writers, as well as by traders and administrators, especially after mobile social surpluses, together with exchange, came into being. The time horizon to which incentives related was short, of course, since most individuals viewed their world as ridden with uncertainty and their probable life expectancy at any age was very low. Yet, within this horizon, material rewards and penalties served to direct men's activities.

While incipient economic motivation, as well as material considerations, was apparently powerful in ancient India and while administrative skill was evident there, India's dominant value system was inimical—so it has been suggested—to economic development, at least after the ascendancy of Hinduism and Hindu institutions (e.g., caste, joint family, transforming social law into sacerdotal law)

---

66. Kramer, *History Begins*, p. 121. On occasion, at least in literature, the "poor man" had his turn. See Oppenheim, *Ancient Mesopotamia*, pp. 274, 301.
67. Ryder, p. 401.
68. Fairsirvis, pp. 80–81; Forbes, p. 44.

during and after the Gupta period.[69] The otherworldliness of Indian religion did not diminish the concern of most Indians with material objectives; yet, Weber believed, it failed to produce something like a Puritan ethic and through it sublimate and rationalize man's acquisitive drive and lead him to find in his economic success evidence of grace and salvation, an end very few apprehended.[70] Mishra concludes that over much of the past three millennia Hinduism was either unfavorable or at best not very favorable to economic development, whereas Buddhism and Jainism were favorable to it on balance.[71]

Today many obstacles to economic development are identified as flowing out of Hindu religion, culture, and personality: "disapproval of material and worldly things, lack of motivation for consumption, acceptance of the status quo, low aspirations, a pervasive sense of pessimism, fatalism, conformity, passivity, distrust, selfishness, and particularism." But as Singh points out,[72] empirical studies have not yet supported the view "that Hindu cultural and religious values weaken economic motivation and hinder economic development and modernization." And he adds that the central question is "whether these barriers stem inherently from the basic core of hinduism and derive their strength of resistance from their religious sanctity or whether they are primarily the products of non-religious factors, such as scarcity, ignorance, governmental inefficiency, low morale, a long period of foreign rule, etc." [73] To this one may add that for more than half a millennium after the Maurya period, merchants continued to support Buddhism and Jainism; yet Hindu merchants played a leading role in extending Indian trade to Indonesia and southeast Asia. In what follows, therefore, no attempt will be made to assess the role of Hindu culture in economic development in general, though the effect of specific obstacles may be noted.

69. Thapar, *History*, chaps. 7–9.
70. Max Weber, pp. 326, 336, 337. Bendix (chap. 6 and p. 268) summarizes Weber's views on India and compares them with his views on other Asian lands. But see M. D. Morris's critique, "Values."
71. Mishra, chaps. 2–3. See also Muranjan. The futilitarian doctrine of sects such as the Ajivikas could not be favorable. Basham, *Ajivikas*.
72. A. K. Singh, p. 16; and cf. also M. D. Morris.
73. A. K. Singh, p. 25. M. D. Morris, "Values," is also highly critical of the evidence purporting to identify the "Hindu value system" as a significant obstacle to economic growth.

Protoeconomics

At least two conditions are essential to the emergence and study of early economic thought, whether in the form of law and regulation or in the form of commentaries on economic matters. These are (i) the development of the art of writing and record keeping,[74] and (ii) a sufficiency of division of labor and exchange. (i) Only if literary records and accounts remain can one infer the ideas present in an ancient civilization. Even then, one must proceed cautiously. Ancient data are apt to be misleading in that some activities generate more data than others and some data survive through the centuries (e.g., coins, pottery, inscriptions), whereas others of perhaps great importance rot or disappear early. Economic as well as other records must often have been of the latter sort. (ii) Exchange gives rise to problems, attempts at whose solution generate discussion. Ideas regarding exchange and related matters probably became manifest only after trade had developed beyond the level of reciprocal gift-giving and "silent" exchange.[75]

Problems of the kind which gave rise to eonomic discussion are analytically traceable to the emergence of an agricultural surplus and population concentrations which made a considerable and varied trade possible. Administrators, statesmen, and military leaders as well as merchants found themselves confronted by logistical, regulatory, and commercial issues requiring judgment, decision, and the establishment of stabilizing rules. While decisions of this sort were not so common in low-energy, agricultural societies, they were present insofar as allocative decisions were required, a system of rewards and penalties was operative, and exchange had to be fallen back on. A price system of sorts, even though a defective one, always tends to come into existence, even in prison camps.[76] A price system can become important, however, only when societies move out of a low-energy stage into a higher-energy stage and acquire a capability to generate a sizable economic surplus.

74. This art was present in the Indus civilization, its script possibly having been derived from the early Elamite script. Singer et al., 1:760. Later Indian scripts were developed after 800 B.C. Ibid., pp. 771–73. On writing see also Gelb; Clauson and Chadwick; Burrow.

75. See, e.g., Marcel Mauss, pp. xiv, 1–5, 69–76, and 53–59 on the theory of the gift in the Hindu classical period; Polanyi et al., pp. 52–53; also Spengler, "Herodotus."

76. E.g., see Radford.

Presumably there was considerable exchange when the Indus civilization was at its height. The society which succeeded it, however, was initially much less urban and much more rural and village-oriented. Yet there were continuities from the Harappan society, among them trade with the West, though not in appreciable volume until Aryan agriculture had risen to and above the Harappan level.[77] With the stabilization and extension of Aryan rule and contact, internal and external trade increased, though irregularly.[78] In its wake came ever-more pressing problems and economic debate resulting in portions of the works discussed in other chapters. By then, of course, economic discussion as such may have been very old, at least in Mesopotamia. Indeed, according to H. Bernardelli, "this proud New Science of Economics really originated within the precincts of Babylonian Temples from metaphysically inspired meditations of very superstitious, pious priests on the mathematical implications of fertility worship." [79]

Two difficulties remain, one analytical and the other historical. First, what appear to be scientific inquiries need to be viewed charily lest they be interpreted to mean more than they actually do. For, as Schumpeter warned, "In economics as elsewhere, most statements of fundamental facts acquire importance only by super-structures they are made to bear and are commonplace in the absence of such superstructures." [80] Moreover, the economic statements put forward must do more than describe behavior; they must function as compressed generalizations respecting much economic behavior.

Second, historians differ respecting when trade was of a form and quality as well as sufficient in quantity to give rise to an economy and undermine what Marx called "community." Is trade really continuing in the country under analysis? "Traits superficially recalling a businessmen's culture may occur independently of

77. "To the complex pattern of the Indian Middle Ages the ancient urban civilization of the Punjab and the Indus surely contributed not a little. . . . The whole character of medieval Hindu society and the structure of its polity and government seem inevitably a reflection of the Bronze Age civilization of Sind and the Punjab." Piggott, *Prehistoric India*, p. 288. See also Thapar, *History*, pp. 36, 114.
78. Thapar, *History*, pp. 61–62, 78, 105–15, 207–10; Adhya, chap. 3. On the considerable volume of internal and external trade, especially in the South, see D. R. Das, chaps. 13–14.
79. Bernardelli, pp. 337–38.
80. Schumpeter, p. 53.

markets and even of the economy altogether." One may, therefore, be dealing not with a real but with a pseudo-economy.[81] Fortunately, this second difficulty may be ignored. The literature discussed in later chapters relates to periods in which trade was sufficiently voluminous and extensive to warrant reference to an Indian economy.[82] In fact, there was more recognition of the role of price and market in some of the Indian writings than in those of Aristotle, viewed by some as the founder of economics.[83]

The development of modern economics may, however, have been retarded in India by the nature of the economy. The assumption of a strictly hedonistic economic man stands up well in a capitalistic society, but not under all the sets of arrangements for distributing income found in Indian society,[84] where both feudal and other rules (e.g., joint-family) were encountered and social variables often influenced economic conduct. Moreover, insofar as overpopulation and underemployment were present, the caste system as well as an excessive bureaucracy must have derived support from the desire of its beneficiaries for job security.

81. Polanyi, "Marketless Trading in Hammurabi's Time," in Polanyi et al., p. 13. The issues involved are treated in chaps. 1–4; also Oppenheim, *Ancient Mesopotamia*, chaps. 1–2. "Commodity exchange begins when community ends," wrote Marx. *Capital*, 1:63.

82. This may have been so even in the Harappan society, though it manifested attributes of the "storage economy" which Oppenheim, *Ancient Mesopotamia*, pp. 89–95, finds in Mesopotamia, namely, an "economy so constituted as to be self-supporting, with a center in either the palace or the temple." After all, there was considerable trade in Mesopotamia at this time. See also Oppenheim, "New Look."

83. See Polanyi, "Aristotle Discovers the Economy," in Polanyi et al., chap. 5; also Kurt Singer.

84. See Georgescu-Roegen; and Chayanov, pp. 1–28, with D. Thorner's introduction, pp. xi, xxiii.

Chapter 3

Arthashastra Economics

> There was hardly anything Chanakya would have re-
> frained from doing to achieve his purpose; . . . yet
> he was also wise enough to know that this very pur-
> pose may be defeated by means unsuited to the end.
>
> JAWAHARLAL NEHRU

> *Chandragupta:* You intrigue me. There are many
>   questions in my head.
> *Chanakya:* Ask them, Your Majesty. There are many
>   answers in mine.
>
> VISHKADATTA

While Hindu thought embodied a strong sense of the past, it placed
less emphasis upon unique events than did Graeco-Roman and
Moslem history, perhaps because wide acceptance had been won
by a cycle theory dominated by a downward trend and unleavened
by a theory of progress. Even so, Hindu ethical thought and social
institutions manifested a remarkable continuity, strongly reinforced by a mass of literature supported by memory and oral tradition.

Continuity characterized economic and political thought as
well [1] and is evident in the economic ideas set down in arthashastra
and dharmashastra literature stretching from ancient to postmedieval times. It was not broken even during the period of Moslem rule
or in the early decades of European ascendancy. "A basic continuity in Indian economic life existed from the agricultural ad-

---

1. On this continuity, see Ghurye; Philips; Gokhale, *Indian Thought,* chap. 1
and pp. 37–47. On continuity in Indian sociopolitical literature, see Kane; Ghoshal,
History, p. 529; Saksena, "Sociology in India," in B. and V. B. Singh, pp. 248–58.
Saksena associates continuity with the abstract component of Indian thought and
its emphasis upon the relation of man to all life and the cosmos.

vances in the later Vedic period into the nineteenth century." [2]
Indian culture, as A. Embree has suggested in an unpublished
lecture, encapsulates rather than absorbs and synthesizes new
strains of thought, allowing them a nondisturbing coexistence and
quality of truth. Marx even asserted in 1853 that "the working of
English steam and English trade . . . produced the greatest, and
. . . the only social revolution ever heard of in Asia." [3]

While my concern in this chapter is the economic content of
arthashastra literature, brief examination of earlier literature will
reveal some of the continuity just mentioned.[4] In this early literature Indian society is pictured as much less complex and less
politically organized than that which had come into existence by
Maurya times. In the Rig-Veda, portions of which date from around
the beginning of the first millennium B.C., one encounters private
property, absence of city life, some democratic political organization, occupational specialization, the beginnings of the caste system,
some slavery, bare references to price bargaining, interest-bearing
loans, an emerging theory of kingship, and a developing concep-
tion of a social order subject to social law (*dharma*) and sustained
by coercive authority (*danda*).[5] In the sutras (manuals of aphoris-
tic instruction adapted to an age in which easily memorized phrases
had to substitute for written instructions) life is described as village-
centered and parochial, landholdings are usually small, and inheritance laws are unsystemized and vary with locality. Property
is protected, and false weights and measures are forbidden. The
king's taxes are generally fixed at between one-tenth and one-sixth
of (net?) farm produce, at smaller rates on other activities, and at

2. Morris and Stein, "Economic History," pp. 180–81, 192–93; B. A. Saletore,
Ancient Karnatka, pp. 475–76. The amount of influence exerted by Moslem and
(after 1500) by early European ideas and practices is easily exaggerated. While
Mohammedan power became ascendant in North India in the late twelfth century,
remaining so until decline set in around 1340, only to be revived and extended
by Akbar in 1536 until by 1691 it embraced much of South India, it did not alter
the basic foundations of the Indian economic agrarian system. See Moreland,
Agrarian System, pp. 17–18.
3. "The British Rule in India," in R. P. Dutt, p. 24. But see n. 48 in chap. 6
below and the associated text.
4. E.g., see Kangle, pt. 3, passim, esp. chap. 3; Kane, passim.
5. *Cambridge History of India*, 1:88–101; Das, vol. 1, chap. 4, esp. pp. 23–24,
58–62, 65–66; Ghoshal, *History*, chaps. 2, 3, 30, and idem, *Agrarian System*,
chaps. 1, 5; Aiyangar, *Aspects*, pp. 56–57, and idem, *Rajadharma*; Macdonnell and
Keith.

one day's work per month for artisans. Trading is permissible to most individuals, and moneylending may be carried on by all but members of the highest caste, with the basic interest maximum fixed at about 1.25 percent per month.[6] In the course of time ideas of asceticism and renunciation, though not parts of early Aryan culture, developed and became parts of Hindu culture, introduced into it from earlier non-Vedic culture.[7] The resulting strain of austerity was already reflected in early poetic discussions of waste.[8]

Early Buddhist writings no more than the early Vedic writings were concerned with analysis.[9] In them the Indian economy is described as overwhelmingly rural and the landholdings as usually small. Pricing is little regulated otherwise than by custom, except in the public sector, though price increases are frowned upon. Money mediates most trade, and moneylending forms (with tillage, trade, and harvesting) one of the four honest callings. Occupations are numerous, sometimes carried on under guild auspices and often pursued in localities specializing therein. Caste characteristics are undeveloped. The lot of the poor is hard and that of the wage earner is described as often little if any better than that of the slave. States are represented as republican, oligarchic, or monarchic

6. *Cambridge History of India,* 1:227–48. See also pp. 267–70, on the epic poems in which local government, light taxes, merchant guilds, and minimum wages for herdsmen are endorsed. For detailed summaries of contemporary views of aspects of the ancient economy of northern India, see A. Bose, vols. 1–2. Bose believes that taxes were usually in kind, based on net rather than on gross output and assessed in the light of quite good estimates of the tax base. Ibid., 1:116–27. See also Bandyopadhyaya, 1:288–90, 306–8; Das, chaps. 5–6; Ghoshal, *Agrarian System,* chap. 1.

7. K. M. Sen, *Hinduism,* p. 18. Kautalya's society was one of enjoyment, arts, merriment, and "few inhibitions." Dwivedi, p. 37.

8. See Kosambi, "Social and Economic Aspects," pp. 203–4, 216–20, 223–24. Diverse economic and political matter was included in the Mahabharata, especially in the twelfth book, Santi Parvan, inserted in the early Christian era.

9. Debt and interest were known from Vedic times. Kosambi, *Introduction,* pp. 139–40. Mrs. C. A. F. Rhys Davids, writing of economic conditions as represented in early Buddhist literature, remarks: "If during, say, the seventh to the fourth century B.C. it had been the vogue, in India, to write treatises on economic institutions, there might have come down to us the record both of conventions and of theories as orderly and as relatively acceptable to the peoples as anything of the kind in, say, the latter Middle Ages was to the peoples of Western Europe." In *Cambridge History of India,* 1:219. See also Rhys Davids, "Economic Conditions"; and Jain. According to Bandyopadhyaya, however, "We have nothing which can help us in showing whether the ancients knew, or cared to know the laws governing demand and supply or production and distribution" (1:308). But cf. A. Bose, 2:471–89, who argues that India's economic history was quite different from that portrayed in Brahmanical and Buddhist literature.

in form, and the economic role of the state as increasing. The king's share of his subject's output is reported fixed at between one-twelfth and one-sixth; mining is described as a royal undertaking.[10] "Property in land was complete and included the right of alienation." Politics and political behavior are subordinated to ethical principles, wisdom is described as superior to wealth, and dharma is made to signify political righteousness and universal ethical principles rather than an enforceable hierarchical order.[11]

Arthashastra vs. Dharmashastra

While this chapter deals with arthashastra matter and the one following with dharmashastra matter, the two overlap. A sharp distinction between economic and political ideas is not made by authors of manuals for rulers and of ethical guidebooks for wider circles of readers. Indeed, Hindu economic ideas were mainly by-products of two concerns: that with ethical and religious rules for the guidance of the behavior of the various social categories composing Indian society; and that with the instruction of the king and his bureaucracy in their rights, duties, and modes of conduct, and of the underlying population in the rules and regulations pertaining to them. Illustrative of the first concern is Manu's code, discussed later, and of the second, the manual ascribed to Kautalya or Kautilya (or Chanakya), Brahman adviser to Chandragupta, founder of the Maurya Empire. Associated with these two concerns were two corresponding types of literature, the dharmashastras and the arthashastras (or nitishastras). The dharmashastras treat dharma as a comprehensive term embracing, as Saletore notes, "law, custom, usage, morality, virtue, religion, duty, piety, justice and righteous conduct" and (as Spellman notes) issuing from a great cosmic dharma corresponding to Western natural law and Chinese *tao*. They "formed essentially a universal code of righteous conduct for all castes and classes"; their content flowed from sruti (vedas), or works of revelation, and from smriti (i.e., shastras and earlier sutras), or works embodying tradition derived from ancient sages and dealing with interpretation of sruti as well as with religious and

10. *Cambridge History of India*, 1:198–219; S. K. Das, chap. 6; Ghoshal, *Agrarian System*, pp. 7–8, 27–28; Wagle, chaps. 2, 4–5.
11. Chanana; Wagle; Ghoshal, *History*, chaps. 4, 14, 19.

civil usage. The arthashastras expounded rules of regal conduct, principles and practices of governmental administration, and regulations relating to many aspects of wealth and its production and use; they apparently evolved in part from the dharmashastra, to whose rules arthashastra rules were considered subordinate in case of conflict. Over time, however, Basham infers, arthashastra was less influential. The arthashastra became differentiated from the dharmashastra in the course of time as the requirements of government, especially in increasingly complex states, made necessary the formulation of guiding principles in treatises on administration and polity; but it continued to embrace legal and political as well as economic matter. Similarly, compliance with and even interpretation of caste rules sometimes varied with the pressure of changing circumstances.[12]

Brahmanical ideology permeated both types of literature, especially the dharmashastra, whose contents were less subject to pressures arising from changing circumstances. The dominant social roles already acquired by the uppermost varnas (social orders), the Brahmans and the Kshatriyas, were reinforced as was the caste system itself, a system that had begun to take shape only toward the end of the Rig-Vedic period. In keeping with this system, quite inferior roles were assigned to the very useful Vaishyas, while contemptible roles were allotted to the lowest of the varnas, the Shudras, as well as to various non-Aryans and outcastes. In practice, however, these roles underwent some modification as did those of the two top orders, and in time in some regions Shudras partially replaced Vaishyas as agriculturalists and rearers of cattle.[13] This

12. Basham, "Ancient Kingship"; Spellman, *Political Theory*, chap. 5; B. A. Saletore, *Ancient Indian Political Thought*, pp. 3, 11–23, 27, 184–90. See also Gokhale, chaps. 2–6; Ghoshal, *History*, pp. 5, 23, 161; Altekar, *State and Government*, and idem, *Sources*; Kane, 3:8–10; Aiyangar, *Indian Cameralism*, p. 50. Aiyangar describes the principles of dharmashastra as "eternal" and hence "discoverable by research and intuition"; in contrast, the method of the arthashastra "is inductive." Ibid., pp. 47–48. The principles received expression, however, in what some have called a police state. "If ever there was a purely police state, it was surely the ancient Hindu state," writes K. A. N. Sastri in Yazdani, p. 386.

13. B. A. Saletore, *Ancient Indian Political Thought*, pp. 187–88; Ghoshal, *History*, pp. 30–31, 35, 59–60, 240, 425–26, 550–52; Basham, *Wonder*, pp. 137–53; Kane, vol. 2, chaps. 2–5; Apte, chap. 1 and pp. 265 ff. See also on the class situation in the times of Kautalya and Manu, Sastri, *Comprehensive History*, 2:458–75, and R. C. Majumdar, *History*, 2:542 ff. The rules relating to varna persisted into and far beyond the Gupta period. Ibid., 3:555–59. In ibid., 4:368–73, for the eighth and ninth centuries, it is indicated that rules relating to Brahmans

class division, together with the duties and privileges assigned to each class, was conceived of as expressed in and reinforced by dharma and later also by the king acting (much as a Physiocratic "despot") in keeping with dharma or under the complementary authority of arthashastra.[14]

More democratic and egalitarian, Buddhist theory seems to have exercised only limited countervailing influence on the class structure, and with the passing of Ashoka, the great Buddhist ruler, Brahman views again became more influential. Even so, Buddhist and Jainist ethics continued to leaven Indian society and make it more gentle and humane than in Kautalya's day—so much so that "in the best days of the Gupta Empire Indian culture reached a perfection which it was never again to attain." [15]

---

remained essentially in the old tradition, while some relating to Shudras were slightly relaxed, and that all foreigners but the Moslems had "been thoroughly assimilated in the Hindu social system." The principle that society was divided into "four primary classes with distinctive status and functions," and with the Brahmans "above all representing the spiritual power in striking dissimilarity to the Kshatriyas who represented the temporal power," Ghoshal states, "dominated the form of Indian social theory through the centuries." Ghoshal, *History*, p. 7. Furthermore, as Kane observes, the concept of dharma evolved until it denoted the duties and privileges of members of the four varnas. Kane, 1:1–4. Even in the Puranas, a branch of sacred literature, a sometimes differently grounded but essentially similar varna ideology is encountered. Ghoshal, *History*, pp. 326–29, 336, 449–50. The great Indian grammarian Panini, who lived in the mid-fifth century B.C., implied that the term Shudra referred to some persons (probably aborigines) who lived outside the pale of Aryan society as well as to persons within the pale. He also indicated the existence of status and occupational differentiation within the Shudra category. See Agrawala, pp. 77–79, and 455–75 on Panini's date. On the beginning of the caste system, see R. C. Majumdar, *Ancient India*, pp. 48–49, 87–89; also H. N. Sinha, *Sovereignty*, pp. 6–10, 38–40, 51–53, 110–14.

14. Ghoshal, *History*, pp. 43–46, 73, 161, 226–27, 407–10. The dharma referred to above is that appropriate to a class and stage in life; there was also dharma, or norm of conduct, for all. See Basham, *Wonder*, p. 137. On the sources and development of dharma and varna rules, see Sen-Gupta, pp. 9, 11, 13–14, 39, 53, 327–31. For an informative comparative account of Vedic and Anglo-Indian law, see Derrett, "Hindu Law." Changes in ethical standards, objectives, and prescriptions are reflected also in Hindu epics. E.g., see Vora; also Gokhale, chaps. 2–6. The Santi Parva of the Mahabharata resembles a treatise on politics.

15. Basham, *Wonder*, p. 66, and pp. 123, 143, on the popularity of Buddhism with peace-loving tradesmen and craftsmen; B. A. Saletore, *Ancient Indian Political Thought*, pp. 107–13, 322–43. On the matters discussed in this paragraph, see Sastri, *Comprehensive History*, 2:364 ff.; Ghoshal, *History*, pp. 157 ff. Buddhists rejected the Brahman theory of a divinely ordained class structure and instead accounted for the emergence of classes and the institution of property in terms of a theory of periodical evolution. Ibid., pp. 62–65, 239, 258–60. They, along with the Jains, looked upon the "science" of politics as antithetical to ethics. Ibid., pp. 66, 260, 297, 339–41, 462–63. Buddhist and Brahmanical education are contrasted in R. K. Mookerji, *Ancient Indian Education*. Despite its superior ethical qualities,

In time, though not notably until the advent of the Moslems in the Middle Ages, the class structure became more rigid, and assimilation into the two uppermost orders became more difficult, in part perhaps because the multiplication of repetitive smritis was accompanied by a tightening of rules and a stagnation of thought.[16] Within each varna, especially the two lowest, identifiable groups (e.g., guilds) emerged as subsets within a set, and many of these finally became castes, membership within which became hereditary and entailed endogamy, commensality, and craft-exclusiveness. But this development proceeded slowly and matured late. In the ancient Indian sources there is much reference to *varna*, class or order, but little to *jati*, which only sometimes designated a rigid and well-defined group; and there is evidence of considerable fluidity and of frequent attainment of economic success by members of lower orders. In time, however, the *jati*, or local endogamous group, became the effective unit.[17] The ordering of the four varnas remained stable, however. The emergence of new castes, together with the transformation of occupational groups into castes, apparently did not diminish intravarna mobility, or signify great increase in accessibility to the higher orders. The standing of the castes fluctuated over time with the importance of their activities, and socioeconomic change sometimes introduced new castes and

---

Buddhism, by the seventh century A.D., had lost its hold on the people. See R. C. Majumdar, *History*, 3:390. Even Jainism, which had been flourishing, declined under the Guptas, whose power, at a peak in A.D. 320–467, came to an end in the sixth century. The hold of the Brahmanical religion became stronger in spite of its gradual transformation. Ibid., pp. xx–xxi, 365, 404, 435 ff. See also R. N. Saletore, *Life*, chaps. 7–8.

16. S. N. Dasgupta, 1:xxv–xxxix; Altekar, *State*, pp. 56 ff., and R. C. Majumdar, *Ancient India*, pp. 469–78, on the possibility that international trade kept southern Indian society more pliable than northern. Roman and perhaps other traders settled in some South Indian towns near the beginning of the modern period. Jairazbhoy, pp. 113–24. Tenney Frank endorses Pliny's estimate that about 50 million sesterces flowed annually from Rome to India. Frank, 5:282–85. For a review of Indian trade from pre-Maurya and Maurya times to the Mughal period, see R. K. Mookerji, *Indian Shipping*. By Kautalya's day the war office included a board of admiralty. Ibid., pp. 73 ff. On Indian commerce from 500 B.C. to 500 A.D., see Hyder; Subrahmanian; A. N. Bose, 2:40–77; Chakraborti; D. R. Das, chaps. 13–14.

17. Basham, *Wonder*, pp. 147–50; Sastri, *Colas*, pp. 546–52. Panini gave *jati*, later the legal term for caste, several meanings. See Agrawala, pp. 75, 91–92, 287, 353. In his book on Patanjali, the grammarian who flourished in the second century B.C. when there was a return to Brahmanical orthodoxy, B. N. Puri refers to castes in his remarks on the division of society, but not particularly in his discussion of occupations. Puri, pp. 89–92, 116–42. See also R. S. Sharma, *Sudras*, and on the role of jati, R. G. Fox.

removed old ones.[18] Persistence of the caste system was greatly assisted, of course, by the Indian economy's remaining agrarian and studded with self-reproducing villages and hence free enough of urbanization that might have weakened the system.

Dharmashastra and arthashastra principles, as already suggested, played a complementary role in the governance of the underlying population, but failed to unify it. India never became a nation, a body of people united by ties of nationalism, patriotism, language, and consciousness of common membership. It never passed completely under single rule to the exclusion of all small states. Their number and extent varied greatly in time, however.[19] The population was of diverse origin, of course, India having undergone many invasions by peoples situated on her borders. In time, however, these peoples, other than those of Moslem persuasion, became quite fully assimilated into the Indian cultural system, which continued to find articulate expression in the fairly stable contents of Dharmashastra and related prescriptive literature (e.g., the puranas) as well as conduct-determining form in prescribed class and caste distinctions, together with supporting religious activities. Even the Moslems underwent some Indianization, including considerable adoption of caste distinctions, which came to be predominantly social in character.[20] National consciousness and patriotism did not emerge, however, in part because a sanctioned and enforced inequality played down the importance of the activities of the most productive elements in the economy, the Vaishyas and the Shudras, and otherwise made for disunity.[21] Within states, moreover, cen-

18. See Basham, *Wonder*, pp. 137–53; Ibbetson, a classic report on the races, tribes, and castes of the Punjab, originally printed in the Census of 1881; Also D. Sharma, chap. 23; and B. P. Mazumdar, chap. 3, pp. 129–33, 184. On the emergence of new castes and subcastes, see Hutton, 1946 ed., pp. 41–46, 97–100.

19. There is no expression in Sanskrit for "citizen," "citizenship," or "economics," Aiyangar notes in *Indian Cameralism*, pp. 126, 129. Panini did give terms for a more localized loyalty. Agrawala, pp. 430–31. And A. S. Altekar points out that Indians felt "great love and patriotism" for their religion, culture, and independence. See Altekar, *State*, chap. 4, esp. pp. 70–72. See also n. 21 below. On the size of states, see B. A. Saletore, *Ancient Indian Political Thought*, pp. 88–90, 99–122, 136, 176–77, 187–88, 378–80, 512–14, 585–86, n. 50; Jayaswal.

20. See Ibbetson; Basham, *Wonder*, p. 151; Tilman.

21. On the lack of a sentiment of nationalism, see Kane, 3:136–37, 235–36. "The fundamental weakness of India has been the spirit of localism," wrote L. J. Barnett in his Introduction (p. xxiii) to B. P. Sinha's *Decline*. See also Derrett, *Introduction*, pp. 227–29. In his account of the decline of the Chauhan kingdoms in the face of Moslem pressure, D. Sharma concludes that the caste system, while it may have helped to preserve Hinduism, prevented fusion of the people into a

trifugal forces were often reinforced by the intensification of tendencies toward feudalism, especially in economic backwaters when trade and imperial controls became weak.[22]

Since ties of nationalism and patriotism could not emerge and fuse India's diverse peoples and areas into a nation-state, the place of these ties had to be taken by a strong and highly centralized administrative system. It was such a system, together with counsel respecting its establishment, extension, and perpetuation, that arthashastra literature expounded; and it was the supposed importance of such a system, given the lack of alternative ties, that helped to maintain interest in this literature. Interest in economic counsel had a similar origin; for a powerful, centralized administrative system can function only if there is a large, dependable, and foreseeable flow of means for its support and if the emergence of serious economic disorder, together with its sequel, political disorder, can be prevented. It was in the productive arts and the economics of bureaucratic control, therefore, and not in free economic inquiry and speculation, that the interest of manuals for rulers was centered. Yet, despite much repetition of this political and economic counsel, together with instruction in implementing wile, sway was extended over much of the subcontinent only three times, and then not for long periods—by the Mauryas, the Guptas, and the Mughals. Only the first of these succeeded in establishing a highly centralized regime. With the weakening of the central power, smaller,

---

nation, kept down the number able to fight, and deprived traders and the oppressesd classes of interest in the perpetuation of the government. D. Sharma, pp. 323–24. A similar view is expressed in the *Cambridge Shorter History of India*, p. 219: "The spirit of caste has for ages ousted the sentiment of nationality." Obsolete military methods contributed repeatedly to the defeat of Indian armies. On the early military system, see B. K. Majumdar, *Military System*, chap. 10. In the arthashastra literature much attention is given to raising and training elephants, despite their limited utility against non-Indian armies. A somewhat different interpretation is put forward by U. N. Ghoshal in his *Studies*, chap. 17.

22. E.g., see D. Sharma, pp. 324–25; Mazumdar, chap. 1, esp. pp. 8–9, 33–35. Quasi-feudalism prevailed throughout much of India's history. See Basham, *Wonder*, pp. 93–96, and p. 128 on how Hinduism encouraged anarchy. Sastri indicates that in South India (where "the individual, as such, did not count," but where there was a great deal of local government and regulation by various local groups), the functions of the numerous bureaucratic governments embraced little more than "the tasks of police and justice," usually without marked distinction between civil and criminal offenses. Villages and temples played major roles in maintaining irrigation works. See Sastri, *Colas*, pp. 460–62, 476–77, 583–84. See also K. M. Gupta. On local and customary regulation, see Kane, 3:158–59, 486–89; R. K. Mookerji, *Local Government*; Altekar, *State*.

localized and more stable power centers emerged only to be reassembled into larger systems during occasional periods of increased centralization. This alternating process was facilitated by the importance of stabilizing local custom, common law, and religious belief.[23]

The absence of stabilizing mechanisms at the state or empire level presented a dilemma not present at the level of the homeostatic, self-sufficing village.[24] The Maurya Empire avoided one horn only to be impaled on the other. Its founders established an apparently powerful but expensive bureaucratic structure [25] and thus avoided the administrative weaknesses of their predecessors by curbing feudal tendencies, predatory nobles, and local rulers. They failed, however, to avoid the economically depressing topheaviness usually associated with a powerful administrative structure. This failure, as Kosambi shows, was manifested both in depreciation of the coinage and in Ashoka's incapacity to extend the Maurya system into less rich or fertile areas. Nor did they succeed in bringing into being a national consciousness and substituting loyalty to the state for popular loyalty to a divinely sanctioned social order. As a result the empire collapsed.[26]

23. See B. A. Saletore, *Ancient Indian Political Thought*, pp. 131–40, 459–73, 530–31. See also R. C. Majumdar, *Corporate Life*, and R. K. Mookerji, *Local Government*. Surajit Sinha describes state formation and the spread of Hindu religious belief. Processes similar to those which Sinha describes must have played a part in the earlier spread of Hindu culture and political organization into non-Hindu areas. In political and related Indian literature the argument for monarchy was usually stated in Hobbesian and Darwinian terms. Authors supposed, even as did Chinese and later Moslem writers, that in the absence of a monarch, anarchy, insecurity, and unremitting strife would prevail. As Sir Edwin Arnold put it in his poetic account of Lord Buddha (bk. 1), life flowed from "mutual murder"; each form of animal life "slew a slayer and in turn was slain," life living upon death. Spellman's *Political Theory*, pp. 4–8, describes Indian fear of anarchy, expressed in the doctrine of *matsyanyaya* (the big fish eating up the little fish) as "almost pathological." Panini referred to the king as solving the evils of kingless society. Agrawala, pp. 411–12.

24. On the homeostatic character of the traditional, self-sufficing, self-perpetuating, unchanging village, wherein the "inhabitants of the country have lived from time immemorial," see the citation from an official report of the British House of Commons on Indian Affairs in 1812 in Marx and Engels, *First Indian War*, pp. 18–19; also Gunnar Myrdal, *Asian Drama*, chap. 23. Prior to the advent of the British, the Indian village was virtually self-subsisting; the towns, engaged mainly in serving military and religious needs along with luxury consumption, were supported by rural tribute. Thorner and Thorner, pp. 51–52.

25. S. N. Eisenstadt compares this structure with that of other empires.

26. Kosambi, *Introduction*, pp. 191–94, 211–12, 221–25; Thapar, *Asoka*, pp. 16–17, 68, 94, 123, 144, 209–12; Kane, 2:138–58; Sastri, *Comprehensive History*, 2:53–65. See also the general account in R. S. Sharma, *Aspects*. There was not present that

Kautalya's Arthashastra

Kautalya's Arthashastra, the last great and only extant work of this genre, has been described as "the most remarkable work on social polity now available in Sanskrit." [27] The identity of the author and the date of the work remain moot, as does the extent of interpolation due to continuators up to the fifth century A.D. Kangle, after reviewing all the evidence, concludes that there is no convincing reason why this work should not be regarded as the work of Kautalya, who helped Chandragupta to come to power in Magadha. [28] Kautalya referred to earlier arthashastra schools as well as to works on dharma, business, agriculture, town planning, architecture, etc., some of which supposedly had been inspired by the Artha-Veda, but he remained quite unaffected by religious bias in dharmashastra literature. [29]

Of the works of Kautalya's acknowledged predecessors, apparently eighteen in number, we have only the short citations or texts found in his own work, in such works as the Nitisara of Kamandaka, perhaps a minister of the Guptas, and in books 12–13 of the Mahabharata. [30] In his own work Kautalya presents many particular views in order to compare them with his own and (often)

---

tribal loyalty which apparently had marked some of the smaller tribal republics over which the Mauryas had triumphed. Thapar, *Asoka,* p. 95. On tribalism and the emergence of earlier states, see Sinha, *Sovereignty,* pp. 55–64, 89–109, 253–60. On the state's response to economic pressure see B. Sen, chap. 10.

27. Aiyangar, *Indian Cameralism,* p. 5. See also Dwivedi. The fullest account of Kautalya's economics is that of B. Sen, which came to my attention after I had completed my study.

28. Kangle, 3:106, Part 2 is Kangle's translation of his new Sanskrit edition of the Arthashastra, which is part 1. The first English translation was R. Shamasastry's; it was based on the text (now superseded by Kangle in his pt. 1) edited and published by Shamasastry in 1909. Kangle lists the various texts and translations in his pt. 3, pp. 285–87. Dwivedi also concluded that Kautalya composed the book "prior to the establishment of the Mauryan empire" (pp. 9, 19, 26–27). Thapar believes that final form was given to Kautalya's text by Visnugupta in the third or fourth century A.D. *Asoka,* pp. 218–25. A. Bose believes that the Arthashastra dates to the first century A.D. (pp. 280–94).

29. Bandyopadhyaya, 1:13–17; Kangle, pt. 3, chap. 3 and pp. 7–9, 67. Kautalya, when discussing education, does not refer to the sixty-four traditional crafts and arts referred to in a number of works. See Mookerji, *Ancient Indian Education,* chaps. 5, 7, 11, 18; S. R. Dongerkery, chaps. 1–2; Keay, chap. 4. On the nonspeculative character of ancient Indian "economic" literature, see G. D. Karwal, "Ancient Indian Economics."

30. Ghoshal, *History,* chaps. 1, 5, pp. 188–201, 210–12; B. A. Saletore, *Ancient Indian Political Thought,* pp. 6–10, 27–39, 54; Kangle, pt. 3, chaps. 1, 3; R. C. Majumdar and Altekar, p. 410; F. Wilhelm, *Polemiken.*

reject them. Because so little of the earlier works exists, it is not possible to determine how much change took place in arthashastra thought. We know that rajaniti, an aspect of arthashastra, consists of laws, rules, and regulations which are subject to change as experience discloses them to be improvable. These rules, etc., thus differ from the fixed and mandatory rules found in dharmashastra and described as of supernatural origin and therefore quite immune to change.[31] Accordingly, arthashastra rules must have yielded more rapidly to the pressure of changing circumstances than did dharmashastra rules, even those relating to economic matters. Yet even the latter could yield. For example, in the eleventh century a distinction (worthy of a casuist) was made between worldly and sacred matter. This allowed relaxation of restraints (e.g., see Manu, VIII, 340, below) upon the right of members of particular varnas (especially Brahmans) to earn a living and acquire property; atonement could now easily be made for having acquired worldly wealth in a spiritually improper way.[32]

Presumably, most of the expositors of arthashastra supposed either that a powerful ruler's sphere of influence included all of India lying south of the Himalayas and within the three surrounding seas, or that northern and southern rulers each had a sphere of influence, one in the north and the other in the south.[33] It is not clear, however, to what extent this sphere of influence was believed to spill over the borders of India proper into surrounding territory.[34]

For expositive convenience, treatment of Kautalya's views on economic matters will be separated from that of his views on political matters. After all, his work is predominantly political, with the political clearly distinguished from the religious. Yet, he is always alert to the economic undergirding of the polity (itself more theoretical in structure than representative of contemporary political structures)[35] and to the importance of economic incentives

31. Pandey.

32. Derrett, "Right to Earn."

33. Sircar, pp. 243, 257, 289, 405. See also Agrawala, chap. 2; D. R. Das, chap. 1.

34. See Sircar's account of India's knowledge of countries outside the Indian subcontinent on pp. 283–92, and 293–334 on the manner in which India and its neighborhood were subdivided by Indian writers. See below, n. 52, and Spellman, *Political Theory*, pp. 165–68 on tributary states.

35. Kangle, 3:64–74. The text, "a theoretical treatise intended for the guidance of rulers in general, . . . does not profess to be a document describing the actual conditions in any particular kingdom." Ibid., p. 67.

and disincentives, especially in the form of fines and monetary re-wards.[36] Of the fifteen books constituting the Arthashastra, nine are almost entirely political; only six contain significant economic as well as political matter. It is thus, as Kautalya himself described it, a compendium of "science" and practice for the acquisition and maintenance of wealth and territory, the joint source of man's livelihood and material and immaterial needs (15.1.1–2).[37] This compendium is presented in conformity with the author's quite detailed description of how and in what style edicts, treatises, communications, and the like, are to be written (2.10; 15).

Kautalya's approach to both economic and political subject mat-ter is practical and empiricistic in that his rules seem mainly to rest, as do his accounts of methods of production, upon past ex-perience. He may thus have reflected a traditionalism apparently emerging in Indian applied science as well as the fact that the Indian polity and economy had long been going concerns.[38] His basic task, however, was not to engage in scientific analysis, but to apply known economic and other information to the realization of preconceived goods, among them "wealth," to which he attached great importance. For while he identified three kinds of goods— spiritual good, material well-being, sensual pleasures—to be en-joyed in suitable proportion, he declared that "material well-being alone is supreme" inasmuch as "spiritual good and sensual pleasures depend on" it (1.7.5–7). This stress upon wealth at the microlevel is present also at the macrolevel and in his account of the power of the state, though subject to the proviso that wealth is to be properly and safely acquired (9.4.5; 9.7.60–64). Thus two of the seven constituents of the state are described as forms of wealth (i.e., the contents of the ruler's treasury and the territory of the state, to-

36. In bks. 2–4 Kautalya lists, besides many offenses against regal law (together with suitable punishments) and custom, some three hundred offenses, together with offsetting fines. The fines served in part to supplement taxes, levied on a "staggering number of items." B. A. Saletore, *Ancient Indian Political Thought*, p. 452.

37. In what follows the first number designates the book, the second the chapter, and the third, after a period, the section within a chapter. Thus 15.1.1–2 designates sections 1–2 in chapter 1 in book 15. When only one number, e.g., 15, is given, it designates the whole of a book (e.g., bk. 15).

38. On scientific knowledge in ancient India, see F. S. Hammett's papers, cited at the close of his "Agriculture and Botanic Knowledge." On opposition to change in Indian culture, see Max Weber, pp. 122–23, 144. On conditions obtaining in Panini's time, see Agrawala. See also below, n. 97 in chap. 5.

gether with its people), and the strength of the other five constituents (ruler, chief minister, army, fortified capital, and friends or allies) is said to depend on wealth (6; 7.1.1–5; 8.1–2).[39] It was important, therefore, for the king to be active in ways giving rise to wealth (1.19).

"Economics" is not defined in a modern sense, though many topics reflecting implicit economic analysis are dealt with. Indeed, there is no Sanskrit term for economics as such. The content of arthashastra economics does not even answer to the title "science" (*shastra*) of "wealth" (*artha*). "Agriculture, cattle-rearing and trade —these constitute economics (which are) beneficial as they yield grains, cattle, money, forest produce and labour" (1.4.1).[40] Thus defined, however, "economics," along with *dandaniti*, or "political science," and two other sciences, or four in all ("philosophy, the three Vedas, economics, and the science of politics"), were to be taught to the king and (when relevant) to his counsellors and to be imbedded in the governmental apparatus. These four sciences, when correctly applied by the king, contributed to the material and spiritual welfare of the people (1.2.2–10): "For the king, trained in the sciences, intent on the discipline of the subjects, enjoys the earth (alone) without sharing it with any other (ruler), being devoted to the welfare of all beings" (1.5.17). It was essential, therefore, that economics and the science of politics (i.e., the wielding of the "rod" by the king) supply guidance, along with philosophy and the three Vedas. The "orderly maintenance of life" depended on "economics," which had for "its purpose the acquisition of (things) not possessed, the preservation of (things) possessed, the augmentation of (things) preserved and the bestowal of (things) augmented on a worthy recipient" (1.4.3; 15.1.1). The king, however, must not overuse or underuse the "rod," merely employ it justly (1.4.7–12,16; 1.5.1–2). Otherwise the "law of the fishes" would prevail and the stronger would swallow the weaker

39. See Kane, 3:17–19, and chaps. 3–9; B. A. Saletore, *Ancient Indian Political Thought*, pp. 249–458; R. S. Sharma, *Aspects*, esp. chap. 2; Spellman, *Political Theory*, chap. 6.
40. The three callings constituted *vartta*, a word derived from *vritti*, "livelihood." Artha is defined as the sustenance or "livelihood" (vritti) of men (15.1.1). Kangle, 3:1–3, 166. Artha is thus one of the three goals of life, along with dharma (virtue) and kama (pleasure); the fourth was moksha, final release from the cycle of rebirth. See Kane, 3:235–41; and Vora, pp. 204 ff., B. Sen, pp. 188–94.

(1.4.13–14; 1.13.5). Kautalya added that a king could not even respond properly to counsel if he did not understand the teachings of politics (1.15.61). Later (8.2) Kautalya deals with situations in which kingship is not working well.[41]

The economy, as conceived by Kautalya, reflected both contemporary actualities and theoretical aspirations; it was predominantly rural, bureaucratic, and centralized and lacked a politically influential middle class or a relatively large number of landowners in the village-studded countryside. Even so, there was much local self-government, conditioned on the economic and military support of the state—in villages and in guilds concerned mainly with trade and handicrafts and engaging most of those not occupied in agriculture or service of state or cult. The economic role of the temple, Kautalya implies, was not yet as large as it became later. The king is described as involved in economic activity, directly in that relating to crownlands and business activities carried on in his name, and indirectly in undertakings conducted by his tenants. He was interested also in improving transport, extending settlement, and regulating diverse economic activities.[42] For these reasons and in order to insure the happiness and material well-being of his subjects including maintenance of children and the aged without support (2.1.26), the king and his counsellors had need of economic knowledge (1.9.1–3; 1.15–61):

> In the happiness of the subjects lies the happiness of the king and in what is beneficial to the subjects his own benefit. What is dear to himself is not beneficial to the king, but what is dear to the subjects is beneficial (to him).
>
> Therefore, being ever active, the king should carry out the management of material well-being. The root of material well-being is activity, of material disaster its reverse.
>
> In the absence of activity, there is certain destruction of what

41. Compare Kangle, "Vyasanas."
42. On the Maurya and the quite similar post-Maurya economies, see Thapar, *Asoka*, chap. 3, and her chapter in Ganguli, *Readings*; R. K. Mookerji, *Chandragupta*; A. N. Bose; Sastri, *Comprehensive History*, 2:70–80, 430–57; B. Sen, passim. In Kautalya's time there were both crown lands and noncrown lands; the latter were under private (usually peasant) ownership, though subject to certain taxes and regulations. See L. Gopal, *Economic Life*, chap. 1, and his "Ownership" and "Quasi-Manorial Rights." With the rise of feudalism and the increase in gifts of land to vassals, temples, officials, and so on, the sovereign's control over land must have declined. See R. S. Sharma, "Origins" and "Land Grants," as well as his *Light*, pp. 52–89, 109–15, and *Aspects*, chaps. 13–14. See also Bandyopadhyaya; Kosambi, *Introduction*, chap. 9. On temples, see Kangle, 3:156–57.

is obtained and of what is not yet received. By activity reward
is obtained, and one also secures abundance of riches [1.19.34–36].

In the two sections below we deal, respectively, with Kautalya's
bureaucracy and its duties and with his "economics." These topics
are treated mainly in books 2–8, the duties and training of the king
and his staff having been outlined in book 1. Books 9–14 deal almost
entirely with military campaigns, logistics, war, and external policy
limited essentially to India as a sphere of influence (9.1.17–19).
He counseled against undertakings in which the prospective gains
did not outweigh the probable loss of men and draft animals,
together with expenses in the form of money and grains (9.4; 9.7.60–
64). Among the incentives to be offered to troops, Kautalya described pecuniary means as very important (10.3.27, 45). He also
stressed the use of incentives when pacifying conquered territory
(13.5). In short, his calculations ran in material terms.

A Brahman, Kautalya supported the four-varna system, apparently
without recognizing its unfavorable impact upon incentive, productivity, dynamic division of labor, and interoccupational balance.
"Studying, teaching, performing sacrifices for self, officiating at
other people's sacrifices, making gifts and receiving gifts" were
the special duties of the Brahman; "studying, performing sacrifices
for self, making gifts, living by (the profession of) arms and protecting beings," those of the Kshatriya. The duties of the Vaishya were
"studying, performing sacrifices for self, making gifts, agriculture,
cattle-rearing and trade"; those of the Shudra, "service of the twice-
born, engaging in an economic calling (viz., agriculture, cattle-
rearing, and trade) and the profession of the artisan and the actor"
(1.3.5–8). It was the business of the king to enforce this system (3.1)
and the duties associated with the four stages (householder, student,
forest anchorite, wandering ascetic) of life (1.3.9–12). Kautalya
stressed the importance of Shudra agriculturalists (2.1.2), however,
and declared a Vaishya or a Shudra army, "when possessed of great
strength," better than Brahman troops (9.2.24). Even so, Brahmans
enjoyed special privileges in respect of land grants, inheritance,
legal treatment, exemptions from various burdens, and social
status.[43]

---

43. On Kautalya on the four varnas, see Kangle, 3:143–56, also 186–88 on the
smallness of the role of the slavery in both Kautalya's India and Indus culture.

Kautalyan Bureaucratic Theory

Kautalya's bureaucratic structure may be divided into three
parts: that closely associated with land settlement and the exploitation of nature, that connected with external relations, and
that connected with regulatory, judicial, and fiscal affairs and hence
manifesting economic rules. Kautalya's elaborate administrative
structure, though it could reflect Western influence present in the
Maurya system, is designed to serve any state that would prosper
rather than the mere needs of the Maurya state; it was essentially
impersonal, whereas the Gupta and later systems were dominated
by the person of the ruler.[44]

Land settlement and its exploitation commanded most attention,
because population and land were considered complements and
essential to a nation's economic and political power (7.11.45; 13.4.5).
Kautalya therefore recommended that unsettled land be peopled
by "bringing in people from foreign lands or by shifting the over-
flow" of the domestic population, these to be settled in villages of
100–500 families and consisting mostly of Shudra agriculturalists
(2.1.1–2). He had new villages in mind (5.3.31–32), not wishing
to disturb established ones. For each 800 villages a large town, or
revenue center, was to be established; a smaller town for each 400
villages, and a yet smaller one for each 200 villages (2.1.4; 2.35.1–6).
He thus implies a ratio of about 115 villages to one town. Given 800
villages averaging 1,500–2,500 persons, and close to 10 percent of
the population living in towns, we should get something like one
town of about forty to sixty-seven thousand, two of twenty to
thirty-three thousand, and four of ten to seventeen thousand.[45]
Arable lands were to be alloted to taxpayers for life and granted to
selected persons on more favorable terms (2.1.7–8). The king should
facilitate the creation of irrigation works (2.1.20), extremely important in monsoon lands subject to wide variation in rainfall (2.24),
establish safe transport and productive nonagricultural activities,
advance grains, cattle, money, and equipment to settlers, and grant

44. Kangle, pt. 3, chaps. 8 and 9–10; Basham, *Ajivikas*, p. 287.
45. Each village included at least five artisans—carpenter, potter, barber, black-
smith, washerman—and often persons of greater skills. Distributions of village plots
imply a cadastral survey. Agrawala, pp. 195, 229–30.

temporary exemptions from burdens (2.1.13–21; 2.36–38).[46] While pleasures are described as refreshing country people and making them work harder (8.4.23), parks or halls for entertainment (2.1.33–35) were not to be permitted, since they would distract workers and tillers of the fields (2.1.10–12). Nonagricultural land was to be allotted for pasture, devoted to the king's recreation, or converted into elephant forests (2.2). Pasture land was to be established in regions between villages (2.34). Suitably situated land was to be made available for cities and villages. Even the construction and situation of dwellings, together with their sale or conveyance and their surroundings, were subject to regulation (3.8–10). It was very difficult, of course, for those settled in the villages to leave (2.34–35); they were, in a sense, tied to the soil.

Land-use policy reflected the conditions of land ownership. Unoccupied land belonged to the king (i.e., the state), but was not a source of taxes and income to the state until occupied and developed. The state also owned settled land—crown land—which was cultivated by tenants or state farms (2.24). Land was also under private ownership and alienable.[47] Gift of land by the ruler to priests and others did not alienate the land but merely made it exempt from taxes and dues or conferred the usufruct (though not tax exemption) upon the donee.[48] The state exercised some control also even over private cultivators.[49] Private cultivators of crown lands usually got one-half the produce if they supplied seed, materials, etc., or one-fourth if the state supplied these, though in some instances cultivators got as little as one-tenth (2.24.16; 3.13.28).

In 2.4 Kautalya describes in detail how forts are to be constructed on the frontier and how a fortified city is to be laid out and equipped with highways and facilities, and how various occupational groups, guilds, merchants, and householders are to be situated within a city. Reserves of various commodities are to be kept on hand in

46. B. Sen, chaps. 2, 5, also pp. 68, 182; D. R. Das, chaps. 3, 6. Great canals and drainage systems were sometimes undertaken. Kosambi, *Introduction*, p. 31. Ashoka settled 150,000 captives on new land. Nikam and McKeon, pp. 27–30.

47. On the land situation, see Adhya, chaps. 1–2; A. N. Bose, 1:38–76; D. R. Das, chap. 2; Kangle, 3:167–71.

48. Kangle, 3:171–72.

49. Kangle, 3:173–75.

sufficient quantities. In 2.5 Kautalya explains how the director of stores is to construct a treasury, a warehouse, a magazine, a store for forest produce, an armory, and a prison house, and how goods of various sorts are to be gathered and stored. In 2.11 the duties of the superintendent of the treasury are described, among them the evaluation of precious articles of all sorts. In 2.36 the rules governing the administration and police of the capital city by the city superintendent are described, among them those relating to fire protection, sanitation, lodging travelers and the needy, curfew, and incarceration. The administration of justice in general is dealt with mainly in books 3 to 5. The superintendent of the magazine (2.15) not only stores agricultural produce but also collects certain taxes in kind and labor (2.15) and administers rations, sometimes after the manner of Cato (2.15.61).

A number of productive activities are described, though with emphasis mainly upon technological details rather than upon managerial practice. Among these are factories and mines, the source of salt, money metals, and the "treasury" (2.12); the workshop of the superintendent of gold (2.13); the gold and silver workshops of artisans superintended by the goldsmith (2.14); the director of forest produce who supervises the gathering and fabrication of all kinds of animal and vegetable products originating in forests (2.17); the superintendents of the armory, of yarn and textile production, and of animal slaughter, courtesans, cattle, horses, elephants, chariots, and pastures (2.18, 23, 26–27, 29–34). Regulation of the production and sale of spiritous liquors, together with methods of their production, is described in 2.25. The director of agriculture regulates, among other matters, sowing, reaping, choice of crop, methods of cultivation, irrigation, water rates, the application of fish fertilizer, and gardeners' wages (2.24). The functions of the superintendent of pasture lands include the development and exploitation of these partly agricultural areas (2.34).

A number of departments of government are concerned with regulatory or fiscal and fiscally related functions. The functions and operating procedures of the administrator of revenue are described in detail (2.6), together with those of the superintendent of the records office (2.7) and procedures for preventing misappropriation or loss of revenue (2.8–9). The activities of departments concerned with the actual collection of taxes, duties, and tolls are described (2.21–22, 28, 31, 35) as are the regulatory activities of the director of trade (2.16) and the controller of shipping (2.28). The standardization of weights and measures is described in chapters dealing with the work of the superintendent of standardization (2.19) and the superintendent of measurement (2.20). The legality of transactions as well as the conveyance of property by sale or in keeping with laws of inheritance is described at length in book 3 on the administration of legal and customary law. Regulation of the activities of artisans and traders, together with taxes and salaries, is dealt with even in accounts of criminal justice (4.1–2; 5.2–3).[50] Books 6–8 deal with foreign policy, though not with its economic implications (but see 8.4.33–50) which, however, crop up here and there in books on military activities (9–14).

Kautalya's Economics

Kautalya's discussion of economic matters falls under three heads: (i) the relation of wealth to a state's power; (ii) the collection of revenue; (iii) the pricing of commodities, of labor, and of capital, together with its regulation. This discussion takes for granted that the state plays a large or even a predominant role in agriculture, industry, and trade, and that enterprise, when private, is usually subject to guild and related control if not also to state control. After all, state control tended to safeguard state income as well as strengthen arrangements making for social peace.[51]

(i) The power of a state, while dependent upon "the power of knowledge" and "the power of valour" (6.2.33; 7.11.45; 8.1.23; 10.6.51), rested mainly upon its wealth, though increase in political power served to augment economic power. To judge by his various observations, Kautalya believed wealth to consist mainly in arable land, mineral and related resources, and the manpower required to cultivate the land, extract raw materials, and fabricate the products of agriculture and other extractive industries (2.1; 6.1.8; 7.10–11; 8.1.19–23, 28; also 2.12, 17, 24). He included among the seven "constituent elements (of the state)" the "treasury" and "the country" (6.1.1). Another element of the state, "the army," is

---

50. Much of Kautalya's discussion of justice in bk. 3 is in keeping with dharmashastra tradition. Kangle, pt. 3, chap. 9, esp. pp. 230–31. See also B. Sen, chaps. 9–12.
51. Kane, 3:184–86, 188; B. Sen, chaps. 4, 6, 13.

brought into being by "the treasury," which "has its source in the mines" and which, in conjunction with the army, constitutes the "power of might" (6.2.23) and obtains "the earth" (2.12.37; 8.1.46–52). The "treasury," moreover, when rich in gold and silver, enables a state to "withstand a calamity even of long duration in which there is no income" (6.1.10) much as an abundance of food reserves cushions the impact of famine (2.15.22; 4.3.17; 8.4.5–7, 46).

Land varied greatly in quality, in part because of great variation in rainfall (2.24). Some was inarable or unhealthy (2.1.36). Its productivity and attractiveness depended upon fertility of the soil, accessibility of water, adaptability of the soil to various crops, and availability and density of population (2.1; 7.10–11, 14). Sparsely settled land might, however, attract gold and population. It was advisable, nonetheless, that the ruler provide (or assist in the provision of) utilizable roads and water transport, reservoirs, other overhead capital, advice or directions respecting choice of crop and mode of cultivation, and (especially in newly settled land) healthy and secure sites for the establishment of villages and towns (2.1; 2.24; 3.9–10; 5.2.3–4).[52] Developed land, while a crucial source of a country's strength, was not the only source:

Possessed of strong positions in the centre and at the frontiers, capable of sustaining itself and others in times of distress, easy to protect, providing excellent (means of) livelihood, malevolent towards enemies, with weak neighbouring princes, devoid of mud, stones, salty ground, uneven land, thorns, bands, wild animals, deer and forest tribes, charming, endowed with agricultural land, mines, material forests and elephant forests, beneficial to cattle, beneficial to men, with protected pastures, rich in animals, not depending on rain for water, provided with water-routes and land-routes, with valuable, manifold and plenty of commodities, capable of bearing fines and taxes, with farmers devoted to work, with a wise master, inhabited mostly by the lower *varnas*, with men loyal and honest,—these are excellences of a country [6.1.8].

Statements of this sort appear in later works.[53] They are applicable to the whole of India or to self-sufficient parts of India.[54] Kautalya's

52. The colonization and settlement to which Kautalya refers seem to have been internal to the empire rather than abroad, though he discusses the naval establishment. Indian colonization of southeast Asia began later, but not "later than the first century A.D." See R. C. Majumdar, *Ancient Indian Colonisation*, pp. 5–6, 13.

53. Kane, 3:132 ff., 177. Compare Agrawala, chap. 2, sec. 4, and pp. 477–91; and Ghoshal, *History*, pp. 482–93, on tenth-century Jain Somadeva's Kautalya-like views of geopolitics and politics.

54. Kane, 3:134–36; B. C. Law. Megasthenes reported autonomous units in the Maurya Empire. Bongard-Levin.

imperial polity apparently relates to India rather than to lands bordering on India.[55] He does not explicitly recognize the tendency to Ricardian diminishing returns implicit in his account of the quite unequally colonizable and unevenly cultivable character of India's lands.

Kautalya did not put forward a population policy beyond that relating to settlement and touched upon in the preceding section. He virtually ignored the role of natural increase except for his reference to unhealthy and inarable lands (2.1.36), marital duties (3.3.1, 12; 3.4.24.31–36), conditions of remarriage (3.2.19–48), and disease, famine, and floods (8.4.5–8). A wife might, with permission of the judges, remarry 3–12 periods after having been deserted by her husband, "for, frustration of the period is destruction of sacred duty" (3.4.31–36). A man was not free to become an ascetic until he had provided for his sons and wife and "lost his capacity for activity" (2.1.29–31). Kautalya emphasized the need of population to exploit land and extractive resources (e.g., 7.11), especially the need for Vaishyas and Shudras (2.1.2; 7.11.21), though he remarked that normally the "number of common men" was "very large." Accordingly, the "loss of chiefs" was a much greater calamity than that of common men; their number was very small and their "spirit and intelligence" were crucial in military and presumably other affairs (8.4.9–12 and 6.2.33–34).

(ii) Given the importance of wealth and the "treasury" (2.8.1), it was essential that the economy be extended, that land and resources be intensively exploited, that the ruler acquire a sufficient share of the output resulting, and that his income base rather than the tax rate be augmented.[56] It was desirable, therefore, that excessive taxation as well as both private and royal waste (8.4.23; 3.17.15–16) be avoided.[57] Kautalya described the king's revenue

55. Kangle, 3:262–65.
56. Causes of treasury increase ("prosperousness of activities, cherishing of customs, suppression of thieves, control over employees, luxuriance of crops, abundance of commodities, deliverance from troubles, reduction in exemptions, [and] presents in cash") and of treasury decrease ("hindrance, lending, trading, concealment, causing loss, use, interchange, and misappropriation") are identified (2.8.3–4). See also on "replenishment of the treasury" (5.2), and on "treasury calamity" (8.1.22–54; 8.4.48–50).
57. On the Brahmanic view of taxation as eating wealth, etc., see Spellman, *Political Theory*, pp. 176–79. "He who causes loss of revenue consumes the property of the king. . . . He who procures double the (normal) revenue consumes the countryside" (2.9.16; 2.1.15–17). "He should take from the kingdom fruits as they ripen, as from a garden; he should avoid unripe (fruit) that causes an uprising, for

(based mainly on land and crown property and secondarily on tolls, imposts, and fines) as amounting to compensation or maintenance for his bringing about order and "the well-being and security of the subjects" (1.13.5–7, 9), a view shared by more recent authors in the West.[58] Kautalya identified about sixty-seven sources and seven categories of revenue, together with eleven types of expenditure (2.6), much of it in kind. He acquiesced in what must have been accepted opinion, that some classes of persons, mainly Brahmans, should remain exempt from taxes and tolls and be favored in respect of inheritance (3.6–7), government grants, use of public capital, etc.

Kautalya's discussion of taxation and expenditure, apparently in keeping with traditional doctrine, gave expression to three Indian principles: taxing power is limited; taxation should not be felt to be heavy or excessive; tax increases should be graduated.[59] One of his main concerns seems to have been the collection and expenditure of revenue in such wise as to build up the permanent revenue-yielding capacity of the economy. While he manifested little knowledge of tax shifting and incidence, he emphasized the long run, cautioned against too heavy taxation in the short run, and noted that a ruler could not tax at his pleasure, particularly in frontier regions whence disgruntled taxpayers could flee to neighboring countries (5.2.3). It therefore behooved the king to collect revenue economically as well as to avoid both unnecessary expenditure and the employment of unneeded servants (5.3.1; 8.4.23). It was essential, however, that the ruler supply sufficient social overhead capital and developmental assistance or encourage it through tax exemption (3.9.33–34), that he direct expenditure into profitable works and properties, and that he keep on hand sufficient reserves of food, clothing, munitions, gold, and other means, to meet needs imposed by calamities, emergencies, war,

---

fear of his own destruction" (5.2.70). Regarding private waste he declared that "the patrimony-squanderer, the immediate-spender and the niggardly" should be kept "in check" (2.9.20–24). See also B. Sen, chap. 10 and pp. 4–7, 36, 78.

58. On the "protection" justification and theory, see Spellman, *Political Theory,* pp. 179–83. St. Thomas Aquinas, in *De regimine Judaeorum,* described the stipends of princes as "their pay." This theory was present in Pali literature of Buddha's period. See Chanana, p. 425, and p. 426 on promoting settlement.

59. Kane, 3:184–89, 192–93. B. A. Saletore, *Ancient Indian Political Thought,* p. 448, describes Kautalya's "theory of public finance" as both "comprehensive" and "probably the world's most ancient." See also Ghoshal, *Contributions;* Panini's report in Agrawala, pp. 413–15; Balkrishna, "Hindu Taxation."

and so on. It was the duty of the "wise" administrator of revenue to "fix the revenue and show an increase in income and decrease in expenditure" and to "remedy the opposite of these" (2.6.28). This entailed (among other things) careful accounting (2.7) and the prevention of embezzlement (2.8–9), of which there were forty forms (2.8.20).

Kautalya distinguished between ordinary rates of taxation and rates temporarily permissible in times of emergency when the king lacked money and grain (7.5.33), was "without a treasure," and faced "difficulties concerning money" (5.2.1). In ordinary times, the king was entitled to one-sixth of the agricultural produce; one-tenth to one-sixth of various animal, etc., catches; 4 to 20 percent on imports except the small number not permitted; sundry other charges on merchants; 5 percent on liquor sales and gambling stakes; taxes on uses of transport facilities; something like two days per month of the earnings of prostitutes; taxes in terms of labor and military service, and various taxes whose meaning and significance are not clear (1.13; 2.15–17, 21–22, 25, 27–28, 34–35; 3.9–10, 20; 5.2). He also enjoyed "accidental" revenue (3.5; 4.1)—numberless fines and shares in treasure troves, findings, escheated property, etc. The king derived additional revenue from tolls (2.28) as well as from irrigation water rates based on the amount of water used (2.24.5, 18); from his share-cropped (2.24.16–17) and other crown land (of whose net yield the king might get as such as 50–80 percent), and from mining and manufacturing activities carried on by his agents or tenants (2.6, 12–17, 23–24, 28). In times of emergency (war, calamity) many of these standard tax rates in money or kind might be temporarily stepped up (e.g., the normal tax on grain stocks and/or yields might become one-fourth or one-third) if necessary, and more people might be made subject to taxation, though even then the tax liability of agriculturalists was to be varied "according to their capacity," while colonizers and developers were to remain particularly favored (5.2) by lower rates or assistance. The rich might be compelled to assist the needy or the king (4.3), and the wealth of the "irreligious" might be seized (5.2). In times of emergency, moreover, many dubious means of raising money were to be approved (5.2.31–69). "A king with a small treasury swallows up the citizens and the country people themselves" (2.1.16).

(iii) Kautalya's views on economic behavior are found mainly in his discussion of pricing and its regulation and secondarily in his treatment of crop sharing (e.g., 2.24). His analysis, of course, was implicit, not explicit; it rested upon the assumption that individual behavior could be controlled in large measure through economic rewards and penalties, particularly when these were commensurate with the action to be encouraged or discouraged (1.8.27–29; 2.23.16; 3.17.5). "Violation of property means loss of livelihood. Not giving (what belongs to the other), taking away, destroying or abandoning property is a violation of property" (8.3.28–29). Accordingly, while Kautalya looked at economic issues through the eyes of an economic administrator, he was aware that rules must fit man's economic propensities and foster rather than repress useful economic activity. For example, in his city plan he recognized the importance of trade and made provision for guilds, foreign merchants, and the transport, display, and sale of goods (2.4.16; 4.2). He recognized the critical economic importance of the two lowest varna, the Vaishyas and the Shudras (7.11.21). He was interested in formulating rules which would contribute to political stability by ensuring something like economic "justice" and preventing transactions which might disturb the existing social order.

While it is not always clear from Kautalya's discussion what he intended, it is apparent that he did not understand the social role of competition and feared that trading profits might be excessive. He was aware that an increase in buyers or their purchasing power tended to augment prices both of settled land [60] and of reproducible commodities. Prices reflected actual or potential scarcity (4.2; 2.21.7–14) as well as the presence of monopolistic arrangements (2.6.10; 4.2.18–19, 28–30). That an increase in prices, by making possible greater profits, might augment supply, and thus finally reduce prices and profits, he usually ignored though he did note that more favorable terms would augment the inflow of desired imports (2.16.11–13, 20; 2.21.18, 31). He recognized, furthermore,

---

60. When immobile property was up for sale, "kinsmen, neighbors and creditors, in this order, shall have the right to purchase landed property (on sale). After that, others who are outsiders (may bid for purchase)." When owners thrice proclaim a dwelling for sale at a specified price, "the purchaser shall be entitled to purchase." However, "in case of increase in price because of competition, the increase in price together with the tax shall go to the treasury. The (successful) bidder at the sale shall pay the tax" (3.9.1–7).

that improvements in transport, especially of land routes, augmented the flow of goods (7.11.17; 7.12, 17–28).

Kautalya seems to have had in mind what amounts to a notion of just price, cost plus reasonable profit, and a distinction between "interest" and "profit." [61] His discussion assumes a director of trade supposedly conversant

with the differences in the prices of commodities of high value and of low value and the popularity or unpopularity of goods of various kinds, whether produced on land or in water (and) whether they have arrived along land-routes or water-routes, (and who) also (should know about) suitable times for resorting to dispersal or concentration, purchase or sale [2.16.1].

This director should allow a price including a reasonable but not excessive profit in respect of exports (2.16.25), imports, and "royal commodities" produced domestically. "A big profit that would be injurious to the subjects" was to be avoided (2.16.4–6). Costs, including interest, must be allowed for when regulating price and fixing profit.

In the case of commodities distant in place and time, however, the . . . expert in fixing prices, shall fix the price after calculating the investment, the production of goods, duty, interest, rent and other expenses [4.2.36].
In foreign territory, however, he should ascertain the price and the value of the commodity (taken out) and the commodity (to be bought) in exchange and should calculate the profit after clearing expenses for duty, road cess, escort-charges, picket- and ferry-dues, food and fodder and [foreign-state's] share [2.16.18].

Apparently in order to facilitate price regulation and the collection of the state's share, commodities were not to be sold "in the places of their origin" but at selected points (2.16.4; 2.22.9–15; 3.12. 25–26). When, upon imports being auctioned, the "competition among purchasers" pushes the price above what presumably is the proper level, "the increase in price together with the duty shall go to the treasury" (2.21.7–9). "If, through fear of a rival purchaser a (trader) increases the price beyond the (due) price of a commodity, the king shall receive the increase in price, or make the

61. At least a century before Kautalya wrote, Panini clearly distinguished between the "capital" invested in an object and the "profit" realized on it when it was sold. Agrawala, p. 240. Kautalya seems to have reasoned likewise (4.2.28; also 2.16.4–6 on interest and profit).

amount of duty double" (2.21.13; also 2.21.10–12).[62] Charging a profit in excess of that allowed was subject to penalty (4.2.28–30). Presumably profit could fall below normal, since gluts of commodities could develop (4.2.31–35) and, if they were perishable, eventuate in lowered prices (2.16.2–3, 7). When prices fell and profit diminished or disappeared, the loss normally did not fall upon an agent but upon his principal (3.12.25–30).

Kautalya deals with allowable weight losses in production as well as with adulteration (2.12–16, 19; 3.15; 4.2). Rules relating to rescission of sale and purchase also served to assure quality (3.15).

Interest is treated in connection with debts and deposits, which are dealt with in book 3, on regal and customary law, the legality of transactions (3.1.6), liability for suretyship, and evidence relating thereto. Debtor-creditor relations, together with interest, were regulated. Of concern here, however, is the fixity of interest rates. Not one but a number of interest maxima were prescribed. Moreover, Kautalya declared, as did Manu and Gautama, that sons and heirs were responsible for repayment of the debts of the deceased (3.11. 13–21).

Differences in these interest maxima reflected differences in risk, uncertainty, and other circumstances surrounding loans of various types (3.11–12). The permissible maxima ranged from the commonly approved 1.25 percent per month on what appear to be secured loans, up through 5 percent on "commercial" loans and 10 percent when borrowers traverse land routes through forests, to 20 percent on loans connected with sea trade, which was considered more risky than land trade (7.11.17; 7.12.20, 25). Even higher rates were sanctioned when risks were still greater or grain was lent. Violators of these rules were subject to punishment (3.11.1–5).[63]

62. A notion of just price was common in the Mesopotamian world. Oppenheim, *Ancient Mesopotamia*, pp. 358, n. 31, 360, n. 56, and pp. 102, 129, 144. On trade and price see B. Sen, chap. 3.

63. "One *pana* and a quarter is the lawful rate of interest per month on one hundred *panas*, five *panas* for purposes of trade, ten *panas* for those going through forests, twenty *panas* for those going by sea. For one charging or making another charge a rate beyond that, the punishment shall be the lowest fine for violence, for witnesses, each one of them, half the fine. If, however, the king is unable to ensure protection, the (judge) should take into consideration the usual practice among creditors and debtors. Interest on grains (shall be) up to half, on the harvesting of crops. . . . Interest on capital (shall amount to) half the profit" (3.11.1–5). Traders advancing supplies to soldiers on expedition and to be paid later were allowed to charge double (5.3.42–44), presumably to cover interest and unusual risk. See B. Sen, chap. 11. On the proverbial perils of sea trade and its uncertain rewards, see D. R. Das, pp. 257–70.

If the lender holding a pledge (say a house) was paid more for its use than the interest due on the pledged house, the excess apparently belonged to the creditor (3.12.15–16). The total amount repayable by a borrower in at least some instances was not to exceed double the principal (3.11). These rates suggest that moneylending was less restricted in India than in Mesopotamia or among the Hebrews.[64]

Moneylending was a lawful occupation in India a century or more before Kautalya wrote, though opprobrium was attached to the charging of excessive or usurious interest, that is, 10 percent or more. The sanctioned level thus rose markedly in the century before Kautalya wrote.[65] Of the six special forms of interest distinguished in ancient India ("compound interest, periodical interest, stipulated interest, corporeal interest, daily interest, and use of a pledged article") Panini referred to all but daily interest. He referred also, as did Kautalya (2.1.13–14; 2.15.3), to interest-free grain loans.[66] He distinguished between the capital invested and the profit earned thereon, as apparently did Kautalya (4.2.29). Indeed, the idea of expressing interest as percent, or so many units per 100, originated in India.[67] Moreover, some of the problems dealt with over the centuries in Indian commercial arithmetic date back to Kautalya's time and earlier and relate to interest.[68] Mathematics was early a part of the educational program for the young and continued to be so.[69] Works on mathematics continued to be produced and studied in the modern era, and commercial arithmetic continued to be a subject of instruction.

Having treated Kautalya's views on commodity prices and interest, I turn to his discussion of the pricing of services. (He said so little about the pricing of land that its implications, outside the realm of administrative rule, are negligible.) His account of the pricing of services may be divided into two parts, that dealing with the salaries of state servants and that relating to other payments for services.

Three criteria governed Kautalya in his prescription of wages

64. Oppenheim, *Ancient Mesopotamia*, pp. 88–89, 102.
65. Agrawala, pp. 274–77.
66. Agrawala, pp. 278–79, and 202–3 on crop loans. See also A. Bose, 2:101–18.
67. B. Datta and Singh, 1:218 and n. 2.
68. B. Datta and Singh, pp. 218–26; W. E. Clark, pp. x–xiii, 38–39. Cf. Leemans, p. 15; Neugebauer, pp. 34, 44, 183.
69. B. Datta and Singh, 1:6; Apte, p. 169. Kautalya declared that after tonsure the prince "should learn the use of the alphabet and arithmetic" (1:5.7).

and salaries for state employees. The loyalty of high-echelon officials needed to be assured (5.3.3–4, 7–10; 5.6.37); efficiency and
effort needed to be evoked (5.3.8, 16, 24, 33; 2.24.29); pay by
occupation needed to be in keeping with an occupation's relative
standing. The aggregate wage and salary bill of the state should not
exceed one-fourth of its revenue (5.3.1). The annual salaries of
upper-echelon bureaucrats were listed at 4,000–48,000 *panas*,
60 of which may have purchased enough to supply a worker's
family with subsistence (5.3.3–11). Astrologers, teachers, learned
men, and various superintendents are listed at 1,000; foot soldiers,
accountants, clerks, at 500; entertainers at 250; artisans and artists
at 120; spies of various sorts at 250–1,000 (5.3.12–16, 22–27). Food
and wages were to be given the wives and sons of those killed in
the line of duty (5.3.28–31). A wage of 60 *panas* per year was
listed for servants, valets, animal-attendants, and similar workers,
to be paid partly in kind if the treasury was short of cash (5.3.17,
31). Kautalya indicates the proper monthly wage for garden
watchmen, cowherds, and laborers to be "food in accordance with
persons dependent on them," and a wage of one *pana* and a
quarter (2.24.28). A family of four would require about 2 *adhakas*
(or about 8 pounds) of rice grains, together with fat, for subsistence in addition to the allowance of 15 *panas* cash for other purposes.[70]

How to fix wages in particular industries, usually in rough keeping with productivity, is indicated in several places (2.23.3–16;
2.24.16, 28–29; 2.29.3), but not the circumstance determining wage
levels. Wages in villages and under other conditions are men-

---

70. It is not clear from the data how badly off workers were. See A. Bose, 2:202–13.
The daily food requirement of a male Arya was put at 3 *prastha* of rice grains,
together with fat; for a minor, 1½; for a woman, 2¼ (2.15.48); hence for a family
of four, at about 8¼ *prastha*—just over 2 adhaka, or about 8 pounds a day (5.3.34,
and Kangle's note thereto). But compare Kangle, 3:209. This daily ration exceeds
the minimum daily requirement estimated by Clark and Haswell, pp. 61–62, at
about 1.4 pounds. According to Pran Nath, pp. 81–83, the support of a Brahman
for a year was the produce of an acre. This comes to around 600 pounds of wheat,
given a gross crop of 15 bushels, with loss and leakage and seed requirements at 5
bushels. According to T. B. Jones and J. W. Snyder, p. 252, unskilled Sumerian
workers were paid a subsistence wage of 9 or more pounds per day, but it is not
clear whether this relatively high wage was for the entire year or only for days
worked. Kane, 3:120–26, believes that Kautalya's wage figures are in copper and
hence monthly, but this is denied by Kangle. On wages and rations see also B. Sen,
chaps. 4, 8–9.

tioned (2.28.23; 3.1.22–23; 3.10–35–36; 3.13, 27–33; 3.14.1–15; 4.1.1–35), together with penalties imposed in the event of nonperformance of work. The law concerning slaves is also described (3.13.1–25). When wages had not been agreed upon in advance, workers were paid in keeping with custom, with what others doing that type of work got, or with what "experts" decided was proper (3.13.26–31, 35, 37). Nonpayment of wages was subject to penalty (3.13.33–34).

Rules for the distribution of remuneration when work was done jointly not only were laid down by Kautalya but also found expression in commercial arithmetic.[71] When workmen, guild members, or others engage in cooperative undertakings, they "shall divide the wages as agreed upon or in equal proportions" (3.14.18). Should a partner to an undertaking have become ill, his share should correspond to the "work as done by him" or by his substitute (3.14.19–22). Voluntary nonperformance of his role subjected a partner to penalty (3.14.23–28).

These rules applied to priests cooperating in a sacrifice. "Sacrificial priests shall divide the fees as agreed upon or in equal shares, excepting objects received for each one's special duties" (3.14.28). Should a priest fall ill, his share was to be fixed according to rule and in keeping with his degree of participation in the sacrifice; some sacrifices lasted "many days" (3.14.29–33). The remaining priests were to perform the duties of those fallen ill (3.14.33–34). Failure on the part of a priest to fulfill his duty if able was punishable (3.14.35–36, 37–38). According to Sen-Gupta (and Kane) the origin of joint-enterprise law in India lies in the distribution of sacrifice fees. "The origin of the entire law regarding joint enterprise was the customary rule of division of the profits of a sacrifice by the several officiating priests, at a time when joint enterprise in trade or other matters was probably unknown to law."[72]

---

71. B. Datta and Singh, pp. 226–29.

72. Sen-Gupta, pp. 243–44. Manu used such division to illustrate partnership distribution (viii, 206–11). Sages whose works appeared soon after Manu's illustrate partnership division in terms of the sharing of trading profits. See, for example, what much-cited Narada and Brihaspati say in their works, forming vol. 33 of the Sacred Books of the East; Sen-Gupta, pp. 244–45; Kane, vol. 3, chap. 18, esp. 469–70. Corporate bodies, partnerships, guilds, etc., were allowed legal personality in Hindu law. See Derrett, *Introduction*, pp. 223 ff.; Mookerji, *Local Government;* R. C. Majumdar, *Corporate Life*. On guild practices and recourse to customary law, see Tirumalachar; Chakraborti, chap. 8.

Aftermath

Kautalya's influence did not disappear. His views apparently had followers for perhaps fifteen centuries after the initial composition of his work. The work underwent little change after 200 A.D. and none after the fourth or fifth century A.D. The arthashastra disappeared from general view in or after 1100–1300 A.D. Around this period dharmashastra views and medieval ideals in politics became ascendant, far beyond the level of emphasis put upon dharma in the arthashastra.[73] In the 1920s, however, scholarly rather than practical interest in Kautalya's work began to grow. Recently Kautalya's "remarkable concept of the Circle of States" was described as being as "close to that of an international system as we could wish." [74]

The Maurya Empire, whose structure and operation were in keeping with Kautalya's image of empire, underwent disintegration after the death in 232 B.C., of Ashoka, Buddhist and India's Marcus Aurelius. The resources required to sustain this empire were no longer forthcoming; expansion was at an end, and contraction in prospect. Ashoka's response, in the form of his policy of *dhamma*,[75] a more inclusive concept than dharma, failed to weld the people into a nation or national community and generate political loyalty. The values Ashoka sought to inculcate in the peoples of his almost India-wide empire did not become sufficiently internalized. Nor was the bureaucracy sufficiently institutionalized and impersonal to supply a unifying alternative. Yet the idea of state was gradually replaced by Dharma or "social order" and political sanctions were partly replaced by divine ones. "Loyalty to the Social Order was actuated at a local level, largely through the institution of caste, and this in turn contributed to an absence

73. Dwivedi, pp. 14, 26, 29. The Kamandakiya Nitisara, a summary of Kautalya's work, was written by a minister of the Guptas. See R. C. Majumdar and Altekar, p. 410.

74. Modelski, p. 665. In the twelfth century the minister to the king of Benares described Kautalya's work as a sixth veda, the Mahabharata having been declared the fifth. Aiyangar, *Indian Cameralism*, p. 30. The famous Indian collection of fables, the Panchatantra, composed in Kashmir about 200 B.C., reflects Kautalya's influence throughout. See Ruben, *Pancatantra*.

75. Thapar, *Asoka;* Nikam and McKeon; Kosambi, *Introduction*, chap. 7; N. R. Ray, pp. 369–76, on conflict between popular sentiments and Maurya administration and values.

of a wider unity." Subsequent attempts at empire never resulted in so much central control and direction as was achieved in the Maurya Empire, since intermediaries possessing a certain degree of autonomy could and did intrude between king and subject.[76]

The empire for which Kautalya contrived his manual and which fell apart after Ashoka's death was not to be replaced for five centuries, and then only partially by the Guptas. Ashoka's dharma, stressing as it did moderation in acquisition and spending, as well as some decentralization of decision making, embodied values at variance with those which had made for empire.[77] Even so, many of his conceptions resembled Kautalya's.[78]

Efforts on the part of smaller states to extend their sway after the disintegration of the Maurya Empire always failed in the end. They had to be satisfied, as Kautalya prescribed on occasion (6.3), with a hegemonic position that, even if imposed for the moment, would be rejected at the first opportunity. Neither the Shunga successor state to the Mauryas nor the more southerly Satavahana state, nor other states emerging between the day of the Mauryas and that of the Guptas could unify much of India politically. India became more unified culturally and perhaps also economically, however, with the spread of Aryan culture to the Tamil South and into border areas and with the development of trade routes within India and between it and the West and East.[79] Basic economic conditions apparently did not change greatly, however, and essentially Kautalyan principles and practices probably remained in vogue. Governments probably continued to absorb perhaps as much as 20–25 percent of the national income, while the common man seldom got more than a poor subsistence.[80] More important, per capita productivity increased little if at all;

76. Thapar, *History*, pp. 90–91.

77. Nikam and McKeon, esp. pp. 58–63. Ashoka ordered wells to be dug every half-mile along roads, together with watering stations and rest houses. Ibid., p. 64.

78. B. A. Saletore, *Ancient Indian Political Thought*, pp. 554–80.

79. Thapar, *History*, chap. 5; R. S. Sharma, *Light*, pp. 70–89; B. Sen, chap. 5; Adhya, pp. 95–178; Sastri, *Comprehensive History*, vol. 2. On the Tamil South, see Subrahmanian, chaps. 8, 9, 13; D. R. Das, passim.

80. The Maurya state must have absorbed close to a fourth or more of the nation's output. See Jha, p. 41; M. H. Gopal. It has been suggested but not demonstrated that the financial burden of government was lower under the Satavahana rulers than under the Mauryas. Sastri, *Comprehensive History*, 2:318. See also Gopalachari. A tax of one-sixth of gross output would approximate at least 18 percent of net output in agriculture. To this amount, other taxes must be added.

this was to be expected in a society in which potential capital was largely consumed and the two uppermost orders were virtually excluded from direct participation in agriculture, industry, and commerce.

It was in a many-state Indian world, therefore, that Manu's work, discussed in the next chapter, took form. Yet this many-state India continued to resemble the single-state world of Kautalya in a variety of respects, despite the decline of empire and of the influence of secular, rationalistic, politicoeconomic ideas. The role and content of law as developed by Kautalya remained influential, though perhaps less so than political organization as such.[81] Comments on Kautalya's economics are reserved to chapter 7.

81. Sen-Gupta, p. 24; Kane, 3:143, and chaps. 12 ff., on the development of civil law in India. See, on the works of lesser Brahman as well as Jain authors more or less in the arthashastra tradition between 400 and 1200 A.D., Ghoshal, *History*, chaps. 21–28.

Chapter 4

Manu's Dharmashastra

> Even when laws have been written down, they ought
> not always to remain unaltered.
>
> ARISTOTLE

Most important of the dharmashastras is the Manusmriti, put into
final form between 200 B.C. and 200 A.D. This work is not to be
confused with a work on *niti* (i.e., politics) by Pracetasa Manu, or
Manavas, to whose arthashastra school and now nonextant works
Kautalya refers several times.[1] The author (whom hereinafter we
shall call Manu) probably was somewhat influenced by Kautalya's
Arthashastra as well as by authors upon whom Kautalya drew.[2]
The Manusmriti is the first of the dharmashastras and one of the
two Instructions in Sacred Law that have come down to us in en-
tirety. The other is Yajnavalkya's Smriti. Manu's work is eclectic,
unconnected with any Vedic school; it incorporates much earlier
material and opinion, sometimes with elaboration or addition of
arthashastra matter. Manu ranged over all of man's activities, view-
ing him as an agent subject to the rule of law and duty. Concerned
primarily with conduct, his work summarized and symbolized
Hinduism; as a result, much of what he said was widely diffused in
his day, repeated (sometimes with greater precision) in later
commentaries and digests, and in some measure internalized and
institutionalized. Many centuries later a seventeenth-century
version of the Institutes of Vishnu embodied much of Manu, and
later still Shukra, author of a work once mistakenly dated to the
Middle Ages, professed to follow Manu.[3]

1. Kangle, 3:14–15, 78–83.
2. Kangle, 3:80–83.
3. Sastri, *Comprehensive History*, 657–58; Ghoshal, *History*, passim; Julius Jolly,
Introduction to the Institutes of Vishnu, in *Sacred Books of the East*, 7:12–48,
189–90.

The period during which the work of Manu took final shape (200 B.C.–A.D. 200) coincides roughly with the period of "the rise of the mercantile community (c. 200 B.C.–A.D. 300)," [4] a rise made possible by the development of roads and uniform administration under the Mauryas, by the emergence of ethical religions (i.e., Buddhism and Jainism) deemed more favorable to trade and development than was Hinduism, and perhaps also by the greater opportunity for private enterprise and guilds to flourish in a society in which the state was no longer so powerful, the demands of empire were less, and Hinduism had not become completely ascendant.[5] In and after the third century A.D., the social structure became more rigid, in considerable part as a result of the increasing authority accorded the social laws laid down by Manu. "The period between A.D. 300 and 500 witnessed the fully developed form of the traditional religion as modified by the developments since 600 B.C."; during it religion "acted as a causal factor in a limited way" only. "The period between A.D. 500 and 800 experienced a reversal of the trend of liberalization of the social structure, a weakening of the emphasis on the codes of behaviour and social relationship and a tendency to depend increasingly upon the supernatural." [6] It was the immobility and "rusticity" that came in the wake of the village, closely identified with Hinduism, which constituted the major obstacle to economic development, Kosambi believes.[7]

Forerunners

Manu drew upon then extant arthashastra literature as well as upon the dharmasutras, the oldest of which was Gautama's Insti-

4. Thapar, *History*, chap. 6; and G. L. Adhya.
5. Mishra believes that except for the doctrines of caste and ahimsa (noninjury to men and animals), traditional religion was not unfavorable and probably was favorable to economic development in the period between 300 B.C. and 300 A.D., during which the social structure was liberalized. During the four hundred years ending about A.D. 100, secular and rationalistic ideas exerted more influence than ever before or thereafter until the nineteenth century. Mishra, p. 26.
6. Mishra, pp. 30, 33; Thapar, *History*, pp. 121–24. See also chap. 3 above, n. 13.
7. The smriti "foreshadows complete victory of the village, with consequences far deadlier than invasion. The hidebound caste system became rigid only within stagnant villages whose chief intellectual product, the *brahman*, was stamped with incurable rusticity elevated to religious dogma." Kosambi, *Introduction*, p. 243. On the village in, under, and after Gupta times, see Altekar, *History*. On the village and stagnation, see Marriott, *Village India*.

tutes of the Sacred Law.[8] Less stress is placed on wealth in these works than in arthashastra literature, Gautama declaring wealth the least of the criteria of social status (vi, 20). The doctrine of the four varnas or "castes" pervades Gautama's Institutes, along with the view that all men "must serve those who belong to higher castes" (x, 66). To each caste he assigned activities or occupations lawful for it (x, 1–4, 44, 49, 56) as well as sets of rights and duties, compliance with which would earn one merit and superior rebirth (xi, 29–30). Gautama relaxed occupational constraints in several ways. Unlike other smriti authors, he permitted a Brahman to play a supervisory or at least sleeping-partner role in agriculture, trade, and moneylending (x, 5–7). Alert also to economic uncertainties, he indicated that "in times of distress" a Brahman might follow the occupations of a Kshatriya or virtually at worst those of a Vaishya (vi, 18; vii, 6–8, 22–23), and a Kshatriya might pursue those of a Vaishya (vii, 26), i.e., "agriculture, trade, tending cattle, and lending money at interest" (x, 49). Shudras, while free to pursue "mechanical arts" (x, 60), were obliged to serve the higher castes and even support them in "distress," though normally each was entitled to support at the hands of his protecting Arya (x, 56–57, 61–63) much as were all employees (x, 34). Shudra status (like caste status generally) affected an individual's liability to punishment, his access to economic advantage (xii), and his rights under the law of inheritance (xxviii). Property could be acquired by all in certain ways (i.e., by inheritance, purchase, partition, seizure, or finding). But a Brahman could acquire it also by gift and a Kshatriya by conquest, whereas a Vaishya or a Shudra had to labor for it (x, 39–42).

Gautama devoted some attention to the king, his duties (among them support of the caste system), and his claims. Among these duties were protection of the taxpayers, the collection of taxes, and apparently, limitation of his personal expenses to what was left of tax revenue after the internal and external security of the kingdom had been provided for (x, 28–30). Cultivators were to pay between one-tenth and one-sixth of the produce as taxes, the actual rate depending upon the nature of the soil and its cultivation (x, 25). A tax of one-fifteenth was imposable upon the stock

8. This work, together with Apastamba's Aphorisms on the Sacred Law, constitutes vol. 2 of the *Sacred Books of the East*. Both works date from around 600 B.C. See also Kane, 1:12–20, 32–46, 135–38.

or increment (?) of gold and cattle, one-twentieth upon merchandise sales, and one-sixtieth upon the output of fruits, herbs, meat, firewood, etc. (x, 25–26). Artisans were subject to corvée; they were required to work a day a month for the king (x, 31). Owners of ships and carts were taxed (x, 33). The king shared in military spoils (x, 22–23), in recovered lost property and treasure trove (x, 36–38, 43–45), and in "the spiritual merit (gained by his subjects)" (xi, 11). While Vedic and related Sacred Law was overriding (i, 1–2, 4; xi, 19), regional and class rules were allowed to govern the behavior of members of local bodies if the rules in question did not run counter to the overriding law (xi, 20–25; xiii, 11). Thus merchants could decide their own disputes, but they had to "give (every month one) article of merchandise for less than the market value" (x, 35).

Gautama says nothing of wages except perhaps to foreshadow a later distributive principle when he observes that "unlearned (coparceners) shall divide (their acquisitions) equally," whereas "what a learned (coparcener) had acquired by his own efforts, he may (at his pleasure) withhold from his unlearned (coparceners)" (xxviii, 34). The normal rate of interest is put at 1.25 percent per month; no interest is to be collected on a pledged loan when the creditor uses the pledge, presumably to earn interest (xii, 29, 32). While repayment of a loan, together with the interest on it, was limited to double the principal (xii, 31), a higher multiple could hold for loans connected with agricultural production (xii, 36). Gautama identified a number of forms of interest (compound, periodical, stipulated, corporal, daily, and use of pledge), but made no application of the distinction (xii, 35).

Several authors, among them Baudhayana and Vasishtha, writing somewhat later than Gautama, agreed with him in basing the interpretation of dharma (which was of divine origin) upon the vedas, traditions (*smriti*), and practices (*shila*) of those versed in the vedas. To these sources were added the customs of virtuous people *shishtas.*[9] As has been noted, however, and as will be noted, different authors allowed more or less autonomy to the customs of economic classes so long as they did not run counter to dharma. There was scope, then, for somewhat enlarging the degree of free-

9. E.g., Spellman, chap. 5, esp. pp. 103–7.

dom of economic behavior. Such enlargement seems not to have continued, however.

In his Dharmasutra,[10] Baudhayana allows greater force to the rule of local custom (I, 1, 2) than did Gautama (XI, 20). Though not necessarily so intended, this view made room for greater freedom of enterprise. Caste (varna) ideology is presented, together with the orthodox allocation of occupations under which Shudras are to serve the higher castes and Vaishyas are to cultivate the soil, pursue trade, and tend cattle (I, 8, 16; I, 10, 18). The significance of caste for inheritance (II, 2, 3) and moneylending is also described. A Vaisya may live by usury, but the interest rate allowed apparently is only 1 percent per month (I, 5, 10). The first two castes were free to "lend (money at interest) to one who neglects his sacred duties, to a miser, to an atheist, or to a very wicked man," though Brahmans could not normally live by trade, usury, crafts, cattle tending, etc. (I, 5, 10). He who acquires "property cheap" and then "employs (it so that it yields) a higher price, is called a usurer, and blamed in all (treatises on) the sacred law" (I, 5, 10).[11] Criminal penalties are not related to usury, however (I, 10, 19).

The king's rights and duties are outlined and the protection theory is endorsed. "Let the king protect (his) subjects, receiving as his pay a sixth part (of their incomes or spiritual merit)" (I, 10, 18). While Brahmans were not required to pay taxes, they had to surrender to the king a sixth part of the spiritual merit which they acquired. The king might impose a duty of 10 percent on goods imported by sea and out of each consignment take an article particularly pleasing to him. He might also "lay just (duties) on other (marketable goods) according to their intrinsic value without oppressing (the traders)" (I, 10, 18). The property of disappearing non-Brahmans passed to the king after he had guarded it for a year (I, 10, 18).

The Vasishtha dharmashastra is not quite as old as the Dharmasutra of Baudhayana.[12] In it as in earlier works the lawful occupations of the Vaishya are said to include "agriculture, trading, tend-

10. This work, together with Vasishtha's, constitutes vol. 14 of the *Sacred Books of the East*.

11. On comparable Jewish and Mesopotamian practice, see Oppenheim, *Ancient Mesopotamia*, p. 88.

12. See the introduction to *Sacred Books of the East*, vol. 2, pp. lii–lx; and Kane, 1:20–32, 50–60. Manu (VII, 140) refers to Vasishtha.

ing cattle, and lending money at interest" and that of the Shudra is defined as serving "superior castes" (II, 19–20). The first two castes could not practice usury (which included "acquiring property cheap" and selling it at "a high price"), though they might "lend to a person who entirely neglects his sacred duties, and is exceedingly wicked" (II, 40–43). The allowable monthly rate of interest is 1¼ percent per month (II, 51), but when no security is given, it may become 5, 4, 3, and 2 percent, respectively, for Shudras, Vaishyas, Kshatriyas, and Brahmans (II, 48), presumably because of differences in risk. The total amount repayable might run double the principal in respect of gold and treble in respect of grain and produce (II, 44–47). Cumulation of interest stopped temporarily when the king died (II, 49–50).

The duty of the king consisted in protecting all beings, in keeping castes and others in their lines of duty (XIX, 1, 7–8), and in insuring correct weights and measures as well as safety (XIX, 13). For performing this duty he obtained "success (in this world and the next)" (XIX, 1). He shared in treasure trove (III, 13–14) and was entitled to a monthly tax on artisans (XIX, 28) as well as "the sixth part of the wealth (of his subjects)" other than Brahmans, who contributed a sixth part of their "merit" (I, 42–44). Several types of tax exemption are indicated (XIX, 23–24, 26, 37) and the taxpayer is declared to be liable only to legitimate taxes (XIX, 14–15). Rules relating to property for whose support the king is responsible are described (XVI). "The (peculiar) laws of countries, castes, and families (may be followed) in the absence of (rules of) the revealed texts" (I, 17).

Apastamba devoted very little attention to economic matter in his dharmasutra. He touched upon the four castes (I, 2, 1) and noted that "trade is not lawful" for a Brahman except in certain products "in times of stress" (I, 7, 20–21; II, 5, 10). He discussed the rules of inheritance (II, 6, 14–15) and the duties of the king; among these he included city building, city and village administration, the appointment of local administrators from the three higher castes, land grants, and the collection of "lawful taxes" (II, 10, 25–26). He indicated that cultivators who failed to perform their tasks were subject to penalty (II, 11, 28). He condemned the usurer (I, 6, 18) but did not discuss the nature of usury. He observed that if one complied with his caste duties, one might be reborn into a higher caste (II, 5, 11), thereby drawing attention to the incentive supplied by the idea of karma.

Manu's Laws

Manu incorporates into his work a great deal of what appeared in the writings of his forerunners and presumably had been tested by experience. Like them, he does not engage in any explicit economic analysis, but he includes much more legal matter, and some of the rules which he includes reflect prior analysis (e.g., the structure of approved interest rates). Of the eighteen sources of lawsuits examined, eleven involve economic transactions (VIII, 3–8).

Manu's rules not only epitomized Hindu economic regulatory thought but also shaped it, though not without modification, and helped to channel economic behavior for centuries. Of particular concern are his attitudes toward wealth and property, occupations, the privileges and duties of the members of the four classes, lending at interest, price and wage fixing, and the collection of revenue. Thus, according to Manu, a man's property is considered to be secure unless he is wicked or a Shudra. Seizure of property normally is forbidden even to the king, who is charged to protect it (VII, 27, 29, 40, 51; VIII, 417; IX, 243–46, 256–57; XI, 13, 18–20); [13] and its transfer is well guarded (VIII, 199–202). Detailed rules are given for determining boundaries to landholdings (VIII, 149, 254–65). Land supposedly belongs to him who clears it (IX, 44), though the king is declared to be "lord of the soil" (VIII, 39). He shares in recovered property and treasure trove and is entitled to half of any treasure concealed in the ground if other than a Brahman has discovered it (VIII, 30–39). [14] Wealth is not to be sought,

13. I have used the translation of G. Bühler, The Laws of Manu, *Sacred Books of the East*, vol. 25. The volume includes many comments of later writers as well as Bühler's long introduction.

14. The king was sometimes incorrectly represented as ultimate owner of land and water, but not of things attached to them. Yet he was proprietor of only crown land. The right of the individual to own and alienate land developed early, though subject to tax unless made tax-free by the king. See L. Gopal, "Ownership"; A. Bose, 1:38–65. While much of the land turned over to religious bodies was made tax-free, these bodies continued to collect the equivalent of taxes and rents from their tenants. The king's tax on the output of privately held (i.e., non-crown) land, commonly one-sixth, was viewed as a rent consonant with his ultimate ownership, though taxes were often described as the king's wages for pro-

nor is pleasure, if its attainment is at the expense of "virtue" (IV, 176; VII, 151–52) (unlike Kautalya, Manu makes piety superior to wealth and wealth to pleasure); when seized through conquest, wealth yields benefits only under certain circumstances (VII, 201–12). Agriculture is sometimes denigrated, as are trade and moneylending (IV, 5–6, 82–89, 91–94; IX, 257), and the pursuit of any one of a variety of occupations serves to exclude a worker from participating in certain sacrifices or from bestowing acceptable food or presents upon Brahmans (III, 152–56, 158–60, 162–66; IV, 84, 210, 212, 215–16, 220–21). "Superintending mines (or factories) of any sort" or "executing great mechanical works" (XI, 64) is described as an offense.

Manu's graduation of occupational activities is associated with his division of society into four varnas, or orders, upon which his societal system rests. To each varna the divine "Brahman" had assigned specific occupational duties, together with privileges (I, 2, 11, 31, 87). These Manu summarizes as follows:

To [Brahmanas] he assigned teaching and studying (the Veda), sacrificing for their own benefit and for others, giving and accepting (of alms).

The Kshatriya he commanded to protect the people, to bestow gifts, to offer sacrifices, to study (the Veda), and to abstain from attaching himself to sensual pleasures.

The Vaisya he commanded to tend cattle, to bestow gifts, to offer sacrifices, to study (the Veda), to trade, to lend money, and to cultivate land.

One occupation only the lord prescribed to the Sudra, to serve meekly even these (other) three castes.[15]

The main economic roles were thus assigned by implication to the Vaishyas and the Shudras. The Brahman's educational role could have become productive only had education been given a produc-

---

tecting his subjects. See, for example, Ghoshal, *History*, pp. 320–21, 324; Maity, pp. 43–52; Aiyangar, *Aspects*, pp. 104–7, 114, 127–29. Spellman points out, however, that the "wage theory of taxation" is not tenable; the king, though a source of protection, was not a servant of the people. See Spellman, "Political Implications." Land transfers were well documented, Maity notes, pp. 47–51, in part because most good land was already occupied in the fourth century A.D., if not earlier, and much fragmented. See also Gonda, pp. 11–24 on the king's economic and related roles.

15. Manu, I, 88–91; see also IV, 2–6 and passim; IX, 317, 319–35, and X, 1–5, 75–131, on varna duties and privileges. On varna intermixture and its consequences, see X, 1–73; on assignment of contemptible occupations, X, 45; on the transcendental origin of the varna, chap. I.

tive turn, and the two upper castes could have become productive only had conditions of distress persisted.[16]

The duties of the Vaishya are detailed. He must be interested in animal husbandry, understand agriculture, know the comparative values of metals, gems, and manufactures, and be prepared to supply men with food and "exert himself to the utmost in order to increase his property in a righteous manner" (IX, 328–30, 333). He must know "the excellence and defects of commodities, the advantages and disadvantages of (different) countries, the (probable) profit and loss on merchandise, and the means of properly rearing cattle" (IX, 331). He must "be acquainted with the (proper) wages of servants, with the various languages of men, with the manner of keeping goods, and (the rules of) purchase and sale" (IX, 332). To him, in sum, were reserved nearly all productive activities other than those assigned to the Shudras.[17]

The specific duties of the Shudras are not detailed by Manu. They consisted generally in serving the higher castes, but particularly the Brahmans (I, 91; IX, 334–35). The status of some Shudras approximated that of slaves (VIII, 413–17). Manu's authority must have contributed notably to the institutionalization of contempt and disability for Shudras and other lower classes.[18] In reality, of course, Shudras sometimes did engage in productive activities and on occasion even became wealthy.[19] They were handicapped even in respect of the acquisition of wealth, since such acquisition would give "pain" to Brahmans (X, 129). According to Manu "there are seven lawful modes of acquiring property, (viz.) inheritance, finding or friendly donation, purchase, conquest, lending at

16. In times of distress a Kshatriya might engage in trade or agriculture, subject to specified constraints; a Vaishya might maintain himself as a Shudra, subject to constraints; and a Shudra might engage in handicrafts of use to the higher orders (X, 77–100). It was "better," however, for a member of a varna to discharge his "duty incompletely" than to live according to the law of another varna and be "instantly excluded from his own" (X, 97). In times of distress a Brahman could even accept a gift from a Shudra (X, 102).

17. Ten "modes of subsistence" are listed: "learning, mechanical arts, work for wages, service, rearing cattle, traffic, agriculture, contentment (with little), alms and receiving interest on money" (X, 116). Gambling was forbidden (IX, 221). The king could learn of trades and professions from the people, not from Brahmans (VII, 43). See also comments on pp. 420–21.

18. Tiwari. A Shudra-ridden kingdom "soon entirely perishes, afflicted by famine and disease," Manu declares (VIII, 22).

19. Basham, *Wonder*, pp. 144, 150. On changes in post-Maurya times, see R. S. Sharma, *Sudras*, chaps. 5–7.

interest, the performance of work, and the acceptance of gifts from virtuous men" (x, 115). The first three modes, commentators held, are lawful for all castes, the fourth for Kshatriyas, the fifth and sixth for Vaishyas (or the fifth for Vaishyas and the sixth for Shudras) and the seventh for Brahmans. Donations were reserved for Brahmans (x, 75–77), probably because they could not charge for teaching (xi, 63). Indeed, even in the celebrated Hindu treatise on love, the Kamasutra (vi, chap. 5) of Vatsyayana, successful courtesans are counseled to give cows to Brahmans as well as to give support to religious and public institutions.

Varna rules served to blunt economic incentive and to keep down interoccupational mobility. The economic ill effects of this policy were somewhat limited, however. Nearly all economically important activities were performed by Vaishyas and Shudras, and downward mobility was permitted to individuals who could not win a livelihood within their own varnas. In the course of time, moreover, the possibility of deferred upward mobility was remarked; an individual's compliance with his varna and other duties might permit him to attain a higher class status in his next life (see, for example, ix, 334–35). It was stressed, however, that the world would be thrown "into confusion" if the two (really productive) varnas "swerved from their duties" (viii, 418; but cf. viii, 22), though not apparently on economic grounds as such. Varna rules also conditioned interpersonal economic rights and relations, among them the security of a person's property (viii, 417; xi, 13), his rights of inheritance,[20] his obligation to repay debts (viii, 177), and his liability to punishment (viii, passim). Varna rules were taken into account also, along with local customs and guild regulations, in the administration of civil and criminal law (vii, 3, 41, 46). Local usage was to be preserved in conquered territory (vii, 203).

The receipt of interest, though sanctioned, was declared subject to various constraints, but provision was made for the collection of debts. A maximum monthly rate of interest of 1.25 percent (viii, 140) was allowed on secured loans, but no interest was required if the pledged property, say land or slaves, yielded ade-

20. A Shudra's right of bequest was limited (ix, 157, 179). Children of a Brahman mother received greater shares than children of non-Brahman mothers from a common Brahman father (ix, 149–56). See also, for rules within varnas, ix, 104–48, and for other rules, ix, 149–219.

quate income to the creditor (VIII, 143). Manu implies that a minimum rate of 2 instead of 1.25 percent may be charged without sinning (VIII, 141). Maximum monthly rates of 2, 3, 4, and 5 percent, respectively, were allowed on unpledged loans to Brahmans, Kshatriyas, Vaishyas, and Shudras (VIII, 142); these differences must have reflected differences in credit standing. Greater risk might justify relatively high rates on sea and perhaps land-voyage loans (VIII, 157). It was not permissible to stipulate for rates in excess of legal maxima or to compound interest or to take at one time more than double the principal (except for loans on produce and animals), but it was permissible to renew a loan after the interest due had been paid or inserted in a new agreement (VIII, 151–55). Overcharging constituted usury (XI, 62). In practice, only a Vaishya was permitted to lend (VIII, 410); a Brahman or a Kshatriya might lend if he were in distress and needed money "for sacred purposes," but even then only "to a very sinful man at a small interest" (X, 117). Rules regarding establishment of proof of indebtedness were quite detailed (VIII, 47–52, 60–61, 107, 176–77); debtors were declared subject to a 5 percent penalty for nonpayment when due (VIII, 139). The qualifications of depositaries, together with their obligations and the depositor's rights of redress, were set down (VIII, 179–202).[21] Indian lending practices were thus more relaxed than those in the Mesopotamian world. Indian interest rates did not, however, differ greatly from those reported in Mesopotamia and the Mediterranean world.[22]

Conditions respecting the rights and obligations of workmen and officers employed by the king and others are laid down. The king was obligated to "fix a daily maintenance, in proportion to their position and to their work" for "women employed in the royal service and for menial servants"; the pay indicated ranged from something like a bare minimum to an amount six times as high (VII, 126–27).[23] Income-yielding land or revenue was allotted

21. Already in Panini's time terms for loans, most of them based on seasonal agricultural activities, were quite varied, often serving to distinguish the purpose of the loan as well as to differentiate between legal and usurious interest. See Agrawala, pp. 274–79; also comments in Manu, pp. 278–84 n.
22. Homer, pp. 29–31, 40–43, 64.
23. "One *pana* must be given (daily) as wages to the lowest, six to the highest, likewise clothing every six months and one drona of grain (rice) every month" (VII, 126). According to Pran Nath a *drona* may have approximated 21 pounds. He believes that the wage of an unskilled day laborer was in the neighborhood of

to local officers.[24] A Brahman was expected to pay his Shudra servant "a suitable maintenance, after considering his ability, his industry and the number of those whom he is bound to support" (x, 124). Workmen who failed to perform their assigned tasks were subject to penalties. The obligations of washermen and weavers (VIII, 396–97) and of operators of land transport (VIII, 156) are specified. Husbandmen and herdsmen were subject to penalty for negligence, in part because it cut down the size of the king's share of the produce (VIII, 235, 240–41, 243). Willful failure on the part of a hired workman "to perform his work according to agreement" made him liable to a fine of about 10 panas (VIII, 215); but failure of an employer to keep an agreement was not correspondingly penalized.[25]

The activities of traders were subject to regulation. They were obligated to behave honestly—i.e., not adulterate products or cheat on prices, and give full weight and measure, etc. (VIII, 203, 403; IX, 257, 286–87), price their goods in keeping with the king's findings,[26] and comply with the king's trading rights and restrictions.[27] Ferry and highway tolls, together with specification of

---

one-half to one copper *pana* a day, which hardly sufficed for a family in Manu's time, when something like two-thirds of a *pana* was required to feed a laborer without difficulty. See Nath, pp. 152–53, and 77, 142–43. On standards and measures, see B. Sen, chaps. 6–7.

24. "The ruler of ten (villages) shall enjoy one kula (as much land as suffices for one family), the ruler of twenty (villages) five kulas, the superintendent of a hundred villages (the revenue of) one village, the lord of a thousand (the revenue of) a town" (VII, 119).

25. In Kautalya's Arthashastra, however, nonpayment of the wages agreed upon subjected an employer to a fine (3.13.33).

26. "Let (the king) fix (the rates for) the purchase and sale of all marketable goods, having (duly) considered whence they come, whither they go, how long they have been kept, the (probable) profit and the (probable) outlay. . . . Once in five nights, or at the close of each fortnight, let the king publicly settle the prices for the (merchants)" (VII, 401–2). He may have had the help of experts, for when fixing upon the amount of toll and duty on merchandise, the king was to limit his impost to "one-twentieth of the (amount) which men, well acquainted with the settlement of tolls and duties (and) skillful in (estimating the value of) all kinds of merchandise, may fix as the value for each saleable commodity" (VIII, 398). Experts were used also in fixing sea-voyage charges (VIII, 157). "All weights and measures" were to be "duly marked, and once in six months" reexamined by the king (VIII, 403). Completed transactions found unsatisfactory were subject to rescission (VIII, 222–23, 228). See Manu, comments, pp. 323–25 nn.

27. "Let the king confiscate the whole property of (a trader) who out of greed exports goods of which the king has a monopoly or (the export of which is) forbidden" (VIII, 399).

persons exempt from these tolls, were set down along with related "miscellaneous rules" (VIII, 404-9) and permission for informed experts to fix the prices of the services of ocean and comparable carriers (VIII, 157, 406). Grounds for rescission of sale and purchase were defined (VIII, 5, 222-28).

The king's obligations to his subjects were various. They included "preventing the confusion" of the varnas, "protecting the weak" in what was essentially a Hobbesian world (VII, 3; VIII, 172), providing security within the country and against its external enemies in accordance with the principles of *niti*, the science of polity (VII, 37, 56-57, 63, 146-83, 205-15, 294-99), resolving interpersonal conflicts and administering civil and criminal justice (VII-IX, passim), supporting Brahmans (VII, 82-85), enforcing varna rules and other regulations and usages (VIII, 1-19; IX, 224-324), among them guild rules (VII, 13; VIII, 219-21), and regulating prices. The king was responsible for selecting exploitable and healthy terrain (VII, 69), for appropriately locating, planning, and constructing his capital city and fortresses (VII, 69-76), for taking into account the superiority of defense to offense (VII, 73-74), and for seeing to it that pasture was ample, accessible, and satisfactorily guarded (VIII, 237-48). In carrying out his obligations he was to make full but just use of coercive authority (*danda*) [28] and of the inclination of man to act in keeping with his self-interest. An exemption from the disposition "to act solely from a desire for rewards . . . is not (to be found) in this (world)" (II, 2, 3-4; and I, 26).[29] Rules for the guidance of royal policy are detailed (VII, 160-215; IX, 294-300).

It was essential that the king claim his due, neither more nor less (VIII, 170-72); tax arrangements should provide that both the king

28. "The whole world is kept in order by punishment, for a guiltless man is hard to find; through fear of punishment the whole world yields the enjoyment (which it owes)" (VII, 22, and 14-21, 23-31). "Of him who is always ready to strike, the whole world stands in awe" (VII, 103). He who does not comply with his duty must not "be left unpunished" (VIII, 335). Barbarous punishments were approved by Manu. See, for example, IX, 276-80, 288, 291-92.

29. Transcendental sanctions strengthened the king's hand against lawbreakers (XII, 70-72); they also hung over unjust kings (VII, 27-29). Individuals had transcendental incentive to behave justly inasmuch as a man's situation in his next birth depended upon what he did currently (XII, 9, 23, 40). A king suffered a sixth part of the demerit of those he failed to protect and gained a sixth part of the merit of those he protected or supported (VIII, 304-5; IX, 23). After death, man's only remaining friend was justice (VIII, 17).

"himself and the man who does the work receive (their due) reward" (vii, 128). While Manu treated the treasury as one of the seven interdependent limbs of the kingdom, he placed much less stress on the importance of revenue than did Kautalya (vii, 156–57; ix, 294–97). When taxing products the king was required to take into account purchase prices, other costs, and selling prices (vii, 127; viii, 398) [30] and to prevent his servants (who "generally become knaves") from seizing the property of others and destroying the source of the income being taxed (vii, 62, 123).[31] The king was advised to limit the customs toll on merchandise to one-twentieth of its value (viii, 398, and 400). He might take one-fiftieth of the increment in cattle and gold, from one-twelfth to one-sixth of crops (with the amount perhaps dependent upon the quality of the soil and labor required), one-sixth of trees, meat, clarified butter, and various other produce, a day of labor per month from mechanics, artisans, and Shudra manual laborers, and a trifling annual tax from small dealers (vii, 130–38). In times of royal or national distress or crisis higher taxes were permissible.[32] The king also collected considerable income in the form of fines (e.g., viii, 129, 138; ix, 229). Moreover, he always had the right to augment his wealth through conquest (vii, 87, 96, 99–101, 204, 206; ix, 251; x, 119), to share in booty, hoards, and unclaimed property (vii, 87; viii, 30–39), and to derive revenue from mines and manufacture (vii, 62). Should the king fail, however, to afford his subjects protection and yet tax and fine them, he would suffer dreadful punishments after death (viii, 307–9).

Insofar as Manu's work dealt with economic matters, it envisaged a more static and less flexible society than did Kautalya. There was

---

30. "Having well considered (the rates of) purchase and (of) sale, (the length of) the road, (the expense for) food and condiments, the charges of securing the goods, make the traders pay duty" (vii, 127).

31. "As the leech, the calf, and the bee take their food little by little, even so must the king draw from his realm moderate annual taxes" (vii, 129). "Let him not cut up his own root (by levying no taxes), nor the root of other (men) by excessive greed" (vii, 139). Law-abiding and trustworthy revenue collectors were essential (vii, 80).

32. A Kshatriya king in great distress could take as much as one-fourth of the crops if he protected "his subjects to the best of his ability" (x, 118). Vaishyas might be required to give one-eighth instead of one-twelfth of their grain and of the profits of trading in grain and one-twentieth of the profits made trading in gold and cattle. Mechanics, artisans, and Shudras were to do additional work for the king or pay a tax on their earnings. See x, 120, and the translator's note.

much less emphasis on capital formation; only the Vaishya's potential contribution thereto was noticed (ix, 333), perhaps because he alone could or would amass wealth. Charity rather than thrift was counseled, though not at the expense of the donor's family (i, 86; ix, 333; x, 68; xi, 6, 9). Extension of settlement was not particularly encouraged, except insofar as possession was conferred upon those cultivating hitherto unexploited land (ix, 44); but the king was enjoined to seek new territory as well as to guard and maintain what he already had (vii, 99, 101), though not through recourse to treachery (vii, 104, 106). Development of his domain was not stressed; presumably, given good government and security of life and property, development would take place automatically (vii, 113). Manu was alert to problems associated with joint undertakings; after noting how cooperating priests should divide sacrificial fees (viii, 206–10), he declared that "these principles" should govern the "allotment of shares" among men "who here (below) perform this work conjointly" (viii, 211). In sum, Manu lay down the rules for a static, quasi-ascriptive society, in which only quite limited scope was allowed economically creative individuals and in which the augmentation of output was assigned only secondary importance.

Manu devoted less attention to the growth and settlement of population than did Kautalya. He was content to condemn abortion (v, 90) and to refer to famine and pestilence (viii, 22). He did, however, describe what constituted optimum territory for a ruler as well as how he was to build a town in this territory and secure it against enemies (vii, 69–76):

Let him settle in a country which is open and has a dry climate, where grain is abundant, which is chiefly (inhabited) by Aryans, not subject to epidemic diseases (or similar troubles), and pleasant, where the vassals are obedient and his own (people easily) find their livelihood [vii, 69].

Manu also described how a local ruling structure was to be set up, but warned that an oppressive king was likely to be deprived of his life whereas "a king who governs his kingdom well, easily prospers" (vii, 110–124). Manu seems to have approved of the king's undertaking conquest, but he urged that what was gained be conserved and augmented (vii, 97–104).

Detailed comparison of Kautalya's work with chapters 7–9 in

Manu's indicates that Manu touched upon many matters dealt with in the Arthashastra. Manu's discussion is less systematic and complete, however. Moreover, his treatment reveals values and a mode of thought less favorable to economic development than Kautalya's. Manu puts greater stress on the hierarchical character of society as reflected in the varna system. He says nothing of the treatment of slaves and looks upon the Shudra as in effect the born slave of the twice-born, especially the Brahman. Kautalya, on the contrary, does not treat the Shudra as a slave, but instead includes him among the Aryas who are forbidden to sell their children into slavery. The two authors agreed largely on some matters—e.g., inheritance rules—but not on others, such as rules relating to marriage. Kautalya is more alert to economic incentive and the practical. Manu must have drawn upon Kautalya's work as well as upon sources whence Kautalya drew.[33]

Aftermath

In the centuries that followed the completion of Manu's work, many more or less comparable works appeared. The economic prescriptions found within them do not differ notably from Manu's. Exemplary are the works of two legal writers whose works appeared in the first half of the first millennium A.D., Narada and Brihaspati.[34]

The older of these, Narada, added little to Manu's structure of interest rates and limitations on repayment or to Gautama's taxonomy of interest, but he stated that if a country had "local usages," special rules according to those usages might apply (I, 105). Interest was not to be charged on loans "made from friendship" (I, 108–10), nor to be charged fully on a pledged loan if the pledge yielded a return to the creditor (I, 127–30). Brihaspati had much on debt but little on interest beyond its classification and acceptance of a noncompounded monthly rate of 1¼ percent as normal (XI, 3–11). A "wretched" man could be charged compound interest until the loan had grown to four to eight times the original, whereas

33. See, for example, Kangle, vol. 3 passim, and his "Manu and Kautilya." See also B. A. Saletore, *Ancient Indian Political Thought*, pp. 184–90, 495–506. On Kautalya and slavery, see B. Sen, chap. 4.

34. The works of these two authors constitute vol. 33 of *Sacred Books of the East*. See Kane, 1:196–213.

on other loans the final amount due could not exceed two to five times the original loan (XI, 12–17). Brihaspati allows the creditor to use a pledge until the cumulated interest equals the principal (XI, 12, 18–27).

Whereas Brihaspati is content to identify seven ways of acquiring immobile property (IX, 2), Narada presents two classifications, one based on caste and the other on source of wealth. Caste limits acquisition only in certain ways, since members of each caste could acquire wealth through inheritance, gifts, and marriage; a Brahman, through alms, sacrificing, and instructing a pupil; a Kshatriya, through taxes, fighting, and fines; a Vaishya, through tillage, tending cows, and commerce; and a Shudra, from what higher castes gave him (I, 50–55). He described as "black wealth" what was got through bribes, gambling, forgery, robbery, fraud, illness, and bearing a message. In contrast, highly favored "white" wealth included that got through sacred study, the "practice of austerities," valor in arms, marriage, inheritance, sacrificing, teaching, and work. "Spotted" wealth was acquired by lending money at interest, tillage, commerce, artistic performance, giving a damsel in marriage, servile attendance, and return for a benefit conferred (I, 45–47). Otherwise neither Narada (I, 56–67) nor Brihaspati (xxv, 26–68) had much to say of the relation of caste to the acquisition of income and wealth.

Price and wage control receive some attention. Narada admonishes merchants to refrain from "dishonest dealings" and to "fix a just price for their merchandise, according to the locality and season," making their "gain" proportional to the price of the merchandise traded (IX, 11–12). Regarding wages, he said that they should be "fixed in proportion" to the "skill" and "the value" of the services of hired servants (v, 22), with soldiers ranked highest, followed by argiculturalists and porters (v, 23). He set down a number of rules for fixing wages and dealing with the nonpayment of wages and nonperformance of obligations (VI, 1–22). Conditions for rescission of purchase are also detailed (IX, 1–16). Rescission of sale and related problems are dealt with by each. Brihaspati's discussion of master-servant relations emphasizes the obligation of each to comply with the agreement to which he is party or which is customary—e.g., that a cultivator get one-third of the crop, or one-fifth plus food and clothing (XVI, esp. 10–14). Both Narada

(III, 1–11) and Brihaspati (XIV, 1–32) discuss the rules of partnership and joint enterprise and the rights and obligations of participating members or priests; the latter in particular prescribed greater remuneration for greater skill and responsibility (XIV, 28–30). Neither Narada (III, 11–14; VII, 6–7) nor Brihaspati (XIV, 13–14) devotes much attention to the king's income. The latter notes that whereas Manu forbade gambling, some legal writers approved it when the king shared in each stake (XXVI). Narada also allowed the king a share in a gambler's winnings and the "house" 10 percent of the stakes (XVII, 2, 8).

The content of Vishnu's Institutes,[35] dated later than Brihaspati, reflects some arthashastra concerns and resembles the works of Manu more closely than those just examined. The duties and accessible modes of livelihood of the castes are enumerated (II, 1–17) along with the duties and rights of a king (III). Somewhat after the manner of Kautalya he advises the king to abide in a district inhabited by many Vaishyas and Shudras (III, 5) and to continue the laws of countries which he conquers (III, 41, 47). The king is entitled to a sixth of a nation's produce and merit for virtuous deeds; 10 and 5 percent, respectively, of commodities sold at home and abroad; and a day of work per month from artisans and Shudras; "the whole produce" of mines; and a share in treasure trove (III, 22–32, 55–63). The king is advised not to "injure his own property (by bootless expenses)" (III, 52). He apparently is responsible for weights and measures (IV).

While "debtors of any caste [may] pay as much interest as has been promised by themselves," the normal rate, in the order of the castes, is put at 2, 3, 4, or 5 percent per month (VI, 2–3, 40). Interest can ordinarily cumulate until it is double to eightfold the original principal, the multiple depending upon the basis of the loan (VI, 7–17), but it may not be charged if a pledge is given and used (VI, 5). The rules of inheritance, together with disabilities of some castes, are described at length (XV–XVIII). While Vishnu discusses sales a number of times, he does not really concern himself with price regulation or with wages except to indicate that employer and employee must comply with their contracts (V, 153–59).

The rules laid down by Manu for economic matters thus seem to have been endorsed on the whole, though with elaboration and

35. Vol. 7 of *Sacred Books of the East.* See Kane, 1:60–70.

eventually some relaxation, by subsequent authors and commentators. They were not always observed, sometimes lower and sometimes higher rates being charged.[36] Guilds and partnerships flourished under the Guptas, and professions and occupations remained
somewhat free of the trammels of caste. Respecting lending at
interest, greater allowance was later made for variations in risk
associated with differences in the sorts of trade carried on and
perhaps also with differences in political conditions. In the stable
Gupta period (say 300–550 A.D.) interest was justified, though
wealth got by lending was termed "spotted." Annual rates ranging
(in keeping with the supposed risk) from 15 percent on secured
loans to 60 percent on unsecured loans to Shudras were allowed,
and the limits put on total amounts repayable were adjusted upward. With the development of the Indian economy there may
have been more need for the clarification of rules relating to deposits, pledges, and indebtedness as well as for elaboration of rules
relating to the division of earnings and liability in joint enterprises
engaged in production or moneylending. Increase in political stability and security resulted in a lowering of actual interest rates.[37]

While an interest rate of 15 percent per year may have been
considered normal, as Nath reports for the tenth and eleventh
centuries, local rates were often higher. Nath found annual rates
ranging between 9 and 30 percent in this period.[38] In the ninth
century, though smriti authors continued to look with disfavor on
agriculture, industry, and trade, monthly interest rates of up to 5
percent were approved under given conditions.[39] In Deccan in the
ninth and the tenth centuries, interest rates ranged between 8 and
50 percent; 12–15 percent was common and rents approximated

36. Concerning interest in 200 B.C.–300 A.D., Adhya writes (p. 100) that "we
have no historical evidence to judge how far these precepts were followed." See
also R. S. Sharma, *Light*, pp. 116–39; Maity, chap. 9; A. Bose, 1:234–55, 281–97;
2:101–11. There is evidence that guilds functioning as banking institutions in the
Deccan paid lower rates to depositors, presumably because the deposits were
considered secure. D. R. Das, chaps. 12, 14.

37. Sen-Gupta, pp. 236–45; Thapar, *History*, pp. 147–48; Kane, 3:418–30,
466–68; Maity, esp. pp. 178–87. Maity notes that until recently annual rates of
75–100 percent were charged even on secured loans in rural India (p. 183). On
caste, business organization, and trade under the Guptas, see R. C. Majumdar and
Altekar, pp. 342–62.

38. Nath, pp. 93–99; Sharma, *Light*, chap. 11; Gopal, *Economic Life*,
pp. 159–78.

39. R. C. Majumdar, *History*, 4:406–7.

25 percent of land value.[40] Rates of 10 to 20 percent are reported for the eleventh century.[41] Loans made by charitable funds tended to fall within a range of 12½–15 percent, though other sources at times got as much as 50 percent.[42] In South India apparently the legal rate stayed at 15 percent even when the northern rate was often 24 percent.[43] B. P. Mazumdar, writing of the eleventh and twelfth centuries, reports monthly rates as high as 2 percent on secured loans and the approval of monthly rates as high as 10 percent on risky loans to traders.[44] In the thirteenth century annual interest rates of 30–33 percent seem to have been common.[45] In practice, the rates charged varied with the conditions prevailing and/or surrounding the loans in question as also at times did the rates permitted.

R. S. Sharma concludes a review of usury in India in A.D. 400–1200 with a number of observations. In early medieval times members of the two upper castes were allowed to lend at interest, whereas in ancient times they could not. While a rate of 15 percent per year continued to be prescribed in legal texts, some lawmakers in the seventh to ninth centuries raised the normal rate to 2 percent per month, apparently in response to the decline of trade and absence of coin after the fall of the Gupta Empire. The association of interest rate chargeable with the varna of the borrower increased. Loans in kind became more frequent in medieval times as the economy became more self-sufficient locally; they seem to have reflected differences in risk. Bodily interest, to be paid by the debtor with his own service or that of his animals or employees, came into greater prominence; it could result in the reduction of the ordinary debtor to the status of semislave. Land became increasingly involved in the lending process as the economy became less monetized; land was mortgaged, or its produce was earmarked for creditors, or the land itself was given on loan to debtors. Debtors

40. Altekar, *Rashtrakutas,* pp. 367–75, 385–86; but see D. R. Das, pp. 210–11 and chap. 14.

41. Yazdani, p. 437.

42. Sastri, *Colas,* pp. 527, 599–601. On the Chola economy in the South, ascendant in the eleventh and twelfth centuries, see Thapar, *History,* chap. 9. In South India temples engaged in moneylending and used the proceeds for religious purposes. R. S. Sharma, *Light,* pp. 120, 123–24, and 138–39 on northern temples. On the role of eleventh-century Chola temples, see Spencer.

43. R. S. Sharma, *Light,* p. 124.

44. Mazumdar, pp. 224–25.

45. D. Sharma, pp. 300–1.

had less protection than in ancient times. "On the whole the laws regarding interest seem to favor the creditors in early medieval times."[46]

Taxation had been oppressive throughout much of India's history, both because it was high and because much of the revenue was put to nonproductive purposes. In Gupta times as in Kautalya's day the output of perhaps as much as one-fourth of the labor force was often absorbed by the traditional land tax of one-sixth (sometimes augmented in an emergency), together with fines and a variety of taxes on cultivators, traders, and others.[47]

Theory and practice differed widely in post-Maurya and Gupta times. The principles of taxation as described "seem to be quite sound, and reveal a fairly advanced stage of financial thinking" for the times, but they were not rigorously observed. The lawbooks "stressed that taxes should be governed by the capacity of the people to pay and should not be oppressive and arbitrary." These principles left scope for fiscal oppression by the king, since he could "override the restrictions imposed on his power of taxation" by the Smritis.[48] In Gupta times "the royal share was at least as much as in Mauryan times, ¼ or more." The "total tax paid" must have "been often oppressive, though perhaps not so oppressive as in the less fortunate periods of Indian history."[49]

The tax burden may have been as great under the Chauhans in and after the ninth century, though this is not clear.[50] In the North in the eleventh and twelfth centuries, the tax burden reached new heights; despite the injunctions of sages that rulers be moderate in their demands, the land tax alone sometimes absorbed close to half the produce.[51] Contemporary southern rulers may have taken as

46. R. S. Sharma, *Light*, pp. 116–44, esp. pp. 142–44.
47. Maity, chap. 3, esp. p. 70. Many of the Gupta taxes were mentioned by Kautalya. In Tamil literature (c. 0–400 A.D.) the king was represented as even less restrained an autocrat than in Sanskrit literature. It is not clear, however, whether the tax burden was heavier in Tamil states. See Sastri, *Colas*, pp. 66–68, 71–72; Subrahmanian, chap. 8.
48. Jha, pp. 34, 203. See also Maity, chap. 3; Niyogi, chap. 7; Gopal, *Economic Life*, chap. 2
49. Maity, p. 70.
50. D. Sharma, pp. 207–12, 219–20, 309–10.
51. Mazumdar, chap. 12, and p. 265. Heavy military expenditures were partly responsible. In the Deccan in the twelfth to the fourteenth centuries the state, seeking to encourage land reclamation, deferred taxes on newly reclaimed land for three to four years, but assumed no direct responsibility for irrigation works. See Yazdani, pp. 687, 680–83. A tax collector's guild was made responsible for tax

much if not more. Under the Cholas taxes may have taken a third or more of the product, but this burden was partly offset by public expenditure on the populace by the government, temples, and wealthy persons.[52] Cultivators of temple property got less than half the produce in the sixteenth century.[53] In the Deccan, according to inscriptions, taxes varied widely, usually in keeping with dharmashastra rules; between 750 and 1000 A.D., the land tax amounted to about 20 percent of the gross product, a rate lower than under the Vijayanagar regime, when over one-third was taken.[54] Moslem rule provided little if any relief. The Moslem sultanate of Delhi took close to half the nation's output; and later Akbar demanded one-third or more of the gross produce alone.[55]

Given the lowness of per worker output—a condition aggravated by the large number of persons not engaged productively—and the heaviness of the tax burden on the productive population, the lot of the cultivator and the worker could not have been other than very hard, as a rule. Waste consumed much of what the worker did not get, with the result that there was little productive investment to elevate his output and alleviate the misery of the many generated by the splendor of the few. Under the Guptas the lot of hired labor seems to have been an unhappy one, sometimes no better than that of forced labor or slaves, and the lot of many cultivators must at times have been nearly as bad.[56] According to Nath, the "standard of comfort of the labouring classes was very low," changing little if at all between the fifth and the eleventh and the sixteenth centuries.[57] D. Sharma notes that while agriculturalists "had enough to eat" in "normal times," they remained subject to periodic fam-

collection and allowed a quite free hand. Ibid., pp. 684–85. On governmental income and expenditure, mainly in 900–1100 A.D., see Niyogi, chap. 7.

52. Sastri, *Cōlas*, pp. 529, 538–41, 641–42; Sundaram, p. 52; Subrahmanian, pp. 207–10.

53. Stein, p. 166. See also Niyogi, chap. 10. On temple property, see Kane, 2:906–16; Thapar, *History*, pp. 158–59, 258–59; Nagaswamy. See also n. 42 above.

54. Altekar, *Rashtrakutas*, pp. 222–23. On taxation in the Deccan up to the sixth century A.D. see D. R. Das, chap. 3.

55. Day, chap. 6; Moreland, *India*, pp. 97–100, 130–36. See also Tripathi; Sadunath Sarkar, p. 177; S. R. Sharma.

56. Maity, pp. 63–64, 84–86, 141–54, 189–90; Nath, pp. 160–62.

57. Nath, pp. 147–53. It will be recalled that Altekar believed people were better off in Deccan in the tenth century than now. *Rashtrakutas*, pp. 395–98. L. Gopal reports poverty in the villages but decidedly higher standards elsewhere. *Economic Life*, pp. 238–53.

ines.[58] B. P. Mazumdar, writing of the eleventh and twelfth centuries, states that "in a feudal society" such as the North Indian, "peasants and artisans are usually condemned to lead a life of poverty." [59]

What is striking in the dharmashastra and related literature described in this chapter as well as in that examined in the early part of the next chapter is the very small amount of feedback between the world of economic reality and the world of the mind reflected in the shastra literature. This lack of feedback is traceable immediately, of course, to the prescriptive approach of the authors of this literature and their lack of interest in fashioning a system of economic analysis, a superstructure in terms of which their individual rules might have taken on theoretical implications. Presumably the rules laid down had at one time had a rational basis and sufficient compatibility with the world of economic reality to conduce to politicoeconomic stability. Moreover, a degree of flexibility had been built into the rules. It was hardly enough, however, to match the variability of conditions within a comparatively static society or to give scope to improvement of the rules. Undoubtedly, therefore, detailed economic inquiry would reveal considerable variation over time in the degree to which actual interpersonal economic relations corresponded to those laid down. This variation, in turn, might have led to economic analysis of sorts, as it did in the postmedieval Western World, but it did not do so. For that matter, analogous variation had little if any more impact in the Graeco-Roman world, where, however, entrepreneurs apparently were freer to carry on as they chose.

58. D. Sharma, pp. 309–10. Traders sometimes enjoyed high incomes, but wasted much of their profits on religious occasions. Sharma refers to the ninth century and after.

59. Mazumdar, pp. 264–65.

Chapter 5

Medieval India: Age
of Transition

All is not Shastra that goes by that name. The Shastras
so called therefore need to be read with much caution.

M. K. GANDHI

The medieval period separating the waning of classical India from
the collapse of Mughal India in and just after the eighteenth century may be described as a transitional one for the development
and crystallization of Indian economic thought, though substantial
changes respecting economic matters did not take place. During
this period much of India passed under Moslem control, with the
result that Moslem administrative rules and practices became influential. Upon the displacement of Moslem rule by the British,
Indian economic thought and practice became subject to British
and Western influence, which slowly made for modernization. In
this chapter, therefore, our concern is twofold—with the overall
state of economically oriented Indian thought and with the Moslem
impact. In neither, of course, do we have explicit, systematic
thought, nor do we encounter great ideational change. Indeed,
much of what appears in the first part of this chapter resembles
what appeared earlier.

Indian Economic Thought

While the distribution of political power among the states composing India changed with the decline of the already relatively
decentralized and prosperous Gupta state after the late seventh
century, there took place little if any change in the fundamental
economic content of arthashastra matter present in dharmashastra

and related literature.¹ Of course, with the decline of Buddhism and the weakening of its appeal to the masses, a harder and more rigid line could be followed by authors of shastras.² Behavior-regulating rules were affected accordingly, but not anything resembling economic analysis. Legal texts could continue in the tradition of Manu, and the hold of the caste and joint-family systems could be strengthened. This tradition became dominant even in the South of India, where decentralized states continued to rise and fall in A.D. 500–1300; it persisted in the North, where political authority became fragmented and something like feudalism emerged between 700 and 1200, facilitating the ascendancy of Moslem power, which began about A.D. 1000 by making inroads that eventuated in the Delhi Sultanate.³ The invasions by Moslem peoples, together with their gradual conquest of India, "threw down a challenge to Hindus" and resulted in the preparation of comprehensive shastras or legal digests, perhaps inspired in part by the desire of the Brahmans, as Thapar notes, "of preserving their exclusiveness." ⁴ Emphasis was placed upon rules directed to the security of spiritual rather than material results, upon dharma rather than artha. Attention was also focused upon the law of inheritance.

This was true of southern as well as of northern India, much of which fell under Moslem control in and after the eleventh century. In the South the institution of caste developed differently than in the North, but, Sastri observes, "was accepted almost universally," and to uphold it remained a primary duty of the ruler. "Economics" (vartta) and "politics" (dandaniti) continued to be studied.⁵ Society was organized for the benefit of the upper classes, the burden of whose extravagance was offset only insofar as expenditures were undertaken for the public and portions of the economy passed into the hands of temples.⁶ The situation of the bulk of the population

1. This literature is described in Kane, vol. 1; also in Ghoshal, *History*, chaps. 21–28.

2. Kane, vol. 5, chap. 24, on the puranas; and 5:913, 922, 932, 939, 947, 949, 1002–30, 1267. See also Ghoshal, *History*, passim; Ibbetson, pp. 2–5.

3. Thapar, *History*, chaps. 8–12; Sastri, *History*, chaps. 8–12, and pp. 322–23 on Sanskrit learning; and L. Gopal, *Economic Life*, pp. xvi–xxiii on sources.

4. Kane, 5:969–70; Thapar, *History*, pp. 303–5; Prasad, pp. 559–60.

5. Subrahmanian, pp. 255–61, on caste in the South; Sastri, *History*, chap. 13, and on earlier polity, chaps. 8–11. See also Mahalingam.

6. Sastri, *History*, pp. 205–6, 306–9, 314–15, 321–32. Under the Vijayangara rulers in the fourteenth and later centuries the proportion of the produce claimed

was no better in areas that passed under Moslem rule. There— because of war—taxes and irregular impositions often absorbed a large share of the produce, beyond what zamindars or similar agents collected and retained. Even under later British rule, often only about one-half of the gross produce was left to the cultivator.[7]

Lessening of emphasis upon arthashastra materials was to be expected. Artha, of course, remained one of the four goals of life, along with dharma, to which artha is inferior, and kama and moksha, the lowest and the highest of man's goals.[8] Moreover, works on dharmashastra continued to deal with at least some subjects included in Kautalya's Arthashastra, with rajashastra (the science of government) and with dandaniti (the rules and controls that keep people in the right paths).[9] Little change took place in the content of dharmashastra literature. "Indian polity has a recorded history of over two thousand years from at least the 4th century B.C. Its growth was gradual but its aims and ideals and its main elements have been the same throughout the centuries."[10] Indian authors continued for two millennia to support the status quo, but without resorting to more than exhortation. They "hardly ever made any fresh approach to the problems of government or stated any rival conceptions or theories," perhaps because their education was literary, there existed no strong middle class to seek change, and there were no statesmen capable of consolidating India's weak small states into more powerful entities.[11] The lack of nationalist sentiment in India, a sentiment not really generated and activated until late in the nineteenth century, must have militated against the creation of large national states, at least outside the region of the Marathas. In any case, little examination of Kautalya's scheme for managing a state economy is to be found in later dharmashastra or legist literature.

---

as revenue "varied from the traditional sixth to as much as half the gross yield"; and there were various other taxes on houses, goods, professions, and domestic and foreign trade, together with fines. Ibid., pp. 306–8, 324–36; Thapar, *History*, pp. 329–30. On the role of the temple in developing irrigation facilities, etc., and on the importance of state donors to the endowment of temples, see Stein, pp. 163–76.

7. Kumar, pp. 6–11, chap. 3 on "agrestic servitude," and pp. 152–57.

8. See, for example, Kane, 2:2–11, 967.

9. Kane, vol. 3, chap. 1.

10. Kane, 3:15. See also Aiyangar, *Rajadharma;* Derrett, *Introduction*, chap. 1.

11. Kane, 3:235–36. The predominance of the traditional village must also have made for societal homeostasis. See, for example, Misra, pp. 55–58.

For expositive convenience, let us postulate three sets of relations —of buyers or sellers to markets, of subject to ruler, and of person to person of similar or dissimilar status. Market conditions change over time as does the capacity of a bureaucracy to regulate prices. For this reason a state, particularly a weak state, could not regulate an economy as Kautalya had proposed. Even the continuing attempt to regulate interest rates had to allow for changes in economic conditions. Similarly, the tax structure underwent change, particularly as political conditions changed. In contrast with these relations, those of person to person, by category, tended to stay put in a relatively static society. It is with relations of this sort that dharmashastra literature dealt in the main. It could therefore continue to repeat, with little or no modification, regulative or legal rules and guides found adequate a millennium or two earlier, especially if the range of allowable interest and taxes was broadened.

This tendency was probably accentuated by the nontheoretical character of early and later Indian economic discussion. As a rule, it is the positing of new theories rather than the emergence of new constellations of facts that changes the direction of discussion, economic as well as noneconomic. This positing did not take place. According to G. D. Karwal, ancient Indians were concerned, not with economic analysis, but with vartta, an art whose aim was practical. "It was intended to afford guidance to the agriculturalist, the cattle rearer, the merchant, the artisan, the director of industry, the statesman and the student to enable them to become practical experts." [12] This concern, as developed at the hands of Kautalya, had shifted emphasis, at least temporarily, from dharma to artha, from escapism and asceticism to meeting material needs. It was "Kautilyanism," Karwal believes, that made the Maurya Empire strong and prosperous.[13] Even if one grants this conclusion, it remains likely that the nonanalytical character of Kautalya's discussion contributed largely to the neglect of even implicit economic analysis in later legist literature.

One does not encounter in these later works the degree of concern with public control of prices found in Kautalya's work. Kautalya had dealt with how rulers had best proceed, whereas the later

12. Karwal, "Ancient Indian Economics," pp. 80–81. See also Balkrishna, "Economics."

13. Karwal, "Kautilyanism."

works dealt mainly with interpersonal relations. It was assumed, as a rule, that buyer and seller had tentatively agreed upon a price. At issue were the conditions making a contract valid or warranting rescission of a sale, and so on.[14] Exchange and trade were always viewed as important, however, though less so than agriculture, the main component of vartta, the source of a people's support and a state's strength.[15] Exchange and trade were therefore less fortified by public investment than was agriculture, which was the beneficiary of irrigation, much of it publicly financed.[16]

Rules regarding the use and disposition of property dominated its discussion over the centuries. The relation of property rights to incentive and economic development is not inquired into, nor is an assessment made of the advantages and disadvantages associated with the joint family as distinguished from the nuclear family. The frequency of land sales was held down by the presence of the joint-family system as well as by village or collective ownership of land and perhaps also by the fact that something like ownership of land was associated with its long-continued cultivation. Ownership itself was important in that the state was entitled to only a share of the crops raised, in exchange for which the state provided the owner with protection.[17] The gift of land, especially by a king, being the most meritorious of all gifts, was made subject to numerous rules.[18]

The rules relating to the acquisition, ownership, and disposability of property, while not formulated in quite the same fashion by all authors, amounted to conventions which gave stability to ownership and its transfer; they did not, however, have to do with economic analysis.[19] The rules underwent some change and im-

---

14. Kane, 3:462, 488–96. Katyayana, who wrote some time after A.D. 400, declared that the adequate price of something (e.g., land, field, house, animals) should fall within a range of plus and minus one-eighth of the value put on this thing by a group of neighbors of the seller. A price lying outside this range would be too high or too low and hence improper. Ibid., 3:493.

15. Kane, 3:50–51.

16. Kane, 3:162–63. Kane refers to an 82 percent reduction in the price of rice consequent upon completion of a vast irrigation project in Kashmir. Ibid. On the early importance of irrigation and its regulation in legal literature, see R. S. Sharma, *Light*, chap. 8; Maity, chap. 4; A. Bose, 1:129–50.

17. Kane, 3:495–97; 2:865–69. Land was owned also by private individuals. Ibid., 3:496–97.

18. Kane, 2:858–65, 915–16.

19. Kane, vol. 3, chaps. 27–31, esp. pp. 317–21, 325–28, 431, 548–54.

provement, including increase in the degree of equality which men enjoyed before the law, especially under English influence, but, Kane wrote in 1946, needed further clarification and accommodation to current conditions.[20]

Rules regarding moneylending continued to be supported, though in practice they were not always adhered to. Moneylending was permissible, so long as excessive interest was not charged, though not on the part of the Brahmans.[21] It was recognized that because of differences in economic conditions and mercantile usages, writers on the law could not fix a set of interest rates to fit all conditions. They fixed rates for a variety of circumstances, much as had been done by Kautalya, Manu, and their immediate successors, but allowed debtor and creditor to agree upon a mutually acceptable rate within the legally sanctioned range. Allowable maximum rates that might be charged varied, as in the past, with a debtor's varna, from 2 percent per month for Brahmans to 5 percent for Shudras. These differences, as noted earlier, reflect differences in risk, together with imposed discrimination. Differences in risk are reflected also in allowances for security as well as for type of pledge (if any), for nature of trade (e.g., forest vs. seafaring vs. ordinary loans), and for the character of the loan when in kind.[22]

Limits continued to be placed on the aggregate amount of interest legally collectable, presumably to guard debtors against being crushed under a constantly growing burden of interest. Normally a creditor could legally collect no more than double the principal. This limitation might be removed through renewal of a loan or the arrangement of a contract; it exceeded a multiple of two when a loan was in kind.[23] Limitation upon the amount of interest collectable has been recognized by Indian courts in modern times under the rule of *damdupat* which in effect replaced the rule of *dvaigunya* of early legists. On this matter and on liability for indebtedness, especially on the part of a son or grandson for the debt of his forebear, modern courts professed "to follow the Hindu Law of the sages and medieval digests." [24]

20. Kane, 3:818–24. See also Derrett, *Introduction*, passim.
21. Kane, 5:417–18; 2:124; 3:417–18, 421.
22. Kane, 3:420–27, and 427–38 on pledges and surety and 454–61 on deposits and their return.
23. Kane, 3:422 ff.
24. Kane, 3:422–25 and n., 427 and n., and 449–54.

Great emphasis was placed upon repayment of debts, in keeping with the general belief (Manu, IV, 257) that each individual was in debt to the gods, the sages, and his ancestors.[25] There was much discussion, therefore, of liability for indebtedness under various circumstances.[26] This liability may have affected even reproductive behavior. A father desired sons in order that they might redeem him from liability for his unrequited earthly and spiritual debts.[27]

It continued to be held that the caste system must be maintained, along with well-established usages relating to castes and to guilds, traders, and other groups.[28] The adverse effects of the caste system, sometimes slightly and temporarily reduced through multiplication of castes, were generally neglected by the legists. The latter not only were interested in maintaining their monopoly of law and education but also failed to appreciate the significance of technological training and the uneconomic impact of discrimination upon occupational composition and performance.[29] In the eleventh century, however, as noted earlier, constraints on the right of members of a particular varna (especially Brahmans) to earn a living and acquire property were somewhat modified by interpretation, a mode of change extendible to other rules.[30]

The later authors of shastras manifested no more insight than earlier authors into various economic effects of the caste system— e.g., its making for underemployment and unemployment, a tendency that increased with the multiplication of castes. Barriers between castes increased much more rapidly than the number of castes. To illustrate: if there are two castes, there is one interface or barrier; if three castes, three barriers; if four castes, six barriers; if five castes ten barriers; and so on: $b = n(n-1)/2$. In other words, if the number of castes increases arithmetically, the number of barriers increases as a simple triangular number. It is not to be expected that the composition of demand might be such as to bring the supply of the services of each caste in balance with the demand

25. Kane, 3:414–16.

26. Kane, 3:416–17, 425, 442–54.

27. Kane, 3:416–17, and 4:570.

28. Kane, 3:566, 630, 843, 860–66, 875, 882.

29. See, for example, the long list of persons not to be invited to a ritual dinner. Kane, 4:393–94.

30. See n. 32 in chap. 3 above. On the growing oversupply of Brahmans relative to the need for priests, see Ibbetson, pp. 3–4.

for those services at quite similar prices. It is likely, therefore, that demand for the services of many castes will be comparatively excessive or deficient. This disparity between supply and demand, by caste, should continually weaken caste barriers.

Kane devotes a chapter to master-servant relations, on the obligations and rights of each, on emergency situations, and on penalties for nonfulfillment of obligations. He relies almost entirely on early authors. There was no economic analysis, but it was indicated that in joint undertakings wages should be shared on the basis of the contribution of each worker.[31] As has been noted, Manu's rule for the distribution of sacrificial fees to participating priests was extended to secular joint undertakings which were more and more emphasized as their number grew.[32] Little if anything was made of Vishnu's condemnation of traders who acted in combination to corner goods and manipulate the prices of commodities.[33]

The basic view that taxes constituted the wages of the king (in exchange for which he supposedly gave protection and allowed the use of his land) continued to be held as did the view that very few adult males were to be exempted from taxation and that in times of emergency tax rates might be increased above the normal levels approved in the smritis.[34] In normal times, at least one twelfth-century author held, the king ought to save a fourth of his revenues.[35] These revenues came from state industry, from tolls, customs duties, fines, taxes on sales and employed persons, and above all, the produce of land—in normal times one-sixth of most produce and in times of emergency one-third. The rates on some types of produce, output, or increment were lower than one-sixth.[36] Excessive taxation was both condemned and described as tending to shrink the tax base.[37]

The Shukraniti, apparently the last of the legal texts purporting to guide bureaucrats, has recently been shown to be of early-nineteenth-century authorship and hence not, as once supposed, of a

---

31. Kane, vol. 3, chap. 20, esp. pp. 477–78; and pp. 466–68. See also Srikantan.
32. Kane, 3:469–70.
33. See Sen-Gupta, p. 243.
34. Kane, vol. 3, chap. 7, esp. pp. 184–85, 189. See n. 58 in chap. 3 above and n. 14 in chap. 4 above.
35. Kane, 3:188.
36. Kane, 3:187, 191–96.
37. Kane, 3:186, 198–99.

date that lets it be applicable to the Hindu period.[38] It does, however, reveal how a pandit might assemble and revise for a local ruler that which early writers had said. After describing governmental functions at some length, the author discusses the role of self-interest as a motivating factor and the almost unlimited importance of wealth. Eight sources of livelihood, among them moneylending, are identified, together with various modes and bases of remuneration and its relation to performance. It is said that profit must be adequate to induce undertakings. The author envisaged a bureaucratic state and provided for the control of many fees and prices which depended largely on cost and utility. He identified ten sources of governmental revenue, but advised that taxation should be kept moderate in normal times. He also described how much the state should save and how expenditures should be distributed. Little economic analysis, other than recognition of economic motivation, is present in the Shukraniti.

A great deal of what the Hindu legists set down with respect to interpersonal relations entered into Hindu law and usage, though with some modification. "Hindu Law proper as it has come down to us is a product of the middle ages, applied and developed by British Indian Courts. Its source books are the great commentaries and textbooks, compiled mostly at a time when the Muslim conquerors were already establishing themselves." [39] The law as it developed was affected by external factors as well as by internal evolution in that shastric texts had to be reconciled with law as practiced in local communities.[40] The British had digests prepared and translated in order to facilitate civil administration.[41] In time treatises which embodied cases came into existence.[42] Although the British in effect continued Mughal practice, inasmuch as smriti law had "continued to be fully recognized and enforced" under Moslem rule,[43] this did not prove easy, J. D. M. Derrett finds.[44]

38. Raghavan; L. Gopal, "The Sukraniti." B. K. Sarkar's English translation was published in Allahabad in 1914. Gopal believes, however, that the text includes much useful information. See his *Economic Life*, pp. xviii–xix.

39. Sen-Gupta, p. 1. See also Lingat; Lipstein.

40. Sen-Gupta, p. 1; Derrett, *Introduction*, pp. 5, 8, 12–16.

41. Probably best known is Colebrooke's *Digest*. Colebrooke was the translator of the digest which was prepared for the British by Jagannatha.

42. For example, Aiyar; Mulla; U. C. Sarkar; Derrett, *Introduction*; Lipstein.

43. Aiyar, p. 4.

44. Derrett, "Hindu Law," pp. 219–21, 239–45; also p. 223 on the corporate rights of guilds, villages, castes, and sects sanctioned by rulers. Derrett expresses

Derrett's account of Hindu law, "the oldest system of law still enforced," and its literature may help to explain why more economic progress was not made. Among the virtues extolled were "fearlessness, freedom from doubt, abstention from undue reflection, intelligent appearance, secrecy, constancy, non-violence, loyalty, abstention from theft, chastity and poverty. Of all virtues generosity and indifference to material things are most praised." [45] Derrett interprets the main function of justice, as conceived within the framework of dharma, to be the protection of the weak against the strong, but in a society based upon a form of inequality with which haphazard social striving for betterment is essentially incompatible.[46] Hindu law itself was "not concerned to justify any rule rationally"; a rule is based upon the assumption that human beings need a rule to guide them.[47] The state was not clearly separated from the people, nor was the creation of loyalty to the national community made an object of dharma.[48]

Moslem Impact

The first contact of Moslems with India, that of seventh-century Arab traders, was succeeded a century later by an Arab conquest of the Sind. Even so, relations proved much more friendly than after the Ghaznavid incursions into India began in the late tenth century [49] and eventuated in the so-called Delhi Sultanate and the extension of Islamic dominion over northern and parts of central and southern India. This dominion, dependent on the heavy use of Hindus in governmental service, collapsed under Tamerlane's late-fourteenth-century invasions. Not until the early sixteenth century and the coming of the Mughals was Moslem dominion again ex-

concern over the recent decline of interest in the study of Hindu law and over the need for its reform and modification. Ibid., pp. 199 ff., 243–45.

45. Derrett, "Hindu Law," p. 211. This list is based on a popular textbook on dharma. "Even cardinal virtues might be evaded by one not conscientiously over-scrupulous," Derrett adds later (p. 232). On the legal system's continuity, see p. 233. On virtues see Basham, *Wonder*, pp. 283–87, 293–94, 338–42.

46. Derrett, "Hindu Law," pp. 230–31. Brahmans were the principal beneficiaries of the king's bounty (p. 227).

47. Derrett, "Hindu Law," p. 239.

48. Derrett, "Hindu Law," pp. 227–28; Kane, 5:1641, 1658, 1662.

49. Jairazbhoy, chap. 8, on the influence of Moslems and Indians on each other. See also E. C. Sachau's Preface to his translation, *Alberuni's India*.

tended over much of India, only to collapse in the first half of the eighteenth century and give way to British dominion.

The introduction of Moslem rule did not significantly modify Hindu economic ideas, though it did stimulate growth of cities, affect division of labor within India, and augment both centralization of administration and the tax burden. While Moslem administrative practice modified existing practice, it seems to have adopted several Indian or organizational practices of Maurya or Kautalyan vintage and continued smriti law in effect.[50] The tax burden, frequently high in Hindu states,[51] must often have been higher under Moslem rulers. Hindu legists fixed the ruler's share at about one-sixth in normal times and one-fourth to one-third in emergency periods, though some rulers took one-third or more. The Ghaznavids, described as not falling behind the Abbasid caliphs in "greed for money," collected mainly tribute and plunder.[52] Under the Delhi Sultanate in and after A.D. 1296, as much as one-half the agricultural produce (based on average yields) was taken, together with other taxes and charges instead of the usual one-fifth; thus the peasant might not retain as much as one-half.[53] "In Muslim India," writes W. H. Moreland, "it may be said in a general way that the claim [of the ruler] usually varied from one-third to one-half; and, in the economic conditions which prevailed, it is probable that the lower proportion was not far short of the danger-point, where production would begin to be checked, while the higher proportion was almost certainly injurious."[54] Moslem jurists held that the state could not

50. Friedrich Wilhelm suggests that efforts of medieval Moslem rulers to check decentralizing tendencies may have echoed arthashastra counsel and that later Mughal efforts to establish royal manufactories and monopolies may have reflected similar counsel or a political tradition going back to the Mauryas. See his "Wirtschaftssystem," esp. pp. 305–8, 311–12; also Sen-Gupta, p. 24; Qureshi, *Mughul Empire*, pp. 162–63; Prasad, p. 535; G. R. Madan, pp. 19–22.

51. See, for example, chap. 4 above; D. Sharma, pp. 207–12, 219–20, 309–10; Mazumdar, chap. 12; Yazdani, pp. 678–85; Kumar, pp. 14, 77, 79.

52. Bosworth, *Ghaznavids*, pp. 71, 75–79, 84, 90, 140.

53. See references in n. 55 of chap. 4, above; Mahajan, pp. 209–10; R. C. Majumdar, *Delhi Sultanate*, p. 450; Qureshi, *Sultanate of Delhi;* Thapar, *History,* pp. 271–75. On the miserable state of the peasants and the excessive expenditure of the ruling class, see Sharif, pp. 93–99, 117–25; and Prasad, pp. 513, 519, 521–22, 532–34, 537; Madan, pp. 18–22.

54. Moreland, "Revenue System of the Mughul Empire," in *Cambridge History of India,* vol. 4 (on the Mughal period), chap. 16, pp. 453, and 457–59, 468–72; Siddiqi, and Ira Klein's comments, "Utilitarianism." In Bengal around 1786 the current rate, down to a third because of price changes, corresponded closely to Ricardian rent. R. M. N. Gupta, pp. 105–6. In the sixteenth and seventeenth cen-

take over one-half, thus assuring the peasant one-half of his average produce.[55] The actual rate under Akbar, usually one-third, varied widely because of variation in the quality and yield of land, conditions taken into account in Sher Shah's reform of the land revenue system.[56] Other exactions than the land tax were imposed by local officials which, though illegal, were hard to prevent, especially before the reforms of the revenue system under Sher Shah and Akbar (1556–1605).[57] These reforms have led Qureshi to declare that the "attitude of the state towards the peasant was one of benevolence" as well as to note that the Mughals wanted to expand agriculture and their export surplus.[58] Indeed, he believes, "the peasant was left with sufficient margin after he had paid the state demand upon his produce to live in modest comfort," given the moderateness of the climate and a tradition "of simple homesteads and meagre furniture."[59]

Some economic matter and much administrative matter are encountered in Abu'l Fazl's *Āin-I-Ākbarī*, a work somewhat remindful of Kautalya's and also quite sympathetic to Hindu thought,[60] much of the third volume being devoted, as was Alberuni's *India*, to an account of Hindu philosophy.[61] The first volume, concerned

---

turies "the annual payment of land revenue alone was nearly half the total sale price" of *zamindari.* I. Habib, "Aspects."

55. *Cambridge History of India,* 4:452–53. Aurangzeb took about one-half if the ryots were not likely to be ruined thereby. See Sadunath Sarkar, p. 177; and S. R. Sharma. On the abuse of peasants even in the prosperous seventeenth century, see R. Mukerjee, pp. 11–18, 68–71, 81–82.

56. Qureshi, *Mughul Empire,* pp. 170–71; Siddiqi. The reform of the land revenue system by Shershah (1536–45), together with his development of transport, reflected Persian influence; it contributed greatly to Akbar's success.

57. *Cambridge History of India,* 4:231–32; Qureshi, *Mughul Empire,* pp. 151–52, 172–73, and pp. 150–53 on the abolition of cesses, some of which could be traced back to Kautalya.

58. Qureshi, *Mughul Empire,* pp. 173–76. Control of granted or other land was sometimes made subject to its effective cultivation. Ibid., pp. 156–58, 175–76, 289.

59. Qureshi, *Mughul Empire,* p. 178. He might have added apparel, for on it too very little was spent. Misra, p. 33. Spear (p. 24) describes the agricultural Hindu as living at the subsistence level in the early sixteenth century, and the condition of northern India at that time as inferior to its condition in the fourteenth century. The lower classes (peasants, artisans, laborers) "were exceedingly poor," a small middle class lived moderately to comfortably, and the upper classes lived magnificently. So finds Moreland, *India,* chap. 7.

60. I have used the three-volume second edition. The author Abu'l Fazl (1551–1602), something of a sycophant, was Akbar's minister and friend. See *Cambridge History of India,* 4:111.

61. In a collection of Akbar's "happy sayings," "sovereignty" is described as consisting "in distinguishing degrees of circumstance and in meting out reward

largely with the operation of the king's household and military establishment and suggesting a large-scale version of the Greek concept of *oikos,* recalls Kautalya's somewhat parallel prescriptions.[62] The country's population is described as being divided into four classes (warriors, artificers and merchants, the learned, and husbandmen and laborers), and later soldiers are ranked above cultivators and cultivators above artisans. Presumably, since the ruler is such by Allah's will, "whatever circumspect rulers exact from their subjects after due deliberation and to subserve the interests of justice and grant to their submissive dependents, has a perfect propriety and is universally in vogue." [63] Taxes on the produce of land, the main source of revenue, should, however, reflect the quality, productivity, and location of the land, while other taxes should be few and nonarbitrary. The collector of revenue should reduce the tax burden somewhat if so doing would encourage production, especially in agriculture, the most basic industry. The grain tax was to be used to to alleviate food shortages as well as to feed the king's animals.[64]

Much of the second volume is devoted to reporting for each subdivision of the kingdom its area, agricultural yields, revenue, armed forces, and main "castes." The duties of various officials are described, together with what ought to be their qualifications. The description of the duties of the *kotwal,* or superintendent of police, reminds the reader of Kautalya's descriptions; one of his many

---

and punishment in proportion thereto." Abu'l Fazl, 3:450. A city is defined as "a place where artisans of various kinds dwell, or a population of such an extent that a voice of average loudness will not carry at night beyond the inhabited limits." Ibid., 3:443. On the growth of cities and urban industry under the Mughals, see Naqvi, *Urban Centres.*

62. This concept, developed in and around Plato's time, seems not to have entered Indian or Mughal thought. *Oikonomia* signifies, as Kurt Singer points out, "administration, management, ordering, ruling a family and its estate (oikos), a pattern of co-ordinated actions conceived both pragmatically and normatively." K. Singer, pp. 54–55. See also Ruben and Fischer.

63. Abu'l Fazl, 2:56. On class structure, see 1:4 and 2:56–67; on the promotion of "rank distinctions" and the conferring of land grants upon worthy persons, 1:278–80. Caste is recognized (2:45). Islam strengthened caste bonds to the advantage of the Brahmans. Ibbetson, pp. 15–16; see also pp. 2, 14–21 on the Punjab, where, according to the village proverb, "As famine from the desert, so comes evil from a Brahman." Ibbetson, p. 218.

64. Abu'l Fazl, 1:12–13, 285–86; 2:58–63, and 46–50 on the duties of the collector of revenue. Exaction of "more than a half" of the land's yield "does not appear exorbitant to a despotic government" (2:59).

duties consisted in setting "the idle to some handicraft." [65] Economic regulation, taxation, and technological matter are dealt with in both volumes. Price fixing is described as insuring honesty and moderateness on the part of sellers; by holding down building costs it also served to facilitate the development of towns. Prices should be fixed in the light of the prospective profits and losses of sellers and in such manner that "both parties are satisfied." [66] Since traders who imported horses for sale to the government showed "large profits," these profits were made subject to taxation.[67]

Economic and technological comments appear here and there. Towns are described as the source of "progress." Money is treated as a medium of exchange and store of value. Trade is said to flourish where justice prevails and rulers are not avaricious. Coin clipping was condemned. Many prices are reported and said to vary with season and otherwise, and economic development is attributed to the introduction of "skilful" foreign "masters and workmen" and their "improved system of manufacture" which in time had brought some prices down.[68] Fines and rewards are described as improving the effectiveness of servants.[69] Officers in need of money were permitted to borrow from an official of the king at zero interest in the first year, 6.25 percent in the second year, 12.5 in the third, 75 in the eighth year and 100 in the tenth year.[70] Some saving is encouraged, to augment property and to provide against "occasional exigencies." These savings should be distributed among coins and wares, land, lending, and speculation on one's own account as well as jointly with others.[71] It is declared also that property can be secure only where autocracy preserves order

65. Abu'l Fazl, 2:44.

66. Abu'l Fazl, 1:232 ff. On fraud and cheating, see 1:134, 141 n., 226–28, 232, 252–53, 268; 2:44.

67. Abu'l Fazl, 1:225, and 140–41. Akbar, *Administration*, pp. 4–6, 53, makes little reference to economic regulations except to the protection of merchants on the highways, the use of escheated property to support public works, and the right of Brahmanic courts to follow their own codes. See also Akbar, *Punjab*.

68. Abu'l Fazl, 1:16–17, 20, 33, 65–68, 93–94, 232. Much of this work was done in imperial workshops (1:93). Rates of pay for various types of servants and prices for a wide variety of products are reported—e.g., 1:69–71, 132, 143–47, 155–56, 159, 161–62, 233–36; 2:75–93, 98–122.

69. Abu'l Fazl, 1:139, 148–50, 226–28. Even cows and buffaloes are fed "in proportion to the quantity of milk they give" (1:158).

70. Abu'l Fazl, 1:275. The term "interest" is not used.

71. Abu'l Fazl, 2:57–59, and 53–55.

and thus protects the people.[72] Some administrative practices of Hindu origin and cultivation, including the accumulation of reserves against emergency, were adopted by the Mughals or their Moslem predecessors.[73]

Various economic changes took place under the Mughals, perhaps in continuation of changes taking place in the fourteenth century in centers of the Delhi Empire. Mukerjee describes seventeenth-century India as "the agricultural mother of Asia and the industrial workshop of the world." In a number of seventeenth-century centers of economic activity, though they were situated in a vast subsistence economy resting upon essentially self-sufficient villages, specialization, exchange, and capital accumulation progressed as economic activities became monetized in part because a third to a half of agricultural produce had to be sold for cash to meet demand for revenue.[74] As a result of changes of this sort, behavior in conformity with Islamic law may have been affected, not by Hindu "economic" thought but by Hindu practice and example. For example, Irfan Habib contends that economic life, monetized already in parts of the Delhi Empire, became more widely monetized under the Mughals, with the result that land revenue was collected largely in money and that demand for credit increased, together with lending at interest in ruling and (later) European circles as well as in the rural economy and in petty and large-scale trade. Most of this lending business, along with much trade, was carried on by Hindus who, though subject to the constraints imposed by Manu and others, were free to lend at interest and to function in a usury-condemning Moslem world much as did Jews and others in the usury-condemning Christian world. Even so, the example of the Hindu, reinforced by growing demands for credit, prompted some Moslems to lend at interest, the state (in effect) to sanction it, and much of the Moslem population to pay it, despite Islamic injunction against the receipt and the payment of interest (*riba*). Moslem moral injunction seems to have been less effective in India than in the Arab world, and perhaps less effective under later than under earlier Moslem rulers

72. Abu'l Fazl, 2:55; 1:247.

73. See, for example, Qureshi, *Mughul Empire*, chaps. 7–8, 12, app. B. It is interesting that Al-Biruni, writing about A.D. 1030, referred to many Indian authors, but not to Kautalya. See Sachau. On administrative theory in the Moslem world, see Bosworth, "Abu Abdullah."

74. See, for example, Mukerjee, pp. i, v–i, xvii, xxiii; Raychaudhuri, "Some Patterns," and "A Re-interpretation," pp. 79–80, 86, 89.

when there seems to have been greater Moslem hostility toward the Hindu business community.[75] Associated with this growth of trade, especially that with England, were capital accumulation [76] and urbanization, concomitants of specialization and monetization.[77] Even so, though real wages were higher around 1650 than around 1600, it is held that the bulk of the population remained in virtually self-subsisting villages, while the towns, supported largely by rural tribute, served mainly royal, military, luxury, and religious "needs." [78]

The masses of the Indian population seem not to have benefited greatly from the progress of monetization. Their standard of living remained low.[79] Productivity was low, waste was great, and the contributions required by the state and its officials were heavy.[80]

75. On the development of the cash nexus under Moslem rule, see I. Habib, *Agrarian System*, "Banking," and "Usury." See also Moreland, *Agrarian System;* Misra, pp. 7–8, 24–28, 57. Moslem dislike of the Hindu business community is very marked in K. Z. Barani's *Fatawa-i-Jahandari* (c. 1358–59). Though cognizant of the opinion that "kings should not strive for price-control and price-fixation, for low prices are contingent upon plenty," Barani condemned regrating and urged the king not only to prevent fraud but also to regulate prices and keep grain and commodities "cheap." Low prices, he said, would hold down the money costs of government and the living expenses of the people, make for political stability, and, by taking the profit out of trading, keep it from attracting artisans and cultivators. Moreover, Moslems would not then be exposed to impoverishment at the hands of Hindus and Magians. See M. Habib and Khan, which includes a translation of Barani's work, pp. 34–38, 140–41, 165, and 127–29, where Hindu exploitation of Moslems is attributed to Hindu counterfeiting of bronze coins. While Barani disliked Hindus and had a low opinion of men in general, he did assert that the state must guarantee people against life-endangering material distress (pp. 43–49, 85, 88, 143). See Prasad, pp. 532–34, on economic misrule and 535–38 on extent of trade in the thirteenth and fourteenth centuries; also Madan, pp. 19–20.

76. Gokhale, "Capital Accumulation," and "English Trade." See also Raychaudhuri, "European Commercial Activity," in Ganguli, pp. 64–77.

77. Naqvi, "Progress of Urbanization." See also I. Habib, "Currency System,"; Kale, "Money Market."

78. D. and A. Thorner, pp. 51–52; Desai, chap 1. Indicative of Mughal waste is Umar. According to R. Mukerjee (chap. 3, pp. 58, 78) real wages rose sharply in 1600–1650, but thereafter fell to levels much below the 1600 level.

79. Misra, p. 56. But see Mukerjee, chaps. 2–4.

80. Before the British came, the share of village crops taken by the rulers ranged from one-sixth or less to one-half; after they came, the share given up by the cultivator was sometimes increased, not to be reduced until 1947. See D. and A. Thorner, pp. 51, 53–54, 62. See also Mukerjee, pp. 11–18, 70–71; Moreland, *Relations of Golconda*, pp. xxvi, 11, 27, 57, 81, on the misery of the heavily taxed and rack-rented inhabitants of Golconda, and his *India*, pp. 97–100, 130–36, and 279–80, 294–300 on progress-retarding and poverty-engendering upper-class waste. Moreland (*India*, pp. 189–93, 269–70) estimated that in 1911 Indian wages did not differ greatly from what they were in Akbar's time. See also Moreland, *Agrarian System;* Mukerjee, p. 58; and Hamilton.

With the collapse of the Mughal Empire in the first half of the eighteenth century, economic conditions worsened and remained worse until some time after the British became ascendant. Even before the collapse, of course, poverty was widespread, generated by low agricultural yields and the high taxes required to finance war and ostentatious waste.[81] Sentiments of loyalty and nationalism, so essential to the functioning of a national economy, were absent; so were values essential to the stimulation of economic growth, even though the Mughal administrative system had "apprenticed [India] to the idea of unity." [82]

To the many references to poverty already made we may add a most depressing picture of poverty in India around the close of the eighteenth century. This picture is supplied by the Abbé J. A. Dubois, who spent three decades (1792–1823) in India, mainly in the Deccan and the Madras Presidency, serving there as a Catholic missionary.[83] He estimated that three-quarters of the population possesed less than £25, mostly less than £10, and spent "about three months of the year . . . on the verge of starvation" even as did their domestic animals. Another 10 percent of the population, agriculturalists with £25–50 of property, lived "in fairly comfortable circumstances" in normal years, but in years of bad harvest often found themselves "reduced to the same state of want as those below them." Indians in distress, Dubois notes, showed great survival power, "a pound a day of millet flour, boiled in water and reduced to a thin gruel" serving to "prevent a family of five or six persons from dying of hunger." The circumstances of the top 15 percent of the population were comfortable or better. Their incomes came from moneylending, commerce, and government posts as well as from agriculture, generally on government or tax-exempt land.[84] Dubois believed that the condition of some of the people had improved somewhat with the substitution of British rule for what had been "arbitrary, oppressive, and tyrannical" rule. He feared, however, that this peaceful rule would so encourage population growth as to prevent much if any improvement in the poorer

81. See, for example, Spear, pp. 18–19, 28, 34, 40–48, 73, 77 97, 112; and Mukerjee's account of the decline, chaps. 3, 6–7.

82. Spear, pp. 35, 37, 47, 50, 70–73, 107, 110–11, 145.

83. Dubois. Most of the manuscript was written before 1806, but finally corrected with additions in 1815.

84. Dubois, pp. 82–91.

classes, particularly with the introduction of labor-displacing machinery.[85]

Postlude on Arthashastra

Returning now to the impact of arthashastra thought upon economic development, one can only infer that it was both favorable and unfavorable. It stressed material considerations and it was calculated to maintain order, a fundamental prerequisite to economic growth and one to which all the more or less universal religions initially (though perhaps unintentionally) gave support.[86] It probably failed, however, particularly in its post-Kautalya form, and despite its avoidance of crippling usury legislation, to give sufficient impetus to capital formation.[87] It may, of course, have been powerless. Much of the wastefulness with which the "social surplus" was used—in military and cultist expenditure and in extravagant consumption on the part of the ruling classes—is not really to be attributed to arthashastra counsel. This waste was indirectly facilitated, however, in that the austerity and asceticism sanctioned in the literature of dharma was not directed toward capital formation but toward depreciation of that very wealth, esteem for which in some form is essential to capital formation. For reasons largely independent of arthashastra counsel, sufficient impetus was not given to invention and innovation—then as now, along with increments in the capital supply, the main source of improvement in living standards. Underlying this lack of sufficient stimulus to saving and invention was the varna system, together with the social immobility and misdirection of talent and inquiry to which this system gave rise or which it accentuated.

The varna system blocked economic development in many ways,

85. Dubois, pp. 93–95, and 592–3. Compare K. Datta.

86. As noted earlier, on several occasions events swamped Kautalya's counsel, with the result that his system was no longer effectively implemented in post-Maurya times, even under the Guptas. By then decentralization or feudalization of the state apparatus had already got under way, and land, revenues, and administrative and judicial rights had been transferred in varying measure to Brahmans, temples, local officers, and so on; responsibility for irrigation was localized and trade became more local in character. While the lot of peasants worsened under some of the donees, that of Shudras improved, many becoming agriculturalists, while slavery diminished. See R. S. Sharma, "Origins"; L. Gopal, "Quasi-Manorial Rights"; and R. S. Sharma, *Aspects*, chap. 14.

87. See Blitz and Long.

especially when it became expanded into a large number of castes. Because it included different dharmas for different groups and stages in life, it could not facilitate the rise of a universalist ethic and the organization of a society founded upon the supposition that men were equal spiritually, potentially, or in some other significant way. So universalism, instrumentalism, emphasis upon achievement, and other elements (among them nationalism) common to dynamic and kinetic societies were ruled out.[88] Instead, divinely sanctioned ascription ruled. Moreover, this ascription did not give weight to the allocation of manpower in accordance with anything like an equimarginal principle; and much of the emphasis upon achievement and reward related, in theory, to the world of rebirth. Theory was somewhat tempered, of course, by the practical rule that man's conduct responds to the prospect of the carrot as well as to the threat of the stick and to the suppositious nature of the demands of transcendental agencies. Yet there was little scope in theory (and not much more in practice) for social mobility and that drive to work and save which tends to emerge in a universalistic achievement society such as arose in western Europe.

The varna system might have produced a beneficial effect, but it seems not to have done so. Presumably membership in the Brahman class was relatively small—in 1931 only 6.4 percent of the Hindu population were Brahmans, though in a number of areas the proportion ranged between 10 and 34.4 percent.[89] Membership in the Kshatriya class must also have been relatively small, especially in areas long under Moslem rule. Moreover, ascent from the Vaishya order into the two higher orders was not permissible. Accordingly, since able and successful entrepreneurs, together with their children, could not move out of the productive Vaishya class into one of the two higher but unproductive classes, one might have expected the Vaishya class to become increasingly skillful and wealthy as did the Japanese mercantile class.[90] Indeed, the success of the Jains in commerce is associated with their exclusion by religious belief and

88. See, for example, T. Parsons, chaps. 3–5; Weber, pp. 143–44; Mishra, *Hinduism;* Kane, 5:1643 on caste, and 1629 ff. on changing beliefs, use of wealth, etc. See also n. 99 below for Morris's views on Indian values.

89. Davis, p. 169; Mishra, *Hinduism,* chap. 7.

90. See Marion Levy, in Kuznets et al., chap. 17, who compares the developing Japanese merchant class with the nondeveloping Chinese merchant class, which was constantly weakened by leakage of its able members into nonmercantile categories.

ritual from many other occupations and with their inclination to save and invest, whereas that of the immigrant Parsis is associated with values expressed in Zoroastrianism.[91] This possible favorable outcome for the Vaishya did not materialize, however, because conditions other than "nonleakage" were not sufficiently favorable.[92]

Among the missing intervening variables one finds failure of the upper classes to appreciate the role of capital formation and invention, together with their marked disesteem for the Vaishyas and the Shudras and their activities. Austerity, when stressed, did not make for saving as among Calvinists and others. Furthermore, while the doctrine of karma (with its emphasis upon reward in the world of rebirth for faithful performance of one's assigned duties) might have been defined to foster hard work, capital formation, etc., at least among the Vaishyas, it was not so defined. At the same time it may be significant that material objectives were emphasized in Indian literature, especially in arthashastra literature, far more than technical progress. Given the persistence of materialist values and the oft demonstrated entrepreneurial ability of businessmen in pre-Mughal India, it is surprising that economic progress was no greater than it seems to have been.

The nonanalytical orientation of the Hindu system of thought reduced its capacity to facilitate economic development. For this system was essentially taxonomic and prescriptive in character and concerned with laying down empirical rules calculated, on the basis of previous experience, to produce concrete economic and political results; it was not an engine of analysis given to inquiry into the genesis, foundation, and adequacy of these rules. It seems to have been implicitly assumed that mundane society was static and hence unlikely to benefit from important changes in rules which were sanctioned by their antiquity and Hindu society's long experience

91. See Kennedy; Kane, 5:1643; Buchanan, chap. 8. The role of the Parsis remains to be assessed adequately; it "has been much exaggerated," Morris and Stein believe, p. 193; Misra, pp. 29–33. There seems to be nothing in the Zend Avesta to prompt a migrating people to achieve commercial success, other than great emphasis upon honesty and the keeping of contracts.

92. In present-day literature the joint family is represented as less favorable to economic development than is the nuclear family. Under some conditions, however, the joint family is potentially more favorable, as the experience of the great late medieval and early modern Italian and German trading families suggests. This could have been true also in India when the joint family was emerging, in Manu's day and earlier. See, for example, Kapadia, chap. 10; Mishra, *Hinduism;* Kane, 5:1672; Madan in V. B. Singh, *Economic History,* pp. 61–73, 82–84.

with them. Hence the rules were repeated from generation to generation and the economic foundations and implications of many of these rules tended to be disregarded. As we noted in chapter 4, for example, several rules set down quite clearly by Narada, largely though not wholly on the basis of Manu's code, were so effectively put that, Jolly found, "upwards of half his work" came to be embodied in medieval and modern compositions "in the province of Sanskrit law." In his discussion of partnership and similar associations Narada laid down rules for the distribution of returns (as had Kautalya and Manu), though he never inquired how these associates might estimate the productivity or contribution on the basis of which they entered into agreements.[93] Similarly, when discussing wages, he said nothing of the skill or productivity according to which workers should be paid.[94] Again, when describing the permissible range of interest rates chargeable and the amounts of credit extendible (1, 98–109), he failed to explain the economic rationale underlying these rates and amounts. That his rules, when initially formulated, had reflected market conditions and constraints, or that such rules were readily enforceable only when they were fairly compatible with market conditions, was not discussed by Narada.[95] Had Narada and others emphasized analysis, the functioning of the Indian economic system would in time have come to be better understood, especially if authors were pressed to develop somewhat modern analytical categories.

It is not easy to assess the degree to which economic development was retarded by the Hindu system of thought in which economically oriented ideas were embedded. So many circumstances were present. There is much evidence of the presence of economic activity and incentive even though traders did not generally invest heavily in

93. Narada wrote (III, 2–3): "Where several partners are jointly carrying on business for the purpose of gain, the contribution of funds towards the common stock of the association forms the basis (of their undertakings). Therefore let each contribute his proper share. . . . The loss, expense, and profit of each partner are equal to those of the other partners, or exceed them, or remain below them, according as his share is equal to theirs, or greater or less." Jolly wrote the introduction to Narada's work.

94. He wrote (v, 22): "Hired servants are of three kinds: highest, middlemost, and lowest. The wages due for their labour are fixed in proportion to their skill and to the value of their services." On other modes of payment, see VI, 3–10.

95. Unlike Manu, Narada was realistic enough to approve public gaming houses (XVII) and a father's right to distribute property among his sons as he pleased (XIII, 15).

fixed capital. The prevailing attitude toward profits was favorable [96] and there was much scope for lending, far more than Islamic and Christian moral literature sanctioned. Indian theoretical and applied science failed to progress despite its favorable early start,[97] perhaps because opposition to change was strong in Indian culture and fortified by segmental ethical relativism associated with the caste system.[98] War and ostentatious consumption must, however, have reinforced whatever development-retarding effects Hindu values exercised; for they gave rise to heavy and variable tax burdens. These burdens in turn were unfavorable to investment in visible and immobile capital as well as innovation.

M. D. Morris has recently questioned the view that Indian "values" have been "a significant obstacle to economic change and growth." On the one hand he finds no single "Indian value system" pervading Brahmanical doctrinal literature," nor a single non-elitist value system animating the underlying population. On the other hand he does not find the pattern of Indian investment to be irrational when examined closely, nor does he find the jati (sub-castes) not to have collaborated within the business sector of the labor force. Indeed, "caste and *jati* seem to be as fluid as change requires," certainly much more so than Manu or anthropologists have allowed.[99] Insofar as Morris's interpretation stands up, other causes of retardation, some of which have been mentioned, have to be assigned greater weight.

96. Even in the celebrated Hindu treatise on love, Vatsyayana's Kamasutra, courtesans are counseled not only to support Brahmans and public and religious institutions but to compute their gains and losses in terms of wealth, pleasure, and religious merit (pt. 6, chaps. 5–6). Compare S. L. Ghosh, esp. chap. 8.

97. In the realm of engineering, Indian technical skill, though great in some crafts and in the field of ironwork and sometimes striking (perhaps because of Western influence) in the field of architecture, did not continue to improve and ramify. See De Camp, pp. 271–77; Niyogi, pp. 169–70, 235, on shipbuilding. The Iron Age began in India between 1000 and 700 B.C., it is now believed. See Kosambi, "Beginning," and S. D. Singh, "Iron." Despite these early beginnings and early achievements in industries and crafts, revolutionary advances did not continue to be made, traditional hereditary skills merely being maintained. Niyogi, p. 235, and Mishra, pp. 39–40, 143. On early Indian science see Maheshwari, and consult n. 38 in chap. 3 above.

98. Weber, pp. 122–23, 143–46.

99. Morris, "Values"; see p. 46 supra.

Chapter 6

Modernization

It is always minorities, . . . provided they are dynamic, that change the shape of nations.

PERCIVAL SPEAR

This chapter, dealing as it does with diverse components of modernization, presents expositive difficulties. We may, of course, present simple indices of modernization. For example, the relative number of Indians literate in English rose from a negligible fraction in 1800 to about 0.5 percent in 1901 and nearly 3 percent in 1941. Average real income, after rising very little (if at all) between around 1800 and the 1850s, seems to have increased intermittently by about 18 percent in 1860–1900 and about 33 percent in 1900–1940.[1] Of greater significance, however, are the circumstances, conflicts, and educational changes underlying the movement of these indicators.

Britain's relation to India underwent a series of changes after the East India Company, initially engaged mainly in trade with India, moved into the power vacuum that emerged in Bengal with the collapse of Mughal rule in the 1750s and subsequently contributed to the extension of British control over India. Some British reaction was unfavorable, initially to the role of the Company,

---

1. M. Mukerji, "National Income," in V. B. Singh, *Economic History*, chap. 25, pp. 701–2. He adds, however, that given the unreliability of the data, "we cannot assert that, today, our level of per capita income is higher than that in 1900 or in 1857" (p. 661). It is this unreliability that is responsible for diversity in income estimates. R. Mukerjee's wage indices (*Economic History*, p. 58) for United Provinces for skilled and unskilled workers show a decline between 1729 and 1850 but some improvement between 1812–1820 and 1850. See also K. Mukerjee's comments in V. B. Singh, *Economic History*, pp. 645–46. S. J. Patel (*Essays*, pp. 36, 44, 48, 49) observes that we cannot even be sure if per capita income has risen in India over the last seventy-five years or so. Whether average income rose in the nineteenth century and what the effects were of British policy are questions discussed by M. D. Morris, B. Chandra, T. Raychaudhuri, and T. Matsui in the *Indian Economic and Social History Review* 5 (March 1969):1–100.

which was brought increasingly under control after 1773, and subsequently to the British crown upon its assumption of control in 1858 after the Sepoy Mutiny in 1857. Economists from Adam Smith on were critical of the mercantilist foundations of Britain's India policy. They would have subscribed both to Eric Stokes's characterization of India as "a military empire in an unimperial age, a vast commitment dubiously balanced by its actual commercial value to English industry" and to Seebohm's description of it as an "imperial phantom in Asia." The Mutiny raised doubts even among those far more sanguine than the economists. These were quelled, however, by Britain's belief that she must contribute substantially to India's economic development and by India's complementary recognition, in the person of its new but growing westernized middle class, that solution for India's economic and related problems was immediately to be found in Western knowledge and industrialization—whence interest in this knowledge (including economic) began to flourish, together with the realization that India's independence lay not far in the future. Even so, the English belief, common to Company officers in their heyday, that British sway would continue into the far distant future, revived in the new imperialistic climate of the closing third of the nineteenth century. It was not foreseen that India would become independent within less than a century of the Mutiny, any more than it was foreseen that economic science in India would finally match the best in the West. After all, who foresaw the two power-shattering Peloponnesian wars that would destroy western Europe's hegemony in the Third World? [2]

Initial Conditions

The first manifestations of economic science in India reflected the state of economic thinking in Britain and India, together with the concrete problems faced in India. The response in India was affected, as will be shown in the next section, by the channels and other factors conditioning communication and response.

2. See Spear, chaps. 11–14; Hutchins; Bearce; S. Bhattacharya. On the rise of the middle class, see Bhatia; Misra. For Stokes's assessment, see his p. xi; and F. Seebohm. See also Patel, "British Economic Thought"; and *Cambridge History of India*, vol. 5, esp. chaps. 10–11, 18, 25–27, 32.

The political economy of Adam Smith was dominant by the time English control of Bengal had become firm. Even so, some influence was exercised in India by James Steuart and the Physiocrats. Moreover, though it was no longer argued that trade with India drained gold and silver out of England, it was about to be argued, by mercantilists and others, that Britain was draining wealth out of India. Still, Smithianism, with its minimization of state control and its emphasis upon economic freedom, was well suited to the ideological needs of both ruler and ruled, of a commercial company obligated to administer a state and of Indian traders and manufacturers interested in achieving freedom from English commercial restrictions, a freedom not really achieved until 1858.[3]

At the time of the Company's establishment of control in Bengal, Western political economy was not at all current there or elsewhere in India. Moreover, as has been indicated, there was no real functional equivalent to be found in indigenous regulatory or other literature. What was known consisted mainly in the wisdom of merchants and administrators, based upon their own experience and the transmitted experience of their predecessors. Western political economy had first to be introduced into India, especially Bengal, there finally to take root and grow, a process initially retarded by the disposition of Indian society to look upon the British as another caste and "withdraw itself even more into the closed circle of its ancient traditions." Not until the early 1800s did the Western impact begin to make itself felt, and it produced a Moslem as well as a Hindu reaction.[4]

While political economy remained virtually unknown, there had for many centuries been provision for training young Indians in commerce and related arts. Secular studies had flourished in Taxila, Kautalya's home. Kautalya made no provision for state support of education, however, presumably because he considered teaching to be a monopoly of the Brahmans and training in the crafts to pass from father to son or from practitioner to apprentice. In and after his time, the education of the two upper varnas apparently dealt

3. Ahmed, pp. 5, 42–43. The Company's fixed policy "till the early part of the nineteenth century had been to avoid interference in the social and religious life of its Indian subjects" (p. 100). On unfavorable effects of British customs, see Rajeshwari Prasad, chaps. 6–7.

4. The quotation is from Basham, *Wonder*, p. 480. On the reaction, see Ahmed, p. 5.

with both the three vedas and the eighteen arts (sippas), among them conveyancing or law, accountancy, agriculture, commerce, cattle breeding, and administrative training.[5] Of the sixty-four arts and crafts sometimes identified in the literature, many dealt with agriculture, industry, or manufacture, though not with trade as such. In village schools, at least later on, commercial subjects were taught.[6] It was only as the caste system became rigid that Brahmans no longer sought training in useful arts and services (e.g., medicine, trade) and that these came to be followed mainly by the Vaishyas. The apprenticeship method continued to be used to fit persons to pursue professions, practice useful arts, and engage in commerce and related activities.[7] Indian literacy, put at about 15 percent around 1800, has been said (presumably with exaggeration) to approximate 30 percent in the Middle Ages and 60 percent in Ashoka's time.[8] Less emphasis was placed upon practical education in the Moslem sector, though Law includes "economics" in a list of "sciences" studied in Mughal times.[9] Akbar himself stressed the importance of practical subjects and urged that every boy read books on such subjects, among them arithmetic, agriculture, household matters, and rules of government.[10] Inasmuch as Hindus filled many posts in the revenue administration, Moslems may have

5. Altekar, *Education*, pp. 215–28, 253; Chaube, pp. 32, 129–32, 136; Keay, chap. 4. On Taxila, see Basham, *Wonder*, p. 164.

6. R. K. Mookerji, *Ancient Indian Education*, pp. 353–63, 468–72 on accountancy, etc., and 349–52 on guild education. Apparently in India as in Mesopotamia and later in the Persian Empire, algebra was needed for the conduct of business and "the Hindu term for the positive quantity, *dhanam*, means . . . 'property, possession, capital.'" Gandz, pp. 273, 275 n. Some commercial training had long been supplied in Hindu village and town schools, J. Ghosh reports, *Higher Education*, pp. 10–12, 105–6 n. See also Apte, *Our Educational Heritage*, pp. 71–72; and K. Datta, chap. 2, pp. 11, 19–22, on continuation over the centuries of reading, writing, arithmetic, and traditional features of education. The 64 arts and sciences are discussed even by Vatsyayana in part I of his treatise.

7. Altekar, *Education*, chap. 5, pp. 351–52. After A.D. 800 the culture of artisans became inferior to what it had been. Ibid., pp. 198–200, 214–18, 347–53. Sanskrit ceased to be intelligible to the common man after around A.D. 900. Ibid., p. 353. See also Chaube, p. 136. Sanskrit learning included only such economic material as was included in the study of law.

8. Altekar, *Education*, pp. 218–19, 352. But see R. C. Majumdar, *British Paramountcy*, pt. 2, p. 19, where adult literacy around 1800 is put at not over 5½ percent. In 1891 literacy among Indian males over ten years of age was 11.4 percent; among women, 0.5 percent. Davis, p. 151.

9. N. N. Law, pp. 161–62. On economic thought in Islam, see my "Economic Thought of Islam." Dongerkerry, p. 13, reports jurisprudence but not "economics" in Moslem syllabi of around 1750.

10. Abu'l Fazl, 1:288–89; and Keay, chap. 7.

had less incentive to prepare themselves for these posts,[11] to the conduct of which Indian education had long been adapted.

Determinants of the Movement of Ideas

The ideas constituting economics flowed from Britain either to Company servants in India or to Indians, directly or via Company representatives. It was, however, the movement to Indians that presented major educational problems, given that important servants of the Company had had some economic education at home. The introduction of British practices into India, of course, presented even greater difficulty than that of ideas, economic and other.

Transfer of Practices

Let us consider first the movement of practices and organizations, themselves institutionalized expressions of ideas. These, if they are to flourish, must be embedded in a matrix of complementary elements. Some of these elements are readily identifiable:

(i) Legal conditions within the receiver country must be suitable, sufficiently stable, and supported by adequate sanctions.

(ii) There must gradually be brought into existence, if it does not already exist, an overhead structure of business-facilitating institutions (e.g., monetary system, price system, banking arrangements, professional or trade organs, and so on).

(iii) Even if the transmitted practice or organization is accompanied by entrepreneurial and/or managerial inputs (e.g., in the form of the famous management agency) as well as by skilled personnel, there is need for indigenously supplied complementary agents of production, labor, specialized and overhead capital, working capital (food and raw materials), complementary small-scale entrepreneurship, and so on. If these are not locally available they will have to be supplied initially from foreign sources and eventually developed domestically.

---

11. Some Hindus prepared books of rules for the guidance of administration. Nadvi, pp. 114–15; Misra, pp. 147–49; Siddiqi. Indeed, the architect of Akbar's revenue system was a Hindu, Raja Todar Mal, a Kayastha of the clerical caste. Moreover, the organization of the land revenue system bore some reesmblance to earlier Hindu systems. Tinker, pp. 38–39, 52. On Indian and Moslem education, see R. C. Majumdar, *British Paramountcy*, pt. 2, pp. 17–21. After around 1500, Hindus studied Persian, the better to participate in Mughal administration. See Metha.

(iv) There must exist, in the receiver country or abroad, at least the prospect of a sufficient demand for the output of goods and services to be made possible by the newly introduced practices and organizations; otherwise men will be without incentive to introduce and establish them.

(v) The cultural milieu of the receiver's country must undergo sufficient transformation to meet the continuing needs requisite to the expansion of the new activities; there must, for example, be provision for adequate education, a growing supply of wage labor, a developing agriculture, enlargement of the budget of typical familial wants, a lengthening of the time horizons underlying economic activities, and scope for the multiplication of indigenous enterprise.[12]

Transmission of Ideas

The movement of ideas, though less difficult than that of practices, also encounters obstacles. The introduction of one country's economic ideas into another, together with their absorption, may, for purposes of analysis, be said to be conditioned by at least four sets of circumstances.

(i) The source of a new set of ideas must command sufficient prestige to warrant progenitors of these ideas—or middlemen—to undertake to transmit them to foreign lands.[13] The English, as conquerors of India, enjoyed something like prestige, with the result that their ideas tended to be viewed favorably, at least by some Indians. The initial agent of the conqueror was the East India Company, which drew upon European political economists for advice as well as performed some educational functions.

Soon after Britain's ascendancy in Bengal, the Indian entrepôt of then modern European ideas, the Company was confronted by two problems. The first consisted in a drain of silver away from Bengal after the victory at Plassey. In 1772 Sir James Steuart was called upon to suggest a solution. This drain differed somewhat from the supposed drain of which critics of British policy in India were to complain after the late 1820s; it was attributable in part

---

12. On the present-day flow of managerial services, see Fforde.

13. Ideas may be transmitted immediately, or stored and subsequently transmitted as were Greek and Roman ideas by the Jews and Arabs. See Coats; and Redlich.

to the deterioration of the currency, though accentuated by a war-generated interruption of exports as well as by the sending of "presents" of silver to Britain. Out of Steuart's report, together with discussions of it by several Company officers, came "the broad principles" which guided "the currency policy of India for the next one-hundred years." [14]

The revenue problem, essentially distributive in nature, was never solved to the satisfaction of those concerned, though it must have acquainted some Indians with European rent and tax theory and some English administrators with the fallaciousness of their belief that one could find in India the analogue of the British or the Physiocratic landlord. After all, before 1760, India was neither feudal nor capitalistic, but a peasant economy dotted here and there by enclaves functioning as towns and supplemented by a variety of arts and crafts. Each year the self-subsisting villages composing this peasant economy paid a share of the crops to a distant Hindu raja or Moslem nawab. An upper limit was set to the size of this share—one-sixth to one-half—by the opportunity an overtaxed peasantry might find to flee to unoccupied or less tax-burdened areas.[15] This alternative, sometimes strengthened by famine (as in 1770, when famine carried away one-third of Bengal's population), grew weaker as population increased, uncultivated area declined, and nonagricultural alternatives failed to keep pace.[16]

Almost from 1760 on the East India Company was under pressure to modify its land-revenue policy, based essentially upon indigenous practice and concern for trade. Land revenues declined despite an apparent increase in the tax burden, "wealth" supposedly was being drained out of Bengal, and the metropole was dissatisfied (e.g., Pitt's India Act of 1784).[17] Yet not until 1793 was a so-called permanent settlement made applicable to Bengal. Somewhat similar provisions were extended eventually to about half of British India.

14. See S. R. Sen, chap. 10; J. C. Sinha. On the drain, see N. K. Sinha, vol. 1, chap. 11; K. Datta, chaps. 6–7; and the views of Alexander Dow and Sir Philip Francis, summarized by Guha, pp. 39 ff., 131 ff. On the origins of the nineteenth-century view, see R. C. Majumdar, *British Paramountcy*, pt. 1, p. 359.

15. D. and A. Thorner, pp. 11, 51–52.

16. D. and A. Thorner, chap. 6. On the degree to which population outstripped the increase of land under cultivation, see Kumar, chap. 7, and Anstey, pp. 100–102.

17. See Huq, esp. pp. 198–99, 258–59, 262; Kumar, pp. 77–78; Misra, pp. 44, 120–28.

Under these, zamindars or comparable intermediaries were made liable in perpetuity for the revenue due the government in fixed cash amounts, while remaining free to make their own terms with their "tenants," whose rights of cultivation remained undefined. In the remainder of India, ryots and others enjoying the right to cultivate were responsible directly to the state for its share of the produce; in time, however, some became "owners," who let out part or all of their land. Neither system made for the hoped-for improvement in agriculture or a lightening of tax and rent burdens. The way was left open for the "growth in power of the moneylender and the absentee landlord." [18]

The system put into effect in Bengal in 1793 resembled closely that submitted by Sir Philip Francis in 1776 only to be rejected. This system reflected mainly Physiocratic influence, with perhaps a touch of the views of Sir James Steuart and Alexander Dow.[19] It was generally agreed that land was the main if not the only source of revenue available, and that security of private property in land was essential to social stability and agricultural and economic progress. It was not recognized how difficult it would be to transform the Indian land system into one resembling the English system and thereby augment the then very low market value of land.[20] It was supposed, therefore, that given stability of land-

18. D. and A. Thorner, pp. 53–54, and pp. 4–5 on the share of the landlord, which in the 1950s amounted to 50 percent or more. See also Anstey, pp. 97–103, 374–78; Kumar, pp. 11–12, 14, 77, 79, 88–90. See also R. C. Majumdar, *British Paramountcy*, pt. 1, pp. 821–22, 1131–33, for critical comments on the system.

19. Dow, a Scottish mercantilist admirer of the Mughals, favored disposing of the Company's land in Bengal in perpetuity for £10 million and an annual revenue of £4 million from the purchasers of the lands. He hoped that as a result private property in land would be securely established, especially among smaller holders. Should the state require more than £4 million, other taxes than land taxes could be resorted to. Dow's work did not, however, exercise much influence upon the formulation of the "permanent settlement." He attributed Bengal's decline mainly to the region's unfavorable balance of trade and a resulting scarcity of money—to a "drain of wealth" to Britain—which adversely affected all sectors of the Indian economy. On Dow's views (in his *Dissertation on the Origin and Nature of Despotism in Hindustan, 1768–1772*), see Guha, pp. 37–42. On the ideas of Francis and Cornwallis and post-1793 doubts, see Guha, chaps. 4–6. See also Natarajan.

20. Anstey, pp. 97–98. Henry Pattullo, Physiocratic author and agronomist, finding in Bengal conditions paralleling those he condemned in France, asserted that agricultural prosperity would transform Bengal into a good market for British products. See his *Essay*, and Guha's summary, pp. 42–50, and pp. 183–86 for a later and somewhat similar English view. It was subsequently noted that to insure an Indian market for British goods, Indian tastes must be modified through Western education. Misra, pp. 152–55.

ownership and/or use, together with moderate taxation and ease of sale of land, Indian agriculture would improve and flourish and with it commerce. Such was Francis's hope and such was the hope of Lord Cornwallis, with whose name is associated the plan finally adopted in Bengal in 1793. While these hopes were not very fully realized, the expectation that more land would be brought under cultivation was satisfied as population grew and the land under cultivation more than doubled.[21]

With the development of Ricardian rent theory and the explicit definition of land rent in an English context, what amounts to a second attempt was made to rationalize the Indian land-revenue system. It was undertaken by James Mill, who assumed his duties in the London headquarters of the East India Company in 1819, after having spent a decade preparing his massive *History of British India* (1817). A close friend of Ricardo, Mill made Ricardo's theory "the lynch-pin of [his] strategy of economic policy for India." Since the absolute rental share would increase in size as the demand for produce rose, the fund whence revenue was drawn would be elastic upward, though not at the expense of wages and profits. Mill therefore found Cornwallis's "permanent settlement" unacceptable, in part because it did not provide a growing source of revenue while at the same time it put no limit upon the demands which zamindars or landowners could make upon cultivators. Ricardo's theory, on the contrary, permitted the construction of an ideal tax system and its extension throughout the Company's domains. The proceeds of the tax, not to exceed a moderate rent, would be used to provide administrative services and maintain law and order and thus, by securing the ryot or cultivator in his property and the returns of his industry, enable agriculture to flourish. There would not, under his system, be a drain of "wealth" to Britain, Mill believed; he supposed, indeed, that India was costing Britain on balance. Though Mill's policy proposals long molded approaches to Indian problems, they were found wanting (especially by Richard Jones and the Earl of Lauderdale) both because the structure of India's landholding system differed so markedly from the British

21. Moreland, "The Ain-i-Akbari," pp. 48, 51; J. C. Ghosh, "Rent," p. 59. Already in Rig-Veda times, Praphuta C. Basu stated, population growth led to the reorganization of agriculture and the emergence of private property in land.

and because the economic relations between England and India were disadvantageous to one or both.[22] Even so, the pressure of circumstances lent support to Mill's view and the eventual giving up, after the early 1880s, of the idea of permanent settlement.[23]

The agricultural prosperity which Mill, together with his predecessors and successors, had anticipated under British rule did not materialize; as a result Indian nationalist economists vigorously condemned the British revenue system. Gross food-crop production did not increase between the early 1890s and the advent of independence in 1947, in part because nonfood crops replaced food crops, and output per capita declined about one-third.[24] Writing at the close of the nineteenth century, W. W. Hunter observed that "throughout large tracts the struggle for life is harder than it was when the country passed into our hands." [25] Some believe, of course, that the agricultural output per capita rose in the nineteenth century, as increase in acreage and output per acre more than offset a low rate of population growth.[26] Even if average output rose, the condition of agricultural labor, of many peasants, and of poorer landlords improved very little, if at all. For with land often becoming fragmented by population growth as well as easily transferable in the course of the nineteenth century, with recurrent agrarian calamities, and with nonagricultural employment failing to absorb excess rural labor, the cultivator often became prey to the moneylender. The early and continuing hope of achieving an agricultural

22. This paragraph is based upon Barber. See also D. and A. Thorner, chap. 10; Stokes, chap, 2; Klein.

23. Klein; Stokes, pp. 118–39; Misra, chap. 9; Black.

24. D. and A. Thorner, pp. 102–7. Output per capita fell to about one-fifth below minimal needs (p. 106). Clark and Haswell, p. 61. On the impact of the development of nonfood crops and their export, see B. M. Bhatia in V. B. Singh, *Economic History*, pp. 123–35.

25. D. and A. Thorner, p. 110. In her study of Madras Presidency, Kumar (pp. 192–93) reports a decline in wages after 1873 but none in 1800–1860, when wages fluctuated around subsistence. V. N. Murti asserts that agricultural and total output lagged behind population under British rule.

26. M. D. Morris "Towards a Reinterpretation," p. 612. Population increased about 140 percent between 1800 and 1901. Total food-grain production did not increase between the first and the fifth decade of this century, though it has since increased nearly 3 percent per year. See *Accelerating India's Food Grain Production*, pp. 2–3. According to George Blyn (*Agricultural Trends*) decline in average agricultural output did not begin until about 1910. Moreover, urban population growth, a sequel to agricultural progress, was at a rate of less than 4 percent per decade in 1881–1931.

middle class of progressive, capital-accumulating, cultivating proprietors was not realized.[27] Of greater importance for this study,
the failure contributed to the attack of Indian economic writers
upon British policy in India and prepared the way for post-1947
agrarian legislation.[28]

The Company was in a position to impart Western economic
learning to its Hindu employees and contacts. Its recruits in training
at Haileybury underwent training in political economy and finance,
among other studies. The attention given to economic learning
probably was too little, however, to convert the recruits into effective bearers of it to India.[29] From this source, therefore, not much
more economic knowledge was acquired than from the controversy
over land revenue. It must, therefore, have been Western mission-
aries and teachers at first and later (after the Mutiny) Western
teachers at the college and university level who, cloaked in British
prestige, were the principal conveyors of political economy to
nineteenth-century India.

(ii) The international diffusion of ideas may depend upon the
vehicle of transmission employed. The medium must be suitable
to the situation. That immediately available, written and spoken
English, was imperfectly suited at first for communication between
the English and Hindus. In the 1790s not many Indians knew English, particularly the English in which classical political economy
was couched; and the English taught hardly met T. B. Macaulay's
expositive stipulations.[30] In time, however, Indian knowledge of
English increased and with it, Indian capacity to symbolize and
order concepts of man's economic universe in both English and the
vernacular.[31] Indeed, to this day the language of economics in

27. Misra, chaps. 5, 9; V. B. Singh, *Economic History*, pp. 146–49; Klein;
Kumar, chap. 11; D. and A. Thorner, pp. 54–60, 77, 102–12; and Darling.

28. D. and A. Thorner, pp. 62–64. S. R. Sharma points out that the British
were slow to develop irrigation, in V. B. Singh, *Economic History*, chap. 7.

29. B. S. Cohn, esp. pp. 113, 117–19, 138–40. Between 1828 and 1849 the
number of Indians in civil posts rose from 1,197 to 2,813. Misra, p. 178.

30. He condemned the darkening of the meaning of rules and legislation "by
gibberish, by tautology, by circumlocution," by "the unnecessary intricacy and
exuberance" of language, when what is needed is to make "meaning" as "trans-
parent as words can make it." Stokes, p. 199. See also F. Machlup; H. A. Innis,
pp. 3–60.

31. The importance of English and English education, most important of the
forces that transformed India, was recognized soon after 1800 in Bengal. R. C.
Majumdar, *British Paramountcy*, pt. 2, chap. 2; and Misra, pp. 147–60, 170, 181,

India has remained predominantly English, now the geographically most widely distributed language in the country. Indian scholars have stressed the communication potential of Sanskrit, suggesting that lack of "suitable" terminology in Indian vernacular languages might be remedied by grafting modern terms on to Sanskrit roots.[32] Even then two barriers would remain—vernacular heterogeneity and lack of an appropriate infrastructure (books, journals, etc.).

(iii) The acceptance of a set of ideas of foreign provenance turns significantly upon their content, its complexity, and its congeniality to the symbolic content of the culture of the land of destination.[33] This congeniality is conditioned above all by the extent to which the content in question is ethically or religiously oriented and permeated by essentially ultimate or noninstrumental values—by the degree to which what is transmitted can serve as an end in the culture of the receiving country. Comprehension of the content of Western economic ideas must long have been handicapped by the traditional character of Indian culture, even though these ideas had to do with means to generally approved material ends rather than with higher values and ethical objectives; for traditional societies attached much less significance to material purposes, rewards, materially oriented motivation, and European forms of organization. Of course, as the ideological content of Western economics changed, becoming more etatist and interventionist in and after the later nineteenth century, it may have become more congenial to traditional cultures in process of change. In the earlier nineteenth century the acceptability of economics as a science in India must have been limited, except among "competition wallahs," those counting upon specialized knowledge—in economics, law, medicine, engineering, or administration—to improve their social and economic condition.

(iv) Acceptance of ideas of foreign provenance depends also upon the potential receiver, together with his political, social, and related milieu, and upon the range of opportunities to which he perceives these foreign ideas to be at least potentially related. More

---

348–49. On linguistic conceptualization, see Whatmough, pp. 82–84, 166, 205; Roger Brown, pp. 229, 260.

32. J. Ghosh, *Higher Education*, pp. 90–91, 217–18; and pp. 105–6 n. on pundits not being opposed to the use of Sanskrit translations of works on commerce.

33. See, for example, E. Cassirer, p. 43; and Hertzler.

particularly if, as was true after 1900, men believe that deliberate-change-producing activities can be institutionalized and given salutary direction,[34] they will tend to accept ideas which give promise of fostering such change. This belief did not begin to have a basis in India until later in the nineteenth century. After all, Warren Hastings believed that "the English as foreigners would rule Indians on Indian lines, largely through Indian agency" and in a supervisory manner rather than through detailed administration. They would, as had the Mughals, "provide a framework for society within which traditional cultures could pursue their ways," commerce and agriculture could proceed unmolested, and society could persist untransformed.[35] Cornwallis, appointed governor-general in 1786, believed in "ruling Indians for their good, but on European rather than Indian lines." He thus anticipated some of his successors, among them spokesmen for the utilitarians and others who were bent upon introducing Western ideas and institutions into India, in the belief that they would take root and grow.[36] In the wake of changes consequent upon these policies, among them importation of a middle-class social order into India, there came into being an Indian middle class, almost nonexistent before the advent of the British. Moreover, it gradually began to flourish, especially after the abolition of the Company's trading monopoly in 1833.[37] It was this middle class, along with those desirous of employment with their new rulers, that stood to profit from a knowledge of English (and in some instances, economics), especially after English had replaced Persian as the official state language in 1835, a substitution recommended earlier by the distinguished Brahman, Ram Mohun Roy (1772–1833), who correctly believed it essential to India's socioeconomic progress.[38]

The hopes of the Anglicists were realized slowly and only in part. Training in English did facilitate the Company's administrative and commercial activities and help to convey Western learning

34. See, for example, Berliner.

35. Spear, 100–101, 118, 121, 125–26; and n. 3 above. Sometimes change took place despite Britain's policy of noninterference. V. B. Singh, *Economic History*, pp. 66–69.

36. Spear, chap. 8; Stokes; Ballhatchet.

37. Misra, pp. 10–17 and pt. 2; N. C. Sinha, *Studies*, chap. 3.

38. B. D. Basu, *History*, passim; N. C. Sinha, *Studies*, pp. 31–96; Ahmed, pp. 130–68, on education in English. Before 1835 few of the Company's Indian uncovenanted servants could speak English. Misra, p. 181.

(including economics but not much Christian doctrine) to India.[39] The case for English was made principally by anti-Orientalists, among them Macaulay, C. E. Trevelyan, and other Company officials.[40] Not surprisingly, already in the 1830s Indian opinion, formerly dependent upon a small vernacular press, was finding expression in Indian-owned English newspapers as well as in a newly flourishing Bengali and Persian press.[41] By the close of the century, when one Indian in a hundred was literate in English, the significance of the role of English was appreciated even by critics of English policy.[42]

While growing knowledge of English contributed notably to the so-called Bengal renaissance, it did not produce linguistic and cultural homogeneity, though in the end it facilitated the emergence of Indian nationalism, and this in turn gave a nationalist orientation to Indian economics. The English-speaking Indian intelligentsia tended to become separated from the masses, to whom, it had been hoped, English would be transmitted and result in the gradual anglicizing of the Hindu population.[43] Knowledge of English early facilitated the learning of political economy, courses in which began to be offered in Hindu College in the 1830s, about a decade after its founding, and in several other colleges, perhaps as early as the 1840s, though not yet in a way to make it bear upon current practical economic issues (e.g., transport).[44] A number of conditions remained relatively unfavorable, however. Educational institutions were too few in number. Some hostility remained to scientific education; and an inexpensive nonscientific education still qualified

39. Ballhatchet, chap. 10; *Cambridge History of the British Empire*, 5:109–19, 355–56; Ahmed, chap. 6; Crane, "Transfer"; R. Sidhanta's chapter in V. B. Singh, *Economic History*, pp. 725–55.

40. See, for example, Trevelyan, esp. chaps. 3–5; B. D. Basu, *History of Education*, pp. 1–96, and 97–121 on the Company's neglect of education through the medium of vernaculars. See also Bijoy Bhattacharya; N. S. Bose, chaps. 1–4. James Mill lay much less stress upon training in English and the immediate role of education. India's need was not for low-salaried administrative positions for English-speaking Hindus, but reform of government, the legal system, and the mode of taxation. Stokes, passim.

41. Ahmed, chaps. 3–4.

42. For example, B. D. Basu, *History of Education*, passim; and R. C. Majumdar's favorable comments upon the developmental impact of English education in *Glimpses of Bengal in the Nineteenth Century*, p. 3; Misra, pp. 347–49.

43. Mayhew, chap. 8; and B. Majumdar, p. 71.

44. J. Ghosh, *Higher Education*, pp. 113, 126 n., and 59–60, 124–26, 131 on cultural resistance to Western ideas; Thomas, p. 333. On transport and other issues see D. and A. Thorner, and D. Thorner, *Investment*.

Hindus for public employment. Above all, a variety of conflicts began to emerge: between the Indian elite and their erstwhile English partners; between missionary and Hindu; between English utilitarian and Hindu intellectual; between Indian businessmen and English traders increasingly interested in selling machine-produced goods rather than in buying Indian products; between the Company and zamindars (against whose excesses Manu's rules were sometimes directed); between the Company as employer and Indians seeking greater access to public employment; and between advocates of the extensive use of English and their opponents.[45] One outcome of the emergence of these cleavages and of the failure of education to filter downward to the masses from the educated elite was a new educational policy, dating from 1854 but accentuated after the Mutiny and the demise of the Company. This policy called for wide support for elementary education and much greater support for professional and scientific education in keeping with the needs of a society undergoing westernization.[46]

By the 1880s employment conditions for the intelligentsia had changed and the educated middle class was beginning to exercise political influence. Despite increasing indianization of the civil service, there were said to be more college graduates than public and professional employment could absorb, and too few appropriately trained for commerce and industry as well as too few businessmen.[47] With the establishment of two more universities in 1882 and 1887 in addition to three established in 1857, the opportunity to study economics increased; one required political economy and another included it among the optional courses. While colleges increased in number from 27 in 1857 to 72 in 1882 and 191 in 1902, they offered little social or natural science. Commerce education, portions of which had been supplied in secondary

45. Some of these conflicts are discussed by Ahmed. See also N. S. Bose, passim. On the nonscientific character of Hindu education, see Crane "Technical Education"; Misra, p. 150; Kane, 5:1123, 1661.

46. Misra, chaps. 6–7, 10; Nurullah and Naik, chaps. 3–6; Crane, "Transfer," pp. 116–20.

47. J. Ghosh, *Higher Education*, pp. 96, 119–21, 146–49, 152, 155, 166–67, 171, 178–87, 238–41 nn., esp. 239 n. on Indian preference for "soft-handed labour"; *Cambridge History of India*, 5:116–18, 342, 349–50; Misra, pp. 348–49. By 1931 of the posts in the administration of India all but 12,000 were filled by Indians. Useem, p. 129.

schools, began in 1886 and at first "showed a strong bias for economics subjects," since the teachers available had studied economics.[48] Now more than ever "English education" could answer to R. C. Majumdar's description of it as the paramount agency of transformation operative in India despite continuing illiteracy.

Increasing interest in political economy, together with greater use of it and increase in the number of eonomists,[49] gave rise to H. S. Jevons's discussion of economic development, a subject of concern to Indian economists, and to a multitude of articles on the content and teaching of economics, together with textbooks and a place for economics in the educational curriculum.[50] There was complaint that too little use was made of Indian economists on commissions of economic inquiry.[51] To these complaints may be added the widespread complaint that economics was not widely included in curricula, that Indian universities had too few economists and too little equipment, and that economic research received little support.[52] B. K. Sarkar added that too often Indian economists were badly trained and inclined to be anti-British.[53] All this changed, especially after World War II, as the demands for economics and economists changed and the advent of independ-

---

48. S. A. Ali, pp. 14, 22–23; Dongerkery, pp. 242–44; Mayhew, pp. 158–59; Nurullah and Naik, chap. 6, and chaps. 4–6 on the period 1800–1854; R. C. Majumdar, *British Paramountcy*, pt. 2, p. 31; Buchanan, pp. 404–8.

49. In 1923–24 there were 163 economists in India. The membership of the Indian Economic Association remained below 200 up to World War II, rising to 249 in 1945–46, at which time nonmember subscribers to the *Indian Journal of Economics* were 286, bringing the total to 535. Members numbered 124 in 1929, 145 in 1934, just over 160 in 1937–42, 173 in 1952, and 507 in 1966.

50. Jevons's essays on economic development appeared in the *Indian Journal of Economics* (of which he was founder and editor) in vol. 2 (1918–19), pages 1–64, 231–64, 329–60, and vol. 3 (1920–22), pp. 306–20. His essay on aspects of economics and economic education appeared in vol. 1 (1916–17), pp. 95–112, 181–218, and 328–50. Discussion of the content and teaching of economics by other authors appeared in vol. 1, pp. 499 ff.; vol. 2, pp. 92–100; vol. 3, pp. 63–83; vol. 5 (1924–25), pp. 308–13; vol. 7 (1926–27), pp. 41–44; vol. 8 (1927–28), pp. 165–69; vol. 9 (1928–29), pp. 608–11, 624; vol. 11 (1930–31), pp. 513–34; vol. 20 (1939–40), pp. 423–504, 645–47, 749–61; vol. 22 (1941–42), pp. 276–89; vol. 27 (1946–47), pp. 331–32, 421–25. See also Pillai.

51. Kale, "Economics in India," pp. 608–11, 624.

52. See Vakil; Krishnaswami; and Calcutta University Commission, *Report*, vol. 11, esp. the replies to questions on subjects omitted from the curricula—pp. 3, 4, 7, 9, 13, 14, 17, 22, 28–30, 32–34, 36, 38–39, 44, 45, 47, 49—and replies to questions on research—pp. 201, 203–7, 219, 227, 234. There is an occasional complaint too that use of English as a medium of instruction greatly limits the diffusion of knowledge. See, for example, ibid., p. 42; B. Majumdar, *History*, pp. 109–10.

53. See S. C. Dutt, pp. 190–92.

ence raised new problems now subject to Indian analyses and solution.

The Development of Indian Economics

Whereas in nineteenth-century Canada and Australia concern with local problems stimulated interest in political economy, in nineteenth-century India it was concern with the acceleration of independence that stimulated interest in economics between (say) 1860 and 1945. How weaken the grip of the British Raj upon the Indian economy? How strengthen the capacity of that economy to supply the bulk of the population with a tolerable standard of living in place of the very widespread poverty allegedly traceable to British misrule? India's economic writers therefore found in economics an ideological tool and a means to problem solution rather than an analytical apparatus, which it finally became after World War II. With the multiplication and specialization of economists, however, and their undertaking of particularized studies, usually with the assistance of newer theory, the dominant approach became less ideological and nationalistic. The approach of independence had a similar effect. Indeed, Datta suggests that the nationalist emphasis ended about 1939 and gave way to an emphasis similar to that found in the West.[54]

One may trace the beginning of political economy in India to the time of Ram Mohan Roy (1772–1833), "Father of Modern India," who will always be remembered for his effort to build bridges between India and the West. Though familiar with Bentham and probably Adam Smith, Roy was not an economist. He was critical, however, of the zamindari and ryotwari systems, under which the cultivators were miserable and few but landholders enjoyed comforts. Under the Settlement, the share of the zamindar had frequently become excessive (often one-half or more of the gross produce), and the value of his property had risen to 10 to 20 times what it had been. Roy recommended, therefore, that the rent of cultivators be reduced and limited. He proposed that, as an offset to the drain of money from India by retiring Europeans, educated Europeans with capital be induced to settle

54. B. Datta. See also B. Chandra, chap. 14. On the state of many concrete problems in India in the 1930s and 1940s, see V. B. Singh, *Economic History*.

permanently in India and bring with them the agricultural and other knowledge, skills, and methods of Europe.[55] He noted that epidemics occasionally thinned the population (which had a great tendency to multiply) and thus improved the condition of surviving laborers. He was critical of the salt monopoly, favored a tax on luxuries if necessary to offset a decline in land revenue, and advocated cutting the cost of government by substituting native for European civil servants and a militia for the expensive standing army. He stressed the importance of private property and a prosperous middle class, while asserting that the government must protect its relatively helpless citizens.[56]

Roy's work did not begin to make a going concern of political economy in India or give rise to "Indian economics." His disciples, together with Hindu College graduates, lay more stress than he upon political, administrative, and social reform (including indianization of the civil service) and less upon economic issues as such (though not to the exclusion of interest in ryots and European settlement).[57]

It was Mahadev Govind Ranade (1842–1901), an early graduate of Bombay University with a residual interest in economic issues, who concerned himself with Indian economic development and gave shape to what was called "Indian economics." [58] Under this system, the student, after doing or reading for a course in the principles of economics, studied "Indian economics" as a separate subject, often from a geographic point of view and usually under the assumption that "peculiar unities"—laws or problems—underlay the Indian economy. This approach became popular and many books bearing the title "Indian Economics" appeared, even though they became increasingly subject to criticism.[59] Swamped as they

55. See B. D. Basu's critical *Colonization*.
56. See S. D. Sarkar, *Rammohun Roy*, pp. 5, 9–10, 21–24, 70–74 on land systems, and 16–18, 74–79, 84–89 on European settlement, 80–83 on salt monopoly, and 62–66, 73, on the state of the population. On economy, taxation, and the role of the state, see B. Majumdar, *History*, pp. 42–49.
57. B. Majumdar, *History*, chap. 4, and chap. 3 on graduates of Hindu College, in whose establishment Roy had a prominent part. See also ibid., chaps. 5–6 for residual reaction to Roy by liberals and their critics, and chap. 14 on Swami Dayananda; J. K. Majumdar; Chanda and J. K. Majumdar.
58. Ranade, "Indian Political Economy," in *Essays*, pp. 1–36. His work is discussed below.
59. Bhatnager, "Bases," who includes under the head of Indian Economy not only Indian geography and economy-affecting laws but also the social customs and

were by India's acute and pressing problems, it is not surprising that India's economists were long concerned mainly with practical issues. Nor is it surprising that some were important *Makers of Modern India,*[60] and among the leaders who built the National Indian Congress Party, political instrument of the rising middle class.[61] Concern with the practical is evident in the content of economic literature, outlets for which increased in the later nineteenth and early twentieth century. For example, economic matters were the subject of about one-sixth of the articles appearing in 1897–1913 in the journal *Dawn,* originally "a vehicle of higher Eastern and Western culture" and later an organ of Indian nationalism.[62] Practical subjects predominated at first in the *Indian Journal of Economics,* India's first professional economic journal, established in 1916.

Foundations for an "Indian economics" designed to place upon Britain major responsibility for the miserable state of India's population were laid by Dadabhai Naoroji (1825–1917), the Grand Old Man of India. Though he spent many years in England, he was twice elected president of the Indian National Congress. In part a follower of J. S. Mill, Dadabhai is best known for his development of the "drain theory," a theme he supplemented with others. This theory, already referred to, had to do with the impact upon the Indian economy of the unilateral transfer of funds from India to England, a subject embodying issues akin to those first effectively discussed in the 1920s when the feasibility of German reparations was under analysis.[63] According to the drain theory, first elaborated in the early 1870s in connection with Dadabhai's study of poverty

religious ideas and ideals of the Indian people. See also his "Religious Base." For critiques, see D. A. Shah's prize-winning critical review of the literature of Indian economics; T. M. Joshi; Butani.

60. Title of a book by T. V. Parvate. See also on "Congress Party Thinking," Madan, chap. 16.

61. Parvate, passim; Desai. The misery of the masses was not overlooked. See Madan, chap. 5, on the speeches of Congress President (in 1901) D. E. Wacha.

62. See Haridas and Uma Mukherjee, chap. 4 and pp. 215, 233. For a 23-page bibliography of Indian economic articles and books in English in 1898–1913, see S. C. Dutt, pp. 8–30.

63. The definitive study of Dadabhai's theory is Ganguli, *Dadabhai Naoroji.* See also B. Chandra, chaps. 1, 13; P. N. Mathur, p. 618; and Masani; also Arun Bose, "Foreign Capital," in V. B. Singh, *Economic History,* chap. 20, pp. 485–92. Bose calls attention to British growth at the expense of India and to the adverse sociological effects of the "drain" upon Indian economic behavior. After 1857, of course, British capital began to flow into India. Ibid., pp. 493 ff.

in India, the failure of the Indian economy to provide the people of India with an adequate subsistence was traceable to the drain of capital out of India and resulting depression of her productive capacity.[64] The drain had its origin in unilateral transfers to England. Of India's income (amounting to about Rs. 20 per head) some 14 percent was absorbed by excessive taxation, a share of the proceeds of which went to England, giving rise, along with other unilateral transfers, to an outflow of £30–40 million per year. The effects of this drain were accentuated, Dadabhai's argument suggests, by the nature of some of the taxes employed (e.g., the salt tax), the heaviness of unproductive military expenditure, the incurring of public debt for unproductive purposes, and reliance upon an expensive foreign civil service. Reasoning as he did, Dadabhai supported the *swadeshi* movement, though he believed that under free and natural conditions trade would be advantageous to both countries.[65]

Dadabhai's contribution consisted in his construction of an anti-imperialist argument that won wide support and strengthened the ideology on which the independence movement might rest. His quite good estimate of India's income and finance manifested a grasp of quantitative economic relations. Even his imperfect grasp of international transfers and their relation to internal finance revealed a sensitivity to macroeconomic aspects of India's economy. B. M. Bhatia rightly comments that it "is simply amazing" that Dadabhai wrote "more than sixty years back." [66]

Dadabhai's main theses found support in the writings of Romesh C. Dutt (1848–1909), Congress president in 1908, economic and social historian, litterateur, and member of the Indian Civil Service in 1869–97. Though critical of British rule, he recognized Britain's contributions to India. The Indian economy had been subject to a continuous unrequited drain which had arrested its development and that of agriculture in particular and thereby prevented significant improvement in average income. India was sub-

64. His findings were more fully developed in Naoroji, *Poverty*, published in London in 1901 simultaneously with William Digby's *Prosperous British India*, in which it is asserted that between 1850 and 1900 Indian average income had declined by more than half.

65. For a brief summary, see Gopalakrishnan; for fuller accounts, see the works cited in the preceding note. See also McLane.

66. See Bhatia's review of Ganguli's work in *Indian Economic Journal* 13 (April–June 1966): 718. His ideas were about ninety years old in 1966.

ject to frequent famine, mainly because of the chronic poverty of cultivators. Accordingly, governmental expenditure, together with the excessive tax burden incident upon agriculture, would have to be greatly reduced and agriculture itself, the principal industry, would have to be modernized and made more productive, in part by giving cultivators greater incentive through reduction of rent and better organization of marketing and rural credit. Industrial development was indicated as well, to absorb excess labor in agriculture, to offset the alleged decay of indigenous industry and shift of its work force to agriculture,[67] and to facilitate the reorganization of agriculture and the conditions under which it was carried on.[68]

Very great influence was exercised upon economics in India by Mahadev Govind Ranade, court justice, a founder of the Congress, advocate of vernacular instruction in the universities, and originator of the Prarthana Samaj, a society resembling the Brahmo Samaj founded by Roy. He was called the Father of Indian Economics, already described and founded upon the supposition that the Indian economy was peculiar and in need of policies fitting its condition. The rules and presuppositions of classical economics, while they may have fitted England, did not suit India's needs. Ranade therefore played a major role in shifting economic thought and policy in India from one based on the ideas of Smith and the classical economists to one based upon the etatistic and/or economic-development-oriented views of Sismondi, Alexander Hamilton, Henry Carey, List, the German Historical School, and (perhaps most of all) Henry Maine, from 1878 when Ranade began to publish economics papers in the journal of the Sarvajanik Sabha.[69] Believing

67. Thorner's data suggest that if "a major shift from industry to agriculture ever occurred during British rule in India, it might have happened some time between 1815 and 1880." It did not take place between 1881 and 1931, when the "industrial distribution of the Indian working force . . . stood still." D. and A. Thorner, p. 77. But see P. C. Joshi.

68. Gopalakrishnan, chap. 5; J. N. Gupta. See esp. R. C. Dutt's *Peasantry*, his *Famine*, and his *Economic History*, two volumes devoted to "early British rule" and "the Victorian Age," respectively; and B. Chandra, passim.

69. See Ranade, *Religious and Social Reform* and his *Essays*; Gopalakrishnan, chap. 3; Karwal, "Mahadev Govind Ranade"; Kale, "Economics in India," pp. 605–28, esp. 624–26. Anantaram; K. N. Sen, "Economic Thinking," esp. p. 693; B. Datta, "Background"; Kellock. J. C. Coyajee acclaims Ranade as "the ablest writer on Indian economics since the days of Kautilya." On Ranade's views on agriculture, see Minocha; and B. Chandra, chaps. 11–12 on Ranade and other nationalists. See also Jagirdar, "Ranade" and *Studies;* Madan, chap. 4.

the solvent of Indian poverty lay in industrialization and some commercialization of agriculture, together with religious and moral reform, Ranade observed that these ends were best attained through capable entrepreneurship, though with such state assistance as was required.[70] He did not, therefore, complain of British investment in India.

While Ranade believed that the state needed to protect the weak against the strong, he supposed that freedom to alienate land facilitated its passage into the hands of the able and prudent. He also urged the creation of new banking institutions to bridge the gulf between savers and investors and facilitate employment. Even then, he believed, emigration abroad as well as planned internal migration was essential to the alleviation of India's uneven population pressure. Though he recognized India's lack of sovereignty, he favored at least temporary protection of native manufactures based upon India's undeveloped resources; in this opinion he had the support of some but not all contemporary and later economists.[71] His stress upon "Indian economic problems," reflected in the frequently used book title, "Indian Economics," persisted in Indian economics-journal literature,[72] though in a form usually unfavorable to the development of empirical, theoretical, and methodological aspects of economic inquiry in India.[73]

In the last third of the nineteenth century, industrialization, state intervention, and protection (sometimes in the form of Swadeshi) had the support of a number of writers who were more concerned with political than with economic issues.[74] Support for laissez-faire was uncommon.[75]

While Ranade's work was continued by V. G. Kale, a careful defender of protection,[76] and G. K. Gokhale (1866–1915), essen-

70. Gopalakrishnan, pp. 104–22; Karve, "Ranade"; Price, pp. 40–52, with H. K. Mazumdar's comments on pp. 53–56; Kellock, pp. 250–55; Coyajee, pp. 309, 316–21, 328–30; Karwal, "Mahadev Govind Ranade."

71. Munshi, esp. pp. 335–38 on the views of G. V. Joshi and R. C. Dutt; Lokanathan; B. Chandra, chap. 4; Thompson.

72. Kellock, pp. 258–60.

73. See comments of D. A. Shah, T. M. Joshi, and Butani.

74. See, for example, B. Majumdar, *History*, pp. 110–11, 202–3, 217–18, 229–31, and 111–12 on Bholanath Chandra (1822–1910), father of the Swadeshi movement, and pp. 128–34, 142–45 on Sisirkumar Ghosh (1840–1911).

75. B. Majumdar, *History*, pp. 120, 122–23, 192–93.

76. See Kale, *Economics and Protection* and his *Introduction*. See also Row: Madan, chap. 8; Thomas; and Karve, "The Late Professor Kale."

tially an opponent of protection and a Congress leader, the latter was perhaps more influential. Moreover, he believed in law and order and opposed noncooperation with the British Raj. He was confident that modern science and technology could transform the India that had lain dormant for centuries. In a sense Gokhale was a latter-day version of men like Ram Mohun Roy who had great faith in the ameliorative effects of westernization. Western ideas, among them the idea of secular progress, were producing change, though hampered by a too centralized foreign civil service, enormous unproductive expenditure on the military and the bureaucracy, and excessive taxation.[77] Gokhale was critical of British policy, therefore, because (he believed) it was deepening poverty in India by weakening native industry, draining wealth out of India, overtaxing agriculture, and pursuing an untenable monetary and fiscal policy. His position, including his views on rural credit, was thus generally similar to that of economist associates in the Congress, over which he presided in 1905.[78] They were "building up a framework of policy grounded upon constructive intervention of the state for the welfare and growth of our economy." [79] Gokhale himself, though a follower of List and a supporter of the Swadeshi principle as well as a strong believer in industrialization, was not an out-and-out advocate of protection. What was needed was judicious protection for certain infant industries, but not duties that would be incident upon the poor.[80]

While the character of economics and the behavior of economists changed after World War I, with the introduction of specialized degree courses in economics at Calcutta (in 1909) and other universities, one legacy of economic nationalism persisted, namely, belief in the necessity of considerable socialization and the transformation of the exploitative economic structure supposedly introduced into India by its alien rulers.[81] Perhaps another was the legacy of an image of the Indian economy out of keeping with

77. A. B. Shah, chaps. 1–3; Hoyland, pp. 73–77, 80–81, 84, 96–100, 116–18; Gopalakrishnan, pp. 128–38; Madan, chap. 7.

78. A. B. Shah, pp. 69–93; Gopalakrishnan, pp. 132–40. Gokhale was "perhaps the first in India to emphasize that governmental expenditure and income should be directed to set right deficiencies in the working of the economic system" (p. 141).

79. A. B. Shah, p. 85.

80. A. B. Shah, pp. 90–92.

81. Chand, pp. 2–3, 13, and passim. On India's slow economic progress under British rule, together with contributing factors, see Buchanan, esp. chaps. 7, 19.

Mahatma Gandhi's emphasis upon the spiritual aspects of economic life and a "philosophy of the isolated individual or of a small group, peasant or artisan, not of the industrial masses." [82]

While provision was made in and after 1909 in some universities for a degree in economics, it may be said that before World War I, "Indian economics" dominated Indian economic thinking. This entailed emphasis upon description and particularities, together with rejection of a general theoretical approach. It also came to involve considerable dependence upon the state as a fomenter of economic development, though without the assistance of models now so fundamental to Indian economic planning. "The Indian economist became an institutionalist without any clear model in his mind of what India ought to become" and without capacity to provide guides for policy.[83] This orientation became self-perpetuating in that economists swamped with particularities are unlikely to induce a woods out of the multitude of trees they observe. The tendency of the state of Indian economic thought to perpetuate itself was greatly accentuated also, Price believes, by the continuing infatuation of typical Hindu students with village life and Hindu doctrine, values, and institutions.[84]

Breakthrough

What may be called the breakthrough in the development of economics in India came after World War I, which clearly presaged the coming of independence from the British Raj. For, given independence, the people of India, acting through agencies of the state, would want the content of the nation's "welfare function" changed from what it was. This would entail the use of economists, particularly since socialism was a component of the Indian nationalist movement and since the critical attitude of Indian writers toward allegedly exploitative British industry generated a belief that much of the private sector was exploitative. Furthermore, Keynesian emphasis upon planning, together with the example of

---

82. Gopalakrishnan, chap. 7, esp. pp. 203–4; Mathur; Anjaria; S. N. Agarwal; S. N. Agarwala. See also S. C. Dutt's contrast of Gandhi's views with the essentially modern development-economic views of Benoy K. Sarkar in S. C. Dutt, *Conflicting Tendencies.* Sarkar's sociological-economic approach is described in B. Dass. Sarkar translated Friedrich List's works into Bengali, 1912 ff.

83. Price, p. 50.

84. Price, p. 50; H. K. Mazumdar rejects Price's explanation. Ibid., pp. 53–55.

Soviet planning, reinforced the belief of those who viewed national planning as essential to India's economic growth.[85]

The interwar period was transitional in a double sense. On the one hand, obstacles to the progress of economic science had to be dissipated. Economics needed to be freed of its negative approach to British policy, wider opportunity for economic training needed to be provided, a complementary relation needed to be established between government and university, and issues of the sort raised by Mahatma Gandhi had to be faced.[86] The gradual coming on to the scene of a new and larger generation of economists helped to overcome these obstacles, despite the pressure of current problems (e.g., the value of the rupee, the role of gold, imperial preference, provincial vs. federal use of fiscal resources, international trade and tariffs). Increasing concern with induced economic growth helped build bridges between state and university as well as accentuate a growing recognition of the importance of theory that was relatively pure and removed from practical realms. Undoubtedly the transition was facilitated by the growing concern of foreign economists with Indian problems and with growth-circumscribing realities. In the 1930s, for example, the population question, generally played down in past searches for causes of poverty attributable to alien rulers, began to command attention that has finally eventuated in a serious fertility-control program. In sum, as Datta observes, "the twenties and thirties were in a sense a spadework period for the real development of economic studies in India." [87]

What I have called a breakthrough has not been confined to Western economics in the orthodox micro- and macroeconomic tradition. It also included leftist and Marxian economics. After all, Marx had devoted much attention to India and its probable future.[88] Marxian economics might, therefore, give impetus and guidance to the business of freeing India from foreign rule and fostering the development of a socialist economy.

85. See, for example, V. B. Singh, *Essays*, chaps. 4, 6–7, and his *Indian Economy*, chaps. 1–2.

86. See H. K. Majumdar, in Price, pp. 53 ff. On Gandhi's views see Mathur; Gandhi, *Industrialize—and Perish;* and n. 82 above.

87. B. Datta, *Evolution*, pp. 32–33.

88. See, for example, R. P. Dutt, *Karl Marx.* Madan, chaps. 17–18 on socialism, and 9 on Narain's views on socialism.

Four sets of conditions have contributed to the increasing popularity of Marxism and Marxian economics in India. First, favorable underlying sentiments have long been present. Marxian economics seemingly explained "colonialism," of which India was a case in point, and thus lent support to exploitative theories such as the drain theory. Second and perhaps as a corollary to the first point, Marxism, being anticapitalistic, drew to itself much of the anticapitalist support which did not find an outlet in Gandhian economic prescriptions. Moreover, Marxian economics, focusing as it did on economic change, could prove an effective analytical instrument in the hands of competent Indian Marxists bent upon modernizing Indian society and economy. Third, growth in the popularity of what passed for Marxian economics in the world outside India must have contributed to its support in India. Fourth, Marxian economics has drawn much support from its identification as a twin of national economic planning, especially in countries such as India, with a considerable tradition of state control and an overwhelming concern to accelerate economic development and escape poverty. This last source of Marxian strength is reinforced, of course, by the disposition of national planners to make use of allocative approaches originating in Western economics.

A problem was presented by the fact that conditions in India were by no means identical with those Marx had observed in the West. M. N. Roy in particular emphasized this point. The class relations found in the West did not correspond closely to those found in India, with its economy still essentially feudal and based upon land, and its capacity for growth thereby limited.[89] It was possible, therefore, that imperialism could help liquidate this feudalism, give release to India's forces of production through industrialization, and thus make a revolution possible.[90] This revolution would initially be bourgeois and democratic in character but would, under appropriate nonproletarian leadership, bring about the transformation of "the hoary structure of Indian society" which had made India the shameful pawn of foreign invaders for a thousand years.[91]

Marxism thus stood at a pole opposite to that of Gandhian eco-

89. M. N. Roy, chap. 3.
90. M. N. Roy, pp. 106–14.
91. M. N. Roy, pp. 115–315. Roy eventually became a revisionist. B. S. Sharma, Dhar; Haithcox.

nomics. The economic observations to which M. K. Gandhi gave expression amounted to an economics of the past—essentially an ideational superstructure resting upon an agricultural and handicraft base. It derived currency and some support, however, from the power role played by Gandhi and his followers in the independence movement.[92]

The development of economics of all sorts in India was slowed down until recently, Dasgupta pointed out in 1960, by the fact that Indian economists were "somewhat allergic to theory." This he found surprising, since "the Indian mind is traditionally speculative and is supposed to lend itself more to abstraction than to crude reality" and nongeneralizable descriptions. The "pioneers of Indian economic thinking" shunned so-called "Western economics." Impatient with the "liberal tenets of classical political economy which were obviously at variance with the requirements of our economy, they repudiated even the tools of analysis that it provided." Conditions have since improved. Research is well supported and soon data will be plentiful. Economics is in demand, with the public in India as elsewhere "perhaps placing more weight upon our science than it ever was designed to bear." Even so, too little attention is being given to techniques of analysis, in part because theoretical economics is undersupported and immediate problems have been allowed to swamp concern with "forces that are persistent and general."[93] D. P. Mukerji had commented in 1954 on "the extent of anti-theory prevalent," a condition he associated in part with the "inadequacy" of Keyneian theory "for the purposes of under-developed economy." What was needed was economic theory in keeping with the "objective situation" of India.[94]

The belief that Indian economics places too little stress upon economic theory is no longer tenable. Within the field of Marxian economics, for example, M. N. Roy's examination of the implication of "imperialism" for India is notable as is V. K. R. V. Rao's work on the limitations to which multiplier analysis is subject in economies like India's with a high ratio of persons of working age

92. On Gandhi's anti-industrial economic views, see his *Economic Thought* and *Industrialize—and Perish*.

93. A. K. Dasgupta, "Tendencies in Economic Theory," in V. B. Singh, *On Political Economy*, pp. 47–51. Indian sociology too has suffered from excessive emphasis on action-oriented research, according to M. B. Clinard and J. W. Elder.

94. D. P. Mukerji, pp. 126–29, 135–37. For other views see Madan, chaps. 11–14.

to factors complementary to labor. Notable also has been the work of the Indian Statistical Institute, with emphasis on both the theoretical and the empirical. Exemplary also has been the long continued empirical work of the Gokhale Institute which, though empirically oriented, is not without a theoretical base.

The sheer size of India's population has contributed to the progress of economic science there. For even though the relative number of economists is very small, the absolute number is large, given a population of some 525 million. Economists are sufficiently numerous, therefore, to support the requisite infrastructure of journals, publications, research institutes, university departments, and ancillary sciences, together with well-developed specialization within economics and ancillary subjects. The number of economists and other professionals is sufficiently large, moreover, to permit use of a scientific lingua franca (i.e., English) that provides ready access to a large fraction of the external world of economists and economics. Another manifestation of the absolute numerousness of Indian economists as of other Indian scientists is the largeness of the number engaged abroad and with international agencies—a consequence both of the lower cost of producing economists in India and of the limited capacity of the contemporary Indian economy to absorb all the economists it turns out.

While my story ends here, that of economics in India does not. Given the large number of economists in India, the richness of Indian life, the great scope for experimentation, and the intensity of competition among Indian economists, it is to be expected that future "Indian economics" will prove an effective blend of pure theory and problem-oriented constructs. For some time to come it will be in what was British India, together with Japan, that a science begun in the West will find an Asian home, perhaps to spread thence to the rest of Asia. Undoubtedly Marxian as well as non-Marxian considerations will be allowed for, together with important and persistent institutional differences. The final outcome will depend, of course, upon what happens to the universities in India and Japan and into whose hands their control passes.

Chapter 7

Overview; Interpretation

The State to be created by the peculiar form of the
Indian Revolution will be correspondingly peculiar.

M. N. ROY

There is no science of "Indian Economics" as apart
from the science of "General Economics."

BRIJ NARAIN

At the start of this study it was remarked that, while men have been
behaving economically for millennia, guided only by slowly ac-
cumulating economic "wisdom," their writings about this behavior
until several centuries ago amounted to no more than protoeconomic
discussion and direction. This description fits Indian materials,
the content of which, however, compared favorably with that
found in contemporary societies. In the Indian case, moreover, the
guidelines laid down, had they not been violated, would have
permitted the quite efficient functioning of the Indian economy
of the day.

In our first two chapters we identified a number of dimensions
of society which set limits to economic behavior at given times
and hence to analysis and prescriptions based on this behavior.
These dimensions did not change markedly over time in India
until in and after the late eighteenth century. Population grew
slowly, albeit intermittently, settlement was extended [1]—quite re-
markably under the Mughals—and urbanization progressed. The
set of options potentially available seems not to have changed
greatly, however, even though the subset actually obtaining at
any given time must have differed from that obtaining at other
times. Great changes began to take place in the nineteenth century,
contemporaneously with the introduction of Western culture, in-

1. See, for example, R. Mukerjee, chap. 1.

cluding Western conceptions of economic behavior and its analysis. Only later in the century, however, did these conceptions begin to make conditions other than they might have been. Even then Gandhi's economics corresponded to an earlier era.

Were it possible to quantify the "progress" of economic thought in India, this progress might be represented by a long-run growth curve resembling those used to depict population growth over the past two or three millennia. Between 300 B.C. and 1750 A.D. the curve would manifest an almost negligible upward trend. Some acceleration would characterize the segment connecting 1750 and (say) 1870. The ensuing hundred years would reveal continuing acceleration, an acceleration perhaps not yet at an end.

While economic matters were discussed quite some time before 300 B.C., nothing worthy of the name "economic science" emerged in India until it was introduced from the West by the British. Then for the first time were the rudiments of price, distributive, and monetary theory apprehended as interrelated elements, the systematic organization of which into an analytical apparatus was recognized as enabling man to explain economic behavior and anticipate consequences of economic action.

It is in arthashastra literature that economic discussion was most highly developed, much more fully than one finds it in classical Greek economics, even though the latter suggests the presence of a more fully developed spirit of analytical inquiry. Early Indian discussion was not only permeated by a greater appreciation of material concerns than was Greek; it also had to meet empirical tests, inasmuch as it provided quite concrete guidelines for economic behavior—guidelines which would have collapsed, thus making for political instability, had they deviated too far from what was in keeping with economic reality. The guidelines laid down must, therefore, have reflected a great deal of experience, and this experience tended to hold for later periods as well so long as the character of the Indian economy did not undergo great change. It may thus be said that the rules, though tending to be habitual and customary in character, had a rational base confirmed by experience.

Conventions pertaining to interpersonal relations that are not predominantly economic in character may vary a great deal more than those pertaining to interpersonal economic relations. Forces operating within the market set limits to how much economic conventions may vary without producing noticeably adverse feedbacks. Variability of essentially noneconomic convention, such as those governing inheritance, though small in the short run, is potentially great, given sufficient time for the modification of law and custom.

Passing now to Kautalya's "economics" in particular, it may be said that little was analytical and that more was in keeping with developing thought and experience.[2] His work demonstrates the presence of much economic information not yet integrated into a systematic body of fact and assumption, and not really to be so integrated until in or about the seventeenth century, in western Europe. Kautalya was, of course, familiar with the general nature of man's response to changes in price and income as well as to changes in the structure of rewards and penalties. This information had been slowly acquired with the partial monetization of India's economy and had become a part of the stock of practical wisdom common to men of affairs. While Kautalya understood how price was influenced by competition and changes in supply and demand, he did not understand the rationing function of price and the tendency for deviations of market price from normal price to be corrected. Living as he did in a static economy, Kautalya took it for granted that experience adequately sanctioned the interest structure which he proposed to legalize. Undoubtedly, his failure to appreciate the allocative role of a competitive price system, together with his apparent assumption of a quite nondynamic economy, led him to place so much stress on the economic role of the state. This stress was reinforced by his awareness of dangers to rulers flowing from the interposition of feudal or other unsalaried intermediaries between the state and the underlying labor force. Presumably, he supposed that the minimal rates of taxation which he recommended in keeping with previous practice fell within the limits of the so-called taxable capacity of the economy. Since later studies put the taxable capacity of modern low-income states below 20 percent,[3] one may infer that taxation was heavy enough to depress private consumption and capital formation. Too little of

2. This is evident from A. N. Bose's valuable historical review of the early Indian economy and prevailing practice. A. Bose, vols. 1–2.

3. According to Brij Narain's estimates, the taxable capacity of British India in the early 1920s was much below 13 percent of gross income. Narain, chap. 28. W. A. Lewis puts at 17 percent of gross domestic product the amount of revenue

the income of the state was diverted to the formation of public capital and the support of economically productive activity. Perhaps symbolic is the fact that a foot soldier was paid at the same rate as an accountant and 8⅓ times as much as a foreman of laborers (5.3. 14, 17).[4]

The works of Manu and other authors of dharmashastra were much less concerned with interpersonal relations that are economic in character and far more concerned with those which are noneconomic. These works therefore imply that Indian society and culture were much less materialistic in nature than they are represented as being in arthashastra literature or in other literature relating to economic conditions.[5] Their point of departure is prescriptive and remained so over the centuries. Even of implicit theory there is very little.

Monetary theory as such received little or no expression in the work of Kautalya, Manu, and others. Adverse consequences were not anticipated from private and state hoarding of coin of domestic and foreign origin, if for no other reason than that in an insecure world hoards cushioned the impact of frequent emergencies. Kautalya insisted on the maintenance of the standard weight of coin (2.12. 24–26) as did Manu (vIII, 403), Vasishtha (xIx, 13), and others, presumably because debasement of coin would modify the pricing guidelines laid down. Rules pertaining to credit did not touch upon its relation to prices.[6]

The introduction of Islamic rule into parts of India was not accompanied by such economic theory as was to be found in the Islamic world to the West.[7] Nor did Islamic writers concern themselves with Hindu literature relating to economic matter, though Moslem rulers made extensive use of Hindu administrative personnel. Kautalya's work is not even mentioned by al-Biruni though he does refer to the work of Manu, Narada, Vishnu, and others, uses

---

needed to meet current aspirations in African countries. Lewis, pp. 115–17, 128–29. After 1947, rents were considered "fair" only if they did not exceed one-sixth to one-fourth of the value of gross produce. A. M. Khusro in V. B. Singh, *Economic History*, p. 390.

4. Aiyangar, *Aspects*, pp. 121–23.

5. See, for example, A. Bose, 2:276–79; Aiyangar, *Aspects*, pp. 72–74; Subrahmanian, pp. 219–21.

6. On banking, exchange, and currency in ancient India, see A. Bose, 2:101–40, and 26–39, 68–70; Aiyangar, *Aspects*, pp. 96–100; B. Sen, chap. 7. Shortage of coin, sometimes mentioned in later times, is not referred to. See Patwardhan, pp. 100–102.

7. See Spengler, "Economic Thought."

"artha" in a noneconomic sense, and is critical of the caste system.[8] His neglect of Hindu economic literature is unfortunate, since he might have set it in a general context. This inference is suggested by his comments on population. For, prompted by Indian cyclical theories and guided by Plato's *Laws* (bk. 3) and Greek explanations (e.g., see *Timaeus*, 22–23) of periodic disaster and man's response thereto,[9] al-Biruni expressed himself much as did Malthus nearly a millennium later, though without anticipating Darwin.[10]

Al-Biruni put forward a natural explanation of the genesis of overpopulation, noted the advent of a stationary population, and then went on to show how Hindu philosophy introduced a corrective external agency:

The life of the world depends upon sowing and procreating. Both processes increase in the course of time, and their increase is unlimited, whilst the world is limited . . . . A single species of plants or animals [will] occupy the earth and spread itself and its kind over as much territory as it can find.

Nature removed surplus growth "to make room for others" as did an agriculturalist, but apparently not in a manner to guide selection. Given inevitable overpopulation, however, corrective action was indicated.[11] It might, some Greeks supposedly held, assume the form of catastrophe (e.g., deluge, earthquake) or disease and pestilence.[12] Under Indian philosophy, however, visitation by an external agent might be counted upon:

If thus the earth is ruined, or is near to be ruined, by giving too many inhabitants, its ruler—for it has a ruler, and his all-embracing cure is apparent in every single particle of it—sends it a messenger for the purpose of reducing the too great number and of cutting away all that is evil.

A messenger of this kind is, according to the belief of the Hindus, Vasudeva, who was sent . . . [at] a time when giants were numerous on earth and the earth was full of their oppression.[13]

Later Islamic writers not only lacked al-Biruni's capacity for generalization but manifested no more concern with Hindu economic discussion or with economic matter. The point of departure of discussion was essentially administrative.

8. Sachau, p. 178, and chaps. 9, 63–64 on castes.
9. Sachau, chap. 43.
10. Wilcynski.
11. Sachau, chap. 47, pp. 400–401.
12. Sachau, chap. 43, pp. 378–79.
13. Sachau, chap. 47, esp. pp. 400–401.

Economics really came to India with the British in the wake of the collapse of the Mughals. Before it could become a part of the body of knowledge at the disposal of an Indian elite, a sufficient number of the population needed to command English and be motivated to acquire a knowledge of economics. Initially motivation flowed from the desire for employment with the British, though stimulated as well by the establishment of several colleges. With the rise of Indian nationalism later on in the nineteenth century, knowledge of economics became a lever in the hands of those seeking independence of the British. It could be used, albeit imperfectly, to fasten responsibility on the British for the economic plight of India and thus strengthen the independence movement. It could also be used to formulate policies conducive to India's economic development much as had been done in English-speaking countries overseas (e.g., the United States, Canada, Australia). Economics in India was long handicapped, however, by an overriding concern with concrete problems and neglect of economic theory. With the spread of English and the multiplication of educational institutions, however, the number of persons with an understanding of economics steadily increased, as did the infrastructure essential to the support of economic study and inquiry.

Marxian economics did not achieve a significant degree of currency in India until the present century. Its support came from those who found it useful in the analysis of the genesis of the Indian economy and in the creation of means to free India of foreign rule and convert its economy into a socialist one.

The really great upsurge in the development and diffusion of economics came, in India much as elsewhere, in the present century. The initial stimulus came from the strengthening of provisions for economic education on the eve of World War I, from the emergence or intensification of problems in the wake of this war, and perhaps from realization that independence lay in the near future. Much more powerful was the impact of World War II and the advent of independence and full responsibility for the planning of the country's future. Striking nonetheless is the magnitude of the post-1940 growth of Indian economics in prestige and quality and of its practitioners in number. Equally striking is the magnitude of the set of economic problems by which India's economists remain confronted.

References

Abu'l Fazl. *Āin-I-Ākbari.* 3 vols. Calcutta, 1939–49. Vol. 1 translated by
H. Blochmann, revised by D. C. Phillott; vols. 2–3 translated by
H. S. Jarrett, corrected and annotated by Sir Jadunath Sarkar.
Accelerating India's Food Grain Production. U.S. Department of Agri-
culture, F.A.E. Report No. 40. Washington, 1968.
Adams, Robert McC. "Agriculture and Urban Life in Early South-
western Iran." *Science* 136 (13 April 1962): 114–15.
———. *The Evolution of Urban Society.* London, 1965.
Adhya, G. L. *Early Indian Economics.* Bombay, 1966.
Agarwal, Shriman Narayan. "Gandhian Economics." *Indian Journal of
Economics* 23 (1942–43): 193–99.
Agarwala, Shri Narayan. "A Critique of the Gandhian Plan." *Indian
Journal of Economics* 25 (1945): 262–70.
Agrawala, V. S. *India as Known to Pāṇini.* Lucknow, 1953.
Ahmed, A. F. Salahuddin. *Social Ideas and Social Change in Bengal,
1818–1835.* Leiden, 1965.
Aiyangar, K. V. Rangaswami. *Aspects of Ancient Indian Economic
Thought.* Benares, 1934.
———. *Indian Cameralism.* Madras, 1949.
———. *Rājadharma.* Madras, 1941.
Aiyar, N. C., ed. *Mayne's Treatise on Hindu Law and Usage.* 1878; 11th
ed. Madras, 1950.
Akbar, Muhammad. *Administration of Justice by the Mughals.* Lahore,
1948.
———. *The Punjab Under the Mughals.* Lahore, 1948.
Ali, Syed Amir. *English Education in India.* Madras, 1902.
Altekar, A. S. *Education in Ancient India.* Benares, 1934.
———. *History of the Village Community in Western India.* Bombay,
1927.
———. *The Rāshtrakutas.* Poona, 1934.
———. *Sources of Hindu Dharma.* Poona, 1952.
———. *State and Government in Ancient India.* Delhi, 1958.
Anantaram, K. "Ranade, the Economist." *Indian Journal of Economics*
22 (1941–42): 387–93.
Anjaria, J. J. "The Gandhian Approach to Indian Economics." *Indian
Journal of Economics* 22 (1941–42): 357–66.
Anstey, Vera. *The Economic Development of India.* 4th ed. London, 1952.
Āpastamba. Aphorisms on the Sacred Law. *Sacred Books of the East,*
vol. 2. Oxford, 1897.
Apte, D. G. *Our Educational Heritage.* Baroda, 1961.

Apte, V. M. *Social and Religious Life in the Griha Sūtras.* Bombay, 1954.

Arnold, Edwin. *The Light of Asia.* Calcutta, 1949.

Bahadur, R. P. "The Economics of Casteism." *Indian Journal of Economics* 36 (1955–56): 325–36.

Balkrishna. "Economics in Ancient India." *Indian Journal of Economics* 2 (1918–19): 629–49.

———. "The Hindu Taxation System." *Indian Journal of Economics* 8 (1927–28): 27–40, 89–117.

Ballhatchet, K. *Social Policy and Social Change in Western India, 1817–1830.* London, 1957.

Bandyopadhyaya, Narayanchandra. *Economic Life and Progress in Ancient India.* Calcutta, 1945.

Banerjee, Gauranga Nath. *Hellenism in Ancient India.* 3d ed. Delhi, 1961.

Banerjee, N. R. *The Iron Age in India.* Delhi, 1965.

Barber, W. J. "James Mill and the Theory of Economic Policy in India." *History of Political Economy* 1 (1969): 85–100.

Basham, A. L. "Ancient Indian Kingship." *Indica* 1 (Sept. 1964): 119–27.

———. *History and Doctrines of the Ājīvikas.* London, 1951.

———. *The Wonder That Was India.* New York, 1954.

Basu, B. D. *The Colonization of India by Europeans.* Calcutta, 1925.

———. *History of Education in India Under the Rule of the East India Company.* Calcutta, 1934.

Basu, Praphuta C. "The Earliest Agricultural Organisation in India and Its Methods." *Indian Journal of Economics* 2 (1918–19): 609–28.

Baudhāyana. *Dharmasūtra.* In *Sacred Books of the East,* vol. 14. Oxford, 1882.

Bauer, P. T., and B. S. Yamey. *The Economics of Underdeveloped Countries.* London, 1957.

Bearce, George D. *British Attitudes Towards India, 1784–1858.* Oxford, 1961.

Bendix, Reinhard. *Max Weber.* Garden City, 1962.

Bennett, M. K. *The World's Food.* New York, 1954.

Berliner, J. S. "The Feet of the Natives Are Large: An Essay on Anthropology by an Economist." *Current Anthropology* 3 (Feb. 1962): 47–61.

Bernardelli, H. "The Origins of Modern Economic Theory." *Economic Record* 37 (Sept. 1961): 320–38.

Bhatia, B. M. "Growth and Composition of the Middle Class in South India in the Nineteenth Century." *Indian Economic and Social History Review* 2 (Oct. 1965): 341–56.

Bhatnager, B. G. "The Bases of Indian Economy." *Indian Journal of Economics* 4 (1923–24): 47–58.

———. "The Religious Base in Indian Economy." *Indian Journal of Economics* 5 (1924–25): 73–86.

Bhattacharya, Bijoy. *Bengal Renaissance.* Calcutta, 1963.

Bhattacharya, Sabyasachi. "Laissez Faire in India." *Indian Economic and Social History Review* 2 (Jan. 1965): 1–22.

Black, R. D. C. "Economic Policy in Ireland and India in the Time of J. S. Mill." *Economic History Review* 21 (1968): 321–36.

Blitz, R. C., and M. F. Long. "The Economics of Usury Legislation." *Journal of Political Economy* 73 (Dec. 1965): 608–19.

Blyn, George. *Agricultural Trends in India, 1891–1947: Output Availability, and Productivity.* Philadelphia, 1966.

Bongard-Lavin, G. "Megasthenes' 'Indica' and the Inscriptions of Asoka." *Indian Studies* 2 (1960–61): 203–11.

Bose, A. N. *Social and Rural Economy of Northern India.* Calcutta, 1961.

Bose, Arun. "Foreign Capital." In *Economic History of India: 1857–1956,* edited by V. B. Singh, chap. 20. Bombay, 1965.

Bose, N. S. *The Indian Awakening and Bengal.* Calcutta, 1960.

Boserup, Ester. *The Conditions of Agricultural Growth.* Chicago, 1965.

Bosworth, C. E. "Abū 'Abdullāh Al-Khwārazmī on the Technical Terms of the Secretary's Art." *Journal of the Economic and Social History of the Orient* 12 (April 1969): 113–64.

———. *The Ghaznavids: Their Empire in Afghanistan and Eastern Iran, 994–1040.* Edinburgh, 1963.

Bowden, Witt, et al. *An Economic History of Europe Since 1750.* New York, 1937.

Braibanti, Ralph, ed. *Asian Bureaucratic Systems Emergent From the British Imperial Tradition.* Durham, N.C., 1966.

Braidwood, R. J. "Near Eastern Prehistory." *Science* 127 (20 June 1958): 1419–30.

———, and G. R. Willey, eds. *Courses Toward Urban Life.* Chicago, 1962.

Brihaspati. Smriti. In *Sacred Books of the East,* vol. 33. Oxford, 1889.

Brown, Lester. *Increasing World Food Output.* Washington, 1965.

Brown, Roger. *Words and Things.* Glencoe, Ill., 1958.

Burrow, T. "Dravidian and the Decipherment of the Indus Script." *Antiquity* 43 (1969), 274–78.

Buchanan, D. H. *The Development of Capitalistic Enterprise in India.* New York, 1934.

Butani, D. H. "The Quality and Perspective of Indian Economic Thought." *Indian Journal of Economics* 22 (1941–42): 280–89.

Calcutta University Commission. *Report,* 1917–1919. Vol. 11. Calcutta, 1919.

The Cambridge Economic History of Europe. Vol. 1, 2d ed. edited by M. M. Postan. Cambridge, Eng., 1966. Vol. 3, 1963. Vol. 6, edited by H. J. Habakkuk and M. M. Postan, 1966.

The Cambridge History of India. Cambridge, Eng., 1922–29.

The Cambridge History of the British Empire. Edited by H. H. Dodwell. New York, 1932.

The Cambridge Shorter History of India. Edited by H. H. Dodwell. Cambridge, Eng., 1934.

Casal, Jean-Marie. *La Civilisation de l'Indus et ses Enigmes,* Paris, 1969.

Cassirer, E. *An Essay on Man.* Garden City, N.Y., 1953.

Casson, Lionel. "Trade in the Ancient World." *Scientific American* 191 (Nov. 1954): 98–104.

Chakadar, H. C. "Aryan Occupation of Eastern India." *Indian Studies* 3 (1961–62): 103–48, 245–312.

Chakraborti, H. *Trade and Commerce of Ancient India (c. 200 B.C.–c. 650 A.D.).* Calcutta, 1966.

Chanana, Dev Raj. "Data on Agriculture in the Dīgha Nikāya." *Indian Studies* 7 (1966): 421–28.

Chand, Gyan. *Socialist Transformation of Indian Economy.* Bombay, 1965.

Chanda, R., and J. K. Majumdar. *Life and Works of Raja Rammohun Roy.* Calcutta, 1938–41.

Chandra, Bipan. *The Rise and Growth of Economic Nationalism in India.* New Delhi, 1966.

Chaube, S. P. *A History of Education in India.* Allahabad, 1965.

Chayanov, A. V. *The Theory of Peasant Economy.* Homewood, Ill., 1966. With Introduction by D. Thorner.

Childe, V. Gordon. *Man Makes Himself.* New York, 1951.

———. *New Light on the Most Ancient East.* New York, 1959.

———. *What Happened in History.* New York, 1946.

Cipolla, C. M. *Money, Prices, and Civilization in the Mediterranean World.* Princeton, 1956.

Clark, Colin. *Conditions of Economic Progress.* 2d ed. London, 1951; 3d ed., 1957.

———. *Population Growth and Land Use.* New York, 1967.

———, and M. R. Haswell. *The Economics of Subsistence Agriculture.* London, 1964.

Clark, Walter E. *The Āryabhatīya of Āryabhata.* Chicago, 1930.

Clauson, Gerald, and John Chadwick. "The Indus Script Deciphered?" *Antiquity* 43 (1969): 200–7.

Clawson, Marion, et al. *Land for the Future.* Baltimore, 1960.

Clinard, M. B., and J. W. Elder. "Sociology in India: A Study in the Sociology of Knowledge." *American Sociological Review* 30 (Aug. 1965): 586 ff.

Coale, A. J., and Paul Demeny. *Regional Model Life Tables and Stable Populations.* Princeton, 1966.

Coats, A. W. "The Historicist Reaction in English Political Economy, 1870–1890." *Economica* 221 (May 1954): 143–53.

Cohn, B. S. "Recruitment and Training of British Civil Servants in India, 1600–1860." In *Asian Bureaucratic Systems,* edited by Ralph Braibanti, pp. 87–140. Durham, N.C., 1966.

Colebrooke, H. T. *A Digest of Hindu Law, on Contracts and Successions,* 3 vols. London, 1797, 1801.

Cottrell, Fred. *Energy and Society.* New York, 1955.

Coyajee, J. C. "Ranade's Work as an Economist." *Indian Journal of Economics* 22 (1941–42): 307–30.

Crane, Robert I. "Technical Education and Economic Development in India Before World War I." In *Education and Economic Development,* edited by C. A. Anderson and M. J. Bowman, pp. 167–201. Chicago, 1965.

——. "The Transfer of Western Education to India." In *The Transfer of Institutions,* edited by W. B. Hamilton, pp. 108–38. Durham, N.C., 1964.

Cunningham, Alexander. *The Ancient Geography of India.* 1871; reprinted, Varanasi, 1963.

Dales, G. F. "The Decline of the Harappans." *Scientific American* 214 (May 1966): 93–100.

Dalton, George. "A Note of Clarification on Economic Surplus." *American Anthropologist* 62 (1960): 483–90.

——. "Economic Surplus Once Again." Ibid., 65 (1963): 389–94.

——. "Theoretical Issues in Economic Anthropology." *Current Anthropology* 10 (Feb. 1969): 63–102.

Darian, S. G. "The Economic History of the Ganges to the End of Gupta Times." *Journal of the Economic and Social History of the Orient* 13 (Jan. 1970): 62–87.

Darling, Sir Malcolm. *The Punjab Peasant in Prosperity and Debt.* Oxford, 1925.

Das, Dipak Ranjan. *Economic History of the Deccan (From the First to the Sixth Century* A.D.). Delhi, 1969.

Das, S. K. *The Economic History of Ancient India.* 2d. ed. vol. 1. Howra, 1937.

Dasgupta, A. K., "Tendencies in Economic Theory." In *On Political Economy,* edited by V. B. Singh, pp. 47–51. Bombay, 1964.

Dasgupta, S. N. *A History of Sanskrit Literature.* Calcutta, 1947.

Dass, Banesvar. *The Social and Economic Ideas of Benoy Sarkar.* Calcutta, 1939.

Datta, Bhabatosh. "The Background of Ranade's Economics." *Indian Journal of Economics* 22 (1941–42): 261–75.

——. *The Evolution of Economic Thinking in India.* Calcutta, 1962.

Datta, Bikhuitibhusan, and A. N. Singh. *History of Hindu Mathematics.* Bombay, 1962.

Datta, K. *Survey of India's Social Life and Economic Condition in the Eighteenth Century (1707–1813).* Calcutta, 1961.

Davis, Kingsley. *The Population of India and Pakistan.* Princeton, N.J., 1951.

Day, U. N. *The Administrative System of the Delhi Sultanat (1206–1413* A.D.). Allahabad, 1959.

Dean, William, H., Jr. *The Theory of Geographic Location of Economic Activities.* Ann Arbor, Mich., 1938.

De Camp, L. Sprague. *The Ancient Engineers.* Garden City, N.Y., 1963.

Derrett, J. D. M. "Hindu Law: The Dharmashastra and the Anglo-Hindu Law—Scope for Further Comparative Study." *Zeitschrift für vergleichende Rechtswissenschaft* 58, Heft 2 (1956): 199–245.

———. *Introduction to Modern Hindu Law.* Oxford, 1963.

———. "The Right to Earn in Ancient India." *Journal of the Economic and Social History of the Orient* 1 (1958): 66–97.

Desai, A. R. *Social Background of Indian Nationalism.* Bombay, 1966.

Dhar, N. *The Political Thought of M. N. Roy, 1936–1954.* Calcutta, 1966.

Dongerkery, S.R. *University Education in India.* Bombay, 1967.

Dube, S. C. *India's Changing Villages.* London, 1958.

Dubois, Abbé J. A. *Hindu Manners, Customs and Ceremonies,* 3d ed. Oxford, 1897.

Dutt, B. B. *Town Planning in Ancient India.* Calcutta, 1925.

Dutt, R. P., ed. *Karl Marx: Articles on India.* Bombay, 1943.

Dutt, Romesh Chandra. *Economic History of British India.* 2 vols. London, 1902–4.

———. *Famine and Land Assessment in India.* London, 1900.

———. *The Peasantry of Bengal.* Calcutta, 1874.

Dutt, Shib Chandra. *Conflicting Tendencies in Indian Economic Thought.* Calcutta, 1934.

Dwivedi, Gautam, N. *The Age of Kautilya.* Agra, 1966.

Eisenstadt, S. N. *The Political Systems of Empires.* Glencoe, Ill., 1963.

Fairsirvis, W. A. *The Ancient Kingdoms of the Nile.* New York, 1962.

Farmer, Virginia. *Roman Farm Management.* New York, 1913.

Fforde, J. S. *An International Trade in Managerial Skills.* Oxford, 1957.

Finley, M. I. "Land, Debt, and the Man of Property in Classical Athens." *Political Science Quarterly* 68 (1953): 249–68.

———. "Technical Innovation and Economic Progress in the Ancient World." *Economic History Review* 18, no. 1 (1965): 29–45.

Flannery, K. V. "The Ecology of Early Food Production in Mesopotamia." *Science* 147 (12 March 1965): 1247–56.

Forbes, R. J. *Man the Maker.* New York, 1950.

Fourastié, J. "De la vie traditionelle à la vie tertiaire." *Population* 14 (1959): 417–32.

Fox, R. G. "Varna Schemes and Ideological Integration in Indian Society." *Comparative Studies in Society and History* 11 (Jan. 1969): 27–45.

Frank, Tenney. *An Economic Survey of Ancient Rome.* Vol. 5. Baltimore, 1940.

Gallion, A. B., and Simon Eisner. *The Urban Pattern.* New York, 1963.

Gandhi, M. K. *Economic Thought.* Edited by J. S. and A. S. Mathur. Allahabad, 1962.

———. *Industrialize—and Perish.* Selected by R. K. Prabhu. Ahmedabad, 1966.

Gandz, S. "The Sources of al-Khowārizmī's Algebra." *Osiris* 1 (1936): 273 ff.

Ganguli, B. N. *Dadabhai Naoroji and the Drain Theory.* Bombay, 1965.

————, ed. *Readings in Indian Economic History*. Bombay, 1964.

Gautama. Institutes of the Sacred Law. *Sacred Books of the East*, vol. 2. Oxford, 1897.

Gelb, I. J. *A Study of Writing*. Chicago, 1952.

George, C. S., Jr. *The History of Management Thought*. Englewood Cliffs, N.J., 1968.

Georgescu-Roegen, N. "Economic Theory and Agrarian Economics." In *Analytical Economics*, chap. 11. Cambridge, 1966.

Ghosh, J. C. "Rent and Land-Revenue in Bengal." *Indian Journal of Economics* 10 (1929–30): 59–80.

Ghosh, Jajneswar. *Higher Education in Bengal Under British Rule*. Calcutta, 1926.

Ghosh, S. L. *Urban Morals in Ancient India*. Calcutta, 1944.

Ghoshal, U. N. *The Agrarian System in Ancient India*. Calcutta, 1930.

————. *Contributions to the History of the Hindu Revenue System*. Calcutta, 1929.

————. *A History of Indian Political Ideas*. Oxford, 1959.

————. *Studies in Indian History and Culture*. Calcutta, 1957.

Ghurye, K. G. *Preservation of Learned Tradition in India*. Bombay, 1950.

Gimbulas, Marya. "The Indo-Europeans: Archaeological Problems." *American Anthropologist* 65 (Aug. 1963): 817–37.

Glob, P. V., and T. G. Bibby. "A Forgotten Civilisation of the Persian Gulf." *Scientific American* 203 (Oct. 1960): 62–71.

Goiten, S. D. *A Mediterranean Society*. Berkeley, Calif., 1967.

Gokhale, B. G. "Capital Accumulation in XVIIth Century Western India." *Journal of the Asiatic Society of Bombay* 39–40 (1964–65): 51–60.

————. "English Trade With Western India." *Journal of Indian History* 42 (Aug. 1964): 329–42.

————. *Indian Thought Through the Ages*. New York, 1961.

Gonda, Jan. *Ancient Indian Kingship From a Religious Point of View*. Leiden, 1966.

Gopal, Lallanji. *The Economic Life of Northern India c.* A.D. *700–1200*. Delhi, 1965.

————. "Ownership of Agricultural Land in Ancient India." *Journal of Economic and Social History of the Orient* 4, no. 3 (1961): 240–63.

————. "Quasi-Manorial Rights in Ancient India." *Journal of the Economic and Social History of the Orient* 6 (1963): 296–308.

————. "The Śukranīti—A Nineteenth-Century Text." *Bulletin of the School of Oriental and African Studies* 25, no. 3 (1962): 524–56.

Gopal, M. H. *Mauryan Public Finance*. London, 1935.

Gopalachari, K. *Early History of the Andhra Country*. Madras, 1941.

Gopalakrishnan, P. K. *Development of Economic Ideas in India (1880–1950)*. Delhi, 1959.

Gordon, D. H. *The Pre-Historic Background of Indian Culture*. Bombay, 1958.

Guha, Ranajit. *A Rule of Property for Bengal.* The Hague, 1963.

Gupta, J. N. *Life and Work of Romesh Chandra Dutt.* London, 1911.

Gupta, K. M. *The Land System of South India Between c. 800 A.D. and 1200 A.D.* Lahore, 1933.

Gupta, R. M. N. *The Land System of Benghal.* Calcutta, 1940.

Habib, Irfan M. *The Agrarian System of Mughal India.* Bombay, 1963.

————. "Aspects of Agrarian Relations and Economy in a Region of Uttar Pradesh During the Sixteenth Century." *Indian Economic and Social History Review* 4 (Sept. 1967): 205–32.

————. "Banking and Mughal India." *Contributions to Indian Economic History* 2 (1963): 1–20.

————. "The Currency System of the Mughal Empire, 1556–1707." *Medieval India Quarterly* 4 (1961): 1–21.

————. "Usury in Medieval India." *Comparative Studies in Society and History* 6 (July 1964): 393–419.

Habib, Mohammad, and A. U. S. Khan. *The Political Theory of the Delhi Sultanate.* Allahabad, n.d.

Haithcox, J. P. *M. N. Roy and Comintern Policy, 1920–1939.* Princeton, 1971.

Halpern, J. M. *The Changing Village Community.* Englewood Cliffs, N.J., 1967.

Hamilton, C. J. "The Fallacy of a Golden Age." *Indian Journal of Economics* 5 (1924): 152–60.

Hammett, F. S. "Agricultural and Botanic Knowledge of Ancient India." *Osiris* 9 (1950): 211–26.

————. "The Ideas of the Ancient Hindus Concerning Man." *Isis* 76 (Feb. 1938): 57–72.

Harris, Marvin. "The Economy Has No Surplus." *American Anthropologist* 61 (1959): 185–99.

Hart, Hornell. *Can World Government Be Predicted by Mathematics?* Durham, N.C., 1943.

————. "The Logistic Growth of Political Areas." *Social Forces* 28 (1948): 396–408.

Heichelheim, F. M. *An Ancient Economic History.* Leiden, 1958.

Heizer, R. F. "Ancient Heavy Transport, Methods and Achievements." *Science* 153 (19 Aug. 1966): 821–30.

Herskovits, M. J. *Economic Anthropology.* 2d ed. New York, 1952.

Hertzler, J. O. "Toward a Sociology of Language." *Social Forces* 32 (Dec. 1953): 109–19.

Hole, Frank. "Investigating the Origins of Mesopotamian Civilization." *Science* 153 (5 Aug. 1966):605–11.

Homer, Sidney. *A History of Interest Rates.* New Brunswick, 1963.

Hoyland, John S. *Gopal Krishna Gokhale, His Life and Speeches.* Calcutta, 1947.

Huq, Mazharul. *The East India Company's Land Policy and Commerce in Bengal, 1698–1784.* Dacca, 1964.

Hutchins, Francis G. *The Illusion of Permanence: British Imperialism in India.* Princeton, 1967.

Hutton, J. H. *Caste in India.* Bombay, 1946; 2d ed., 1951.

Hyder, L. K. "Early Commerce of India." *Indian Journal of Economics* 4 (1923–24): 59–72.

Ibbetson, Sir Denzil. *Panjáb Castes.* Lahore, 1916.

Innis, H. A. *The Bias of Communication.* Toronto, 1951.

Jagirdar, P. J. "Ranade and the Historical School of Economics." *Indian Journal of Economics* 35 (1954): 195–201.

———. *Studies in the Social Thought of M. G. Ranade.* Bombay, 1963.

Jain, Jagish C. *Life in Ancient India as Depicted in the Jain Canons.* Bombay, 1947.

Jairazbhoy, R. A. *Foreign Influence in Ancient India.* London, 1963.

Jasny, N. "The Daily Bread of the Ancient Greeks and Romans." *Osiris* 9 (1950): 227–53.

Jawad, A. J. *The Advent of the Era of Townships in Northern Mesopotamia.* Leiden, 1965.

Jayaswal, K. P. *Hindu Polity.* 3d ed. Bangalore City, 1955.

Jha, Dwijendra Narayan. *Revenue System in Post-Maurya and Gupta Times.* Calcutta, 1967.

Johnson, E. A. J. *Predecessors of Adam Smith.* New York, 1937.

Jones, A. H. M. *Athenian Democracy.* Oxford, 1957.

Jones, T. B., and J. W. Snyder. *Sumerian Economic Texts From the Third Ur Dynasty.* Minneapolis, 1961.

Jones, William O. "Economic Man in Africa." *Food Research Institute Studies* 1 (May 1966): 107–34.

Joshi, P. C. "The Decline of Indigenous Handicrafts in Uttar Pradesh." *Indian Economic and Social History Review* 1 (1964): 24–35.

Joshi, T. M. "A Critique of 'Indian Economics.'" *Indian Journal of Economics* 22 (1941–42): 276–79.

Kale, V. G. "Economics in India." *Indian Journal of Economics* 9 (1928–29): 608 ff.

———. *Economics of Protection in India.* Poona, 1929.

———. *Introduction to the Study of Economics.* Poona, 1918.

———. "The Money Market in Maharashtra Two Centuries Ago." *Indian Journal of Economics* 17 (Jan. 1937): 241–48.

Kane, P. S. V. *History of Dharmasastra.* 5 vols. Poona, 1930–62.

Kangle, R. P. *The Kautilīya Arthaśāstra.* 3 vols. Bombay. 1965.

———. "Manu and Kautilya." *Indian Antiquary* 1 (1964): 48–54.

———. "The Vyasanas According to Kautilya." *Indian Antiquary* 1 (1964): 145–53.

Kapadia, K. M. *Marriage and Family in India.* 2d ed. Bombay, 1959.

Karve, D. G. "The Late Professor V. G. Kale of Poona." *Indian Journal of Economics* 27 (1946–47): 335–38.

———. "Ranade and Economic Planning." *Indian Journal of Economics* 22 (1941–42): 235–44.

Karwal, G. D. "Ancient Indian Economics." *Indian Journal of Economics* 43 (Oct. 1962): 65–84.

———. "Kautilyanism." *Indian Journal of Economics* 46 (April 1966): 370–95.

———. "Mahadev Govind Ranade: His Economic Views." *Indian Journal of Economics* 13 (1932–33): 643–68; 14 (1933–34): 53–78.

Keay, F. E. *Indian Education in Ancient and Later Times.* London, 1938.

Kellock, James. "Ranade and After: A Study of the Development of Economic Thought in India." *Indian Journal of Economics* 22 (1941–42): 245–60.

Kennedy, R. E., Jr. "The Protestant Ethic and the Parsis." *American Journal of Sociology* 68 (1962): 11–20.

Keyfitz, Nathan. "The Interlocking of Economic and Social Factors in Asian Development." *Canadian Journal of Economics and Political Science* 25 (1959): 34–46.

Klein, Ira. "Utilitarianism and Agrarian Progress in Western India." *Economic History Review* 18 (Dec. 1965): 576–95.

Kosambi, D. D. "The Beginning of the Iron Age in India." *Journal of the Economic and Social History of the Orient* 6, no. 3 (1963): 309–18.

———. *An Introduction to the Study of Indian History.* Bombay, 1956.

———. "Social and Economic Aspects of Bhagavad Gīta." *Journal of the Economic and Social History of the Orient* 4 (1961): 198–229.

Kramer, Samuel N. *History Begins at Sumer.* New York, 1959.

———. *The Sumerians.* Chicago, 1963.

Krishnaswami, A. "Marshall's Contribution to Indian Economics." *Indian Journal of Economics* 15 (1934–35): 898–907.

Kumar, Dharma. *Land and Caste in South India.* Cambridge, Eng., 1965.

Kuznets, S., W. E. Moore, and J. J. Spengler, eds. *Economic Growth: Brazil, India, Japan.* Durham, N.C., 1955.

Law, B. C. *Historical Geography of India.* Paris, 1954.

Law, N. N. *Promotion of Learning in India During Muhammadan Rule (by Muhammadans).* Bombay, 1916.

Leemans, W. F. *The Old-Babylonian Merchant.* Leiden, 1950.

Lewis, W. A. *Development Planning.* New York, 1966.

Lingat, Robert. *Les sources du droit dans le système traditionnel de l'Inde.* Paris, 1957.

Lipstein, K. "The Reception of Western Law in India." *International Social Science Bulletin* no. 9 (1957): 85–96.

Lokanathan, P. S. "The Economics of Gokhale." *Indian Journal of Economics* 22 (1941–42): 225–34.

Lopez, R. S., and I. W. Raymond. *Medieval Trade in the Mediterranean World.* New York, 1955.

Macdonell, A. A., and A. B. Keith. *Vedic Index of Names and Subjects.* 2 vols. Naranasi, 1958.

Machlup, F. *Essays on Economic Semantics*. Englewood Cliffs, N.J., 1963.

MacIver, Robert M. *The Web of Government*. New York, 1947.

McLane, John. "The Drain of Wealth and Indian Nationalism at the Turn of the Century." *Contributions to Indian Economic History* 2 (1963): 21–40.

Madan, G. R. *Economic Thinking in India*. New Delhi, 1966.

Mahajan, W. D. *The Sultanate of Delhi*. Delhi, 1962.

Mahalingam, T. V. *Economic Life in the Vijayanagar Empire*. Madras, 1955.

Maheshwari, P., ed. *The History of Sciences in India*. New Delhi, 1963.

Maity, Sachindra K. *Economic Life of Northern India in the Gupta Period*. Calcutta, 1957.

Majumdar, Bimanbehari. *History of Indian Social and Political Ideas from Rammohun to Dayananda (1821–1884)*. Calcutta, 1967.

Majumdar, Bimol Kanti, *The Military System in Ancient India*. 2d ed. Calcutta, 1960.

Majumdar, J. K. *Raja Rammohun Roy and Progressive Movements in India*. Calcutta, 1941.

Majumdar, R. C. *Ancient India*. Delhi, 1960.

———. *Ancient Indian Colonisation in South-East Asia*. Baroda, 1955.

———, ed. *British Paramountcy and Indian Renaissance*, 2 parts. Bombay, 1963, 1965, Vols. 9–10 in *The History and Culture of the Indian People*.

———. *Corporate Life in Ancient India*. Calcutta, 1922.

———, ed. *The Delhi Sultanate*. Bombay, 1960.

———. *Glimpses of Bengal in the Nineteenth Century*. Calcutta, 1960.

———, ed. *The History and Culture of the Indian People*. Bombay, 1951 ff.

———, and A. S. Altekar. *The Vākātaka Gupta Age (c. 200–550 A.D.)*. Delhi, 1960.

Mallowan, M. E. L. "Civilized Life Begins: Mesopotamia and Iran." In *The Dawn of Civilization*, edited by Stuart Piggott. New York, 1961.

Manu. The Laws of Manu. Translated by G. Bühler. *Sacred Books of the East*, vol. 25. Oxford, 1886.

Marriott, McKim, ed. *Village India*. Chicago, 1955.

Marx, Karl. "The British Rule in India." In *Articles on India*, edited by R. P. Dutt. Bombay, 1943.

———, and F. Engels. *The First Indian War of Independence, 1857–1859*. Moscow, 1959.

Masani, R. P. *Dadabhai Naoroji: The Grand Old Man of India*. London, 1939.

Mathur, P. N. "Gains in Economic Growth From International Trade—A Theoretical Exploration of Leontief's Paradox." *Kyklos* 16 (1963): 583–96.

Mauss, Marcel. *The Gift*. Glencoe, Ill., 1954.

Mayhew, Arthur. *The Education of India.* London, 1926.

Mazumdar, B. P. *The Socio-Economic History of Northern India, 1030–1194 A.D.* Calcutta, 1960.

Mehta, Sumant. "Cultivation of Persian by Hindus." *Journal of the Oriental Institute* 15 (Dec. 1965): 127–34.

Michell, H. *The Economics of Ancient Greece.* Cambridge, Eng., 1940.

Millon, R. "Teotihuacán: Completion of Map of Giant Ancient City in the Valley of Mexico." *Science* 170 (4 December 1970): 1077–82.

Minocha, V. S. "Ranade on the Agrarian Problem." *Indian Economic and Social History Review* 2 (1965): 357–66.

Mishra, Vikra. *Hinduism and Economic Growth.* Bombay, 1962.

Misra, B. B. *The Indian Middle Classes.* London, 1961.

Mode, Heinz. *Indische Frühkulturen.* Basel, 1944.

Modelski, George. "Comparative International Systems." *World Politics* 14 (1962): 665.

Mookerji, Radhakmund K. *Ancient Indian Education.* Delhi, 1960.

———. *Chandragupta Maurya and His Times.* Delhi, 1960.

———. *Indian Shipping.* Bombay, 1957.

———. *Local Government in Ancient India.* Oxford, 1920.

Moreland, W. H. *The Agrarian System of Moslem India.* Cambridge, 1929.

———. "The Ain-i-Akbari: A Baseline for the Economic History of India." *Indian Journal of Economics* 1 (1916): 44–53.

———. *India at the Death of Akbar.* London, 1920.

———. *Relations of Golconda in the Seventeenth Century.* London, 1931.

———. "The Revenue System of the Mughul Empire." In *The Cambridge History of India,* vol. 4 (on the Mughul period), edited by Richard Burns, chap. 16, p. 453. Cambridge, 1937.

Morley, S. G. *The Ancient Maya.* Stanford, 1946.

Morris, Morris D. "Towards a Reinterpretation of Nineteenth-Century Indian Economic History." *Journal of Economic History* 23 (Dec. 1963): 606–618.

———. "Values as an Obstacle to Economic Growth in South Asia." *Journal of Economic History* 27 (Dec. 1967): 588–607.

———, and Burton Stein. "The Economic History of India: A Bibliographic Essay." *Journal of Economic History* 21 (1961): 179–207.

Mukerjee, R. *The Economic History of India, 1600–1800.* Allahabad, 1967.

Mukerji, D. P. "An Economic Theory for India." In *On Political Economy,* edited by V. B. Singh, pp. 126 ff. Bombay, 1964.

Mukherjee, Haridas, and Uma Mukherjee. *The Origins of the National Education Movement (1905–1914).* Calcutta, 1957.

Mukherjee, T. B. *Inter-State Relations in Ancient India.* Delhi, 1966.

Mulla, D. F. *Principles of Hindu Law.* Edited and enlarged by S. T. Desai. 13th ed. Bombay, 1966.

Munshi, M. C. "Protectionism and Indian Economic Thought." *Indian Journal of Economics* 22 (1941–42): 331–56.

Muranjan, S. K. "Hinduism and Economic Growth." *Indian Economic Journal* 11 (Oct.–Dec. 1963): 243–48.

Murti, V. N. "Indian Economy During the British Rule." *Indian Journal of Economics* 41 (1960–61): 331–36.

Myrdal, Gunnar. *Asian Drama.* New York, 1968.

Nadvi, Syed Sulaiman. *The Education of Hindus Under Muslim Rule.* Karachi, 1963.

Nagaswamy, R. "South Indian Temple—As an Employer." *Indian Economic and Social History Review* 2 (1965): 367–72.

Naoroji, Dadabhai. *Poverty and Un-British Rule in India.* London, 1901.

Naqvi, Hameeda Khatoon. "Progress of Urbanization in United Provinces, 1550–1800." *Journal of the Economic and Social History of the Orient* 10 (July 1967): 81–101.

———. *Urban Centres and Industries in Upper India, 1556–1803.* Calcutta, 1968.

Nārada. The Institutes of Narada. In *Sacred Books of the East,* vol. 33. Oxford, 1889.

Narain, Brij. *Indian Economic Life, Past and Present.* Lahore, 1929.

Natarajan, B. "Economic Ideas Behind the Permanent Settlement." *Indian Journal of Economics* 22 (Jan. 1942): 708–23.

Nath, Pran. *A Study in the Economic Condition of Ancient India.* London, 1929.

Nef, John U. *War and Human Progress.* Cambridge, Mass., 1952.

Neugebauer, O. *The Exact Sciences in Antiquity.* Providence, 1957.

Nikam, N. A., and Richard McKeon. *The Edicts of Aśoka.* Chicago, 1959.

Niyogi, Puspa. *Contributions to the Economic History of Northern India.* Calcutta, 1962.

Nurullah, Syed, and J. P. Naik. *A Student's History of Education in India (1800–1965).* Bombay, 1964.

Olmstead, A. T. *History of the Persian Empire.* Chicago, 1948.

Oppenheim, A. L. *Ancient Mesopotamia.* Chicago, 1964.

———. "A New Look at the Structure of Mesopotamian Society." *Journal of the Economic and Social History of the Orient* 10 (July 1967): 9–10.

Pandey, K. G. "Rājanīti or Politics." *Indian Antiquary,* 3d ser. 1 (April 1964): 90–103.

Parsons, Talcott. *Social System.* Glencoe, Ill., 1951.

Parvate, T. V. *Makers of Modern India.* Delhi, 1964.

Patel, S. J. "British Economic Thought and the Treatment of India as a Colony." *Indian Journal of Economics* 27 (1946–47): 367–71.

———. *Essays on Economic Transition.* Bombay, 1965.

Patten, S. N. *The Development of English Thought.* New York, 1899.

Patten, S. N. *Essays in Economic Theory.* Edited by R. G. Tugwell. New York, 1924.

Pattullo, Henry. *An Essay Upon the Cultivation of the Lands, and Improvements of the Revenues of Bengal.* London, 1772.

Patwardhan, Appa. *Chalanashuddhi, or Nature Forging Towards Sarvodaya.* Ahmedabad, 1967.

Pearson, F. A., and F. A. Harper. *The World's Hunger.* Ithaca, N.Y., 1945.

Philips, C. H., ed. *Historians of India, Pakistan and Ceylon.* London, 1961.

Piggott, Stuart. *Ancient Europe.* Chicago, 1968.

————. *Prehistoric India.* Harmondsworth, 1950.

Pillai, V. R. "Reflections on the Teaching of Economics in India." *Indian Economic Journal* 10 (1963): 209–30.

Polanyi, Karl, C. M. Arensberg, and H. W. Pearson. *Trade and Market in Early Empires.* Glencoe, Ill., 1957.

Postan, M. M. "Investment in Medieval Agriculture." *Journal of Economic History* 27 (Dec. 1967): 576–87.

Prasad, Ishwari. *History of Medieval India.* Allahabad, 1966.

Prasad, Rajeshwari. *Some Aspects of British Revenue Policy in India, 1773–1833.* Delhi, 1970.

Price, Ralph. "M. G. Ranade's Theory of Development and Growth." *Explorations in Entrepreneurial History* 4 (1966): 40–52.

Puri, B. N. *Cities of Ancient India.* Calcutta, 1966.

————. *India in the Time of Patañjali.* Bombay, 1957.

Quigley, C. *The Evolution of Civilizations.* New York, 1961.

Qureshi, I. H. *The Administration of the Mughul Empire.* Karachi, 1966.

————. *The Administration of the Sultanate of Delhi,* 4th ed. Karachi, 1956.

Radford, R. A. "The Economic Organization of a P.O.W. Camp." *Economica* 12 (Nov. 1945): 189–201.

Raghavan, V. "Sukraniti." *Rajavidya,* no. 1 (April 1964): 5–14.

Ranade, Mahadev Govind. *Essays on Indian Economics.* Madras, 1898; 1920.

————. *Religious and Social Reform.* Bombay, 1902.

Ray, Amita. *Villages, Towns, and Secular Buildings in Ancient India.* Calcutta, 1964.

Ray, N. R. "Maurya and Śunga Art." *Indian Studies* 5 (1964): 319–76.

Raychaudhuri, Tapan. "European Commercial Activity and the Organization of India's Commerce and Industrial Production, 1500–1700." In *Readings in Indian Economic History,* edited by B. N. Ganguli, pp. 64–77. Bombay, 1964.

————. "A Re-interpretation of Nineteenth-Century Indian Economic History." *Indian Economic and Social History Review* 5 (1965): 77–100.

————. "Some Patterns of Economic Organization and Activity in 17th-

Century India." *Second International Economic History Conference,* Aix-en-Provence, 1965–66.

Redlich, Fritz. "Ideas: Their Migration in Space and Transmittal Over Time." *Kyklos* 6 (1953–54): 302–4.

Rhys Davids, Caroline A. F. "Economic Conditions in Ancient India." *Economic Journal* 11 (Sept. 1901): 305–20.

Rostovtzeff, M. *Social and Economic History of the Ancient World.* Oxford, 1941.

———. *Social and Economic History of the Hellenistic World.* Oxford, 1953.

Row, B. Govinda. "V. G. Kale: His Industrial Outlook." *Indian Journal of Economics* 27 (1946–47): 323–30.

Roy, M. N. *Scientific Politics.* Calcutta, 1942.

Roy, Ram Mohan. *Rammohun Roy on Indian Economy.* Edited by S. C. Sarkar. Calcutta, 1965.

Roy, Satischandra. *An Essay on the Economic Causes of Famines in India.* Calcutta, 1909.

Ruben, Walter. *Das Pancatantra und seine Morallehre.* Berlin, 1959.

———. "Rgveda and Homer's Epics." *Journal of the Royal Oriental Institute* 15 (March–June 1966): 314–21.

———, and K. Fischer. *Der Maurya und der Mogul Staat.* Berlin, 1965.

Russell, J. C. "Late Ancient and Medieval Population." *Transactions of the American Philosophical Society* 48 (1958): 37–101.

———. "The Metropolitan City Region of the Middle Ages." *Journal of Regional Science* 2 (1960): 55–70.

Ryder, Arthur W. *Panchatantra.* Chicago, 1955.

Sachau, E. C., trans. *Alberuni's India (c. 1030 A.D.).* London, 1914.

Saksena, R. N. "Sociology in India." In *Social and Economic Change,* edited by B. Singh and V. B. Singh. Bombay, 1967.

Saletore, B. A. *Ancient India Political Thought and Political Institutions.* London, 1963.

———. *Ancient Karnātka: History of Tuḷava.* Poona, 1936.

Saletore, R. N. *Life in the Gupta Age.* Bombay, 1943.

Sankalia, H. D. "Middle Stone Age Culture in India and Pakistan." *Science* 140 (16 Oct. 1964): 365–75.

Sarkar, Sadunath. *Studies in Mughal India.* London, 1920.

Sarkar, S. D., ed. *Rammohun Roy on Indian Economy.* Calcutta, 1965.

Sarkar, U. C. *Epochs in Hindu Legal History.* Hoshiarpur, 1958.

Sastri, K. A. N. *The Cōlas.* 2d ed. Madras, 1955.

———, ed. *A Comprehensive History of India.* Calcutta, 1957.

———. *A History of South India.* 3d ed. Madras, 1966.

Sawyer, J. S., ed. *World Climate from 8000 to 0 B.C.* London, 1967.

Sawyer, Jack. "Dimensions of Nations: Size, Wealth and Politics." *American Journal of Sociology* 73 (1967): 145–72.

Say, J. B. *A Treatise in Political Economy.* 4th ed. Philadelphia, 1841.

Schumpeter, J. A. *History of Economic Analysis.* New York, 1954.

Seebohm, F. "Imperialism and Socialism." *The Nineteenth Century* 7 (1880): 725–36.

Seebohm, M. E. *The Evolution of the English Farm*. Revised 2d ed. London, 1952.

Sen, Benoychandra. *Economics in Kautilya*. Calcutta, 1967.

Sen, K. M. *Hinduism*. Baltimore, 1961.

Sen, K. N. "Economic Thinking in the Indian National Congress." *Indian Journal of Economics* 22 (1941–42): 689–707.

Sen, S. R. *The Economics of Sir James Steuart*. Cambridge, 1957.

Sen-Gupta, N. C. *Evolution of Ancient Indian Law*. Calcutta, 1953.

Shah, A. B., ed. *Gokhale and Modern India*. Bombay, 1966.

Shah, D. A. *The Indian Point of View in Economics*. Bombay, 1920.

Shamasastry, R., trans. *Kauṭilya's Arthaśāstra*. 1st ed. Mysore, 1915; 6th ed., 1960.

Sharif, K. M. *Life and Conditions of the People of Hindustan*. Delhi, 1959.

Sharma, B. S. *The Political Philosophy of M. N. Roy*. Delhi, 1965.

Sharma, Dasharatha. *Early Chauhān Dynasties*. Delhi, 1959.

Sharma, Ram Sharan. *Aspects of Political Ideas and Institutions in Ancient India*. 2d ed. Delhi, 1968.

———. "Land Grants to Vassals and Officials in Northern India (c. A.D. 1000–1200)." *Journal of the Economic and Social History of the Orient* 4, no. 1 (1961): 70–105.

———. *Light on Early Indian Society and Economy*. Bombay, 1966.

———. "The Origins of Feudalism in India (c. A.D. 400–650)." *Journal of the Economic and Social History of the Orient* 1 (1957): 297–328.

———. *Śūdras in Ancient India*. Delhi, 1958.

Sharma, Sri Ram. *Mughal Government and Administration*. Bombay, 1951.

Siddiqi, N. A. "Land Revenue Demand Under the Mughals." *Indian Economic and Social History Review* 2 (Oct. 1965): 373–80.

Singer, Charles, et al. *A History of Technology*. New York, 1954.

Singer, Kurt. "Oikonomia: An Inquiry Into Beginnings of Economic Thought and Language." *Kyklos* 11, no. 1 (1958): 29–55.

Singh, A. K. "Hindu Culture and Economic Development in India." Reprinted from *Conspectus*, no. 1 (1967), p. 16.

Singh, B., and V. B. Singh, eds. *Social and Economic Change*. Bombay, 1967.

Singh, S. D. *Ancient Indian Warfare, With Special Reference to the Vedic Period*. Leiden, 1965.

———. "Iron in Ancient India." *Journal of the Economic and Social History of the Orient* 5, no. 2 (1962): 212–16.

Singh, V. B., ed. *Economic History of India: 1857–1956*. Bombay, 1965.

———. *Essays in Indian Political Economy*. New Delhi, 1967.

———. *Indian Economy Yesterday and Today*. New Delhi, 1964.

———, ed. *On Political Economy*. Bombay, 1964.

Sinha, B. P. *The Decline of the Kingdom of Magadha.* Patna, 1954.

Sinha, H. N. *Sovereignty in Ancient Indian Polity.* London, 1938.

Sinha, J. C. "Economic Theorists Among the Servants of John Company (1766–1806)." *Economic Journal* 35 (March 1925): 47–49.

Sinha, N. C. *Studies in Indo-British Economy a Hundred Years Ago.* Calcutta, 1946.

Sinha, N. K. *The Economic History of Bengal.* Calcutta, 1961.

Sinha, Surajit. "State Formation and Rajput Myth in Tribal and Central India." *Man in India* 42 (1962): 35–80.

Sircar, D. C. "Cosmography and Geography in Early Indian Literature." *Indian Studies, Past and Present* 7 (April–June 1966): 234–348, 353–428.

Sjoberg, Gideon. "The Origin and Evolution of Cities." *Scientific American* 213 (Sept. 1965): 54–63.

———. *The Preindustrial City.* Glencoe, Ill., 1960.

Smith, Adam. *An Inquiry Into the Nature and Causes of the Wealth of Nations.* Modern Library edition. New York, 1937.

Solecki, R. S. "Prehistory in Shanidar Valley, Northern Iraq." *Science* 129 (18 Jan. 1963): 179–93.

Sovani, N. V. *Urbanization and Urban India.* New York, 1966.

Spear, Percival. *A History of India.* Harmondsworth, 1965.

Spellman, John W. "Political Implications of the King's Vetana." *Journal of the Economic and Social History of the Orient* 5 (Dec. 1962): 314–20.

———. *Political Theory of Ancient India.* Oxford, 1964.

Spencer, George W. "Temple Money-Lending and Livestock Redistribution." *Indian Economic and Social History Review* 5 (1969): 277–93.

Spengler, Joseph J. "Economic Thought of Islam: Ibn Khaldūn." *Comparative Studies in Society and History* 6 (April 1964): 268–306.

———. "Herodotus on the Subject Matter of Economics." *Scientific Monthly* 81 (Dec. 1955): 276–77.

Sperber, Daniel. "Costs of Living in Roman Palestine." *Journal of the Economic and Social History of the Orient* 13 (Jan. 1970): 1–15.

Srikantan, S. K. "Labour in Ancient India." *Indian Journal of Economics* 20 (1939–40): 639–43.

Stein, Burton. "The Economic Functions of a Medieval South Indian Temple." *Journal of Asian Studies* 19 (1960): 163–76.

Stokes, Eric. *The English Utilitarians and India.* Oxford, 1959.

Stolper, Wolfgang. *Planning Without Facts.* Cambridge, Eng., 1966.

Subrahmanian, N. *Sangam Polity.* New York, 1966.

The Śukranīti. Translated by B. K. Sarkar. Allahabad, 1914.

Sundaram, K. *Studies in Economic and Social Conditions of Medieval Andhra.* Madras, 1968.

Taeuber, C., and I. B. Taeuber. *The Changing Population of the United States.* New York, 1958.

Thapar, Romila. *Aśoka and the Decline of the Mauryas.* Oxford, 1961.

Thapar, Romila. *A History of India.* London, 1966.

Thomas, P. J. "The Late Professor V. G. Kale." *Indian Journal of Economics* 27 (1946–47): 333–34.

Thompson, C. D. "Modern Mercantilism in India." *Indian Journal of Economics* 2 (1918–19): 507–19.

Thompson, D'Arcy W. *On Growth and Form.* Abridged and edited by J. T. Bonner. Cambridge, Eng., 1961.

Thorner, Daniel. *Investment in Empire.* Philadelphia, 1950.

——, and Alice Thorner. *Land and Labor in India.* Bombay, 1962.

Tilman, Robert O. "The Influence of Caste on Economic Development." In *Administration and Economic Development in India,* edited by Ralph Braibanti and Joseph J. Spengler, pp. 202–23. Durham, N.C., 1963.

Tinker, Hugh. "Structure of the British Imperial Heritage" In *Asian Bureaucratic Systems Emergent from the British Imperial Tradition,* edited by Ralph Braibanti, pp. 23–86. Durham, N.C., 1966.

Tirumalachar, B. "Economic Organisation in Ancient India." *Indian Journal of Economics* 15 (1934–35): 758–84.

Titus, M. T. *Indian Islam.* London, 1930.

Tiwari, Chitra. *Śūdras in Manu.* Delhi, 1963.

Trevelyan, Sir Charles E. *On the Education of the People of India.* London, 1838.

Tripathi, R. P. *Some Aspects of Muslim Administration.* Allahabad, 1956.

Umar, Muhammad. "Life of the Mughal Royalty in India During the Eighteenth Century." *Medieval India Quarterly* 4 (1961): 137–54.

Useem, John, and Ruth Hill Useem. *The Western-Educated Man in India.* New York, 1955.

Vakil, C. N. "The Formation of Economic Opinion in India." *Indian Journal of Economics* 15 (1934–35): 758–84.

[Vaśiṣṭha]. Dharmashastra. In *Sacred Books of the East,* vol. 14. Oxford, 1882.

Vatsyayana. *Kamasutra.* Paris, 1962.

Vishnu. Institutes of Vishnu. *Sacred Books of the East,* vol. 7. Oxford, 1900.

Vora, D. P. *Evolution of Morals in the Epics (Mahābhārata and Rāmāyana).* Bombay, 1959.

Wagle, Narenda. "Patterns of Settlements at the Time of the Buddha." *Indian Antiquary* 1 (1964): 219–53.

——. *Society at the Time of the Buddha.* Bombay, 1966.

Warmington, B. H. *Carthage.* Baltimore, 1964.

Weber, Max. *The Religion of India.* Glencoe, Ill., 1958.

Whatmough, J. *Language: A Modern Synthesis.* New York, 1957.

Wheeler, Sir Mortimer. *The Indus Civilization.* Cambridge, Eng., 1968.

——. "Ancient India." In *The Dawn of Civilization,* edited by Stuart Pizzott, pp. 229–52. New York, 1961.

Wilcynski, J. C. "On the Presumed Darwinism of Alberuni Eight Hundred Years Before Darwin." *Isis* 50 (1959): 459–66.

Wilhelm, Friedrich. *Die politische Polemiken im Staatslehrbuch des Kautalya.* Wiesbaden, 1960.

———. "Das Wirtschaftssystem des Kautaliya Arthasastra." *Journal of the Economic and Social History of the Orient* 2 (1959): 294–312.

Woolley, L. "The Urbanization of Society." *Journal of World History* 4 (1957): 236–72.

The World Food Problem. President's Science Advisory Committee. Washington, 1967.

Woytinsky, W. S., and E. S. Woytinsky. *World Population and Production.* New York, 1933.

Yazdani, G., ed. *The Early History of Deccan.* London, 1960.

Zeuner, Frederick. *A History of Domesticated Animals.* New York, 1963.

Name Index

Subject Index